NORTHEASTERN ILLINOIS UNIVERSITY

3 1224 00492 2711

D1444595

WITHDRAWN
NORTHEASTERN ILLINOIS
UNIVERSITY LIBRARY

Children's Books about Religion

Children's Books about Religion

Patricia Pearl Dole

WITHDRAWN
NORTHEASTERN ILLINOIS
UNIVERSITY LIBRARY

1999
Libraries Unlimited, Inc.
Englewood, Colorado

Copyright © 1999 Libraries Unlimited, Inc.
All Rights Reserved
Printed in the United States of America

No part of this publication may be reproduced, stored in a retrieval system, or transmitted, in any form or by any means, electronic, mechanical, photocopying, recording, or otherwise, without the prior written permission of the publisher.

Libraries Unlimited, Inc.
P.O. Box 6633
Englewood, CO 80155-6633
1-800-237-6124
www.lu.com

Production Editor: Kevin W. Perizzolo
Copy Editor: Jason Cook
Proofreader: Felicity Tucker
Indexer: Nancy Fulton
Typesetter: Michael Florman

Library of Congress Cataloging-in-Publication Data

Dole, Patricia Pearl, 1927-   6-26-01
    Children's books about religion / by Patricia Pearl Dole.
    xii, 230 p. 17x25 cm.
    Includes bibliographical references and index.
    ISBN 1-56308-515-1 (cloth)
    1. Religions--Juvenile literature--Bibliography. 2. Christian literature for children--Bibliography. I. Title.
Z7759.D65 1998
[BL92]
016.2--dc21   98-33707
                                                                CIP

Ronald Williams Library
Northeastern Illinois University

Contents

Acknowledgments

As there are no research collections in the area of children's religious books, with the exception of one begun by the Library Science department of Baylor University in the mid-1980s, gathering material for this bibliography would not have been possible without the cooperation and generosity of the following publishers in supplying review copies of their most recent books: Abrams, Augsburg, August House, Ave Maria, Baker, Bantam Doubleday Dell, Peter Bedrick, Bethany House, Blackbirch, Boyds Mills, Candlewick, ChariotVictor, David C. Cook, Crabtree, Dharma, Dorling Kindersley, William B. Eerdmans, Enslow, Farrar Straus & Giroux, Firefly, Grolier, Herald, Holiday House, Holt, Houghton Mifflin, Ideals, Jewish Lights, Jewish Publication Society, KarBen, Lee and Low, Lerner, Little Brown, Liturgy, Millbrook, Morehouse, Morrow, Nilgiri, North-South, Parvardigar, Pelican, Penguin, Pinata, Pitspopany, Putnam and Grosset, Raintree Steck-Vaughn, Rigby, Roper, Smith and Kraus, Gareth Stevens, Troll, Tundra, and Tyndale.

In addition, my heartfelt appreciation goes to the children's bookstore Narnia in Richmond, Virginia, whose owners graciously allowed me to examine the religious books on their shelves, and to the Jewish Community Center library for sharing its excellent collection. Other sources of appropriate materials were the county and city public libraries, church libraries, and bookstores in the area.

Introduction

Since I first began to write on this subject as a master's degree project in 1980, trends in religious publications have changed in interesting ways. The earlier books dealt largely with Bible story collections, prayers, Noah's ark, the Nativity, baby Moses in his basket and other well-known biblical personages, lives and teachings of Jesus, good reference material in the form of encyclopedias, dictionaries, and such, and some fine works on comparative religion. There have always been books of excellent quality in this area; it is by no means limited to didactic, saccharine, or doctrinaire material. Outstanding authors who have written in these fields include Barbara Cohen, Isaac Bashevis Singer, Warwick Hutton, Marguerite De Angeli, Maude Petersham, Barbara Cooney, Tasha Tudor, Sholem Asch, Peter Spier, Tomie dePaola, Miriam Chaikin, and Pearl Buck, among many others. Trade publishers have always been active in this area, and included were Atheneum, Harper and Row, Random House, Lothrop, Lee & Shepard, Thomas Y. Crowell, Doubleday, Macmillan, Viking, Holiday House, Putnam, Harcourt Brace, Scribner's, Franklin Watts, and Prentice-Hall, as well as religious publishing houses. Although some of these survive as individual entities, many have been absorbed into conglomerate operations, but the good religious output remains. The first Caldecott Medalist was *Animals of the Bible, A Picture Book* by Dorothy P. Lathrop, published by J. B. Lippincott in 1937, and the most recent, as of this writing, was *The Golem* by David Wisniewski, published by Clarion in 1996.

Until recently the Nativity has been the source of some of the most creative work, including books such as William Kurelek's *A Northern Nativity*, which shows the Holy Family in many ethnic forms appearing in all areas of Canada at the time of the Depression; Julie Vivas' *The Nativity*, in which Mary and Joseph are young, awkward, exuberant teenagers; *The Nativity Play* by Nick Butterworth and Mick Inkpen, which portrays every jerry-built, heartfelt school Christmas pageant in all its hilarity; and *What a Morning! The Christmas Story in Black Spirituals*, edited by John Langstaff and illustrated by Ashley Bryan, which depicts the principals in African American folk art. Now the subject is generally treated more conventionally, although still with great beauty and meaning. Noah and the Flood, with its great potential for humor and winningly-portrayed animals, continues strongly, but there are fewer prayer books and good reference material. Outstandingly beautiful books about Creation have come to the forefront, as have excellent, big, beautiful, brilliantly-illustrated works about comparative religion. The use of reproductions of Renaissance paintings to illustrate topics such as prayer and Bible stories has become popular, particularly with Simon and Schuster. Most biographies continue to be laudatory, with the exception of those dealing with Father Junipero Serra, in which the mission movement is criticized for its treatment and displacement of Native Americans in California. Jewish books have always been good but are now expanding delightfully into holiday material, with authors such as Eric Kimmel, David Adler, Malka Drucker, Nina Jaffe, and Barbara Diamond Goldin. But the most exciting change in religious publishing has been the great increase in books, both informational and fictional, about other than Judeo-Christian religions.

Since religion and spirituality are an integral part of every culture in the world, access to information on all types of faiths should be freely available to readers of all ages. Good literature on these topics will help develop understanding, tolerance, and interest about other peoples, discourage chauvinism and prejudice, and promote global harmony.

In past publications I have discussed extensively religious books published before 1990; and since I do not want to repeat old material, and because books tend to go in and out of print very rapidly, I have limited my bibliography to publications from 1990 forward and to those with overt religious themes. At the end of each section, however, I have named additional, older resources that I consider valuable.

In the cases of variations in spelling, such as Hanukkah and Chanukah, I have followed the form used in the book.

Chapter One

Religions

Comparative Overviews

1.   Birdseye, Debbie Holsclaw, and Tom Birdseye. **What I Believe: Kids Talk About Faith**. New York: Holiday House, 1996. 32p. $15.95. LC 96-11240. ISBN 0-8234-1268-7.

Six articulate twelve- and thirteen-year-olds of the Hindu, Buddhist, Muslim, Jewish, Christian, and Native American faiths tell about their concepts of God and right living. Despite the differences in religious practices, the underlying ethics are the same, reinforcing the ecumenical values of learning about others' spirituality. Good color photographs show the young people in everyday activities in the United States. A reading list is included.

2.   Breuilly, Elizabeth. **Religions of the World: The Illustrated Guide to Origins, Beliefs, Traditions, and Festivals**. New York: Facts on File, 1997. 160p. $29.95. LC 97-22829. ISBN 0-8160-3723-X.

For middle school and up, this superb overview is written in a scholarly but interesting and lucid manner. Discussion includes the history, development, worship, and celebrations for the Abrahamic faiths of Judaism, Christianity, and Islam; the Vedic faiths of Hinduism, Buddhism, and Jainism; and the other major traditions of Shintoism, Taoism, Sikhism, and Bahaism. Color photographs, maps, charts, calendars, and drawings illustrate this attractively formatted book, and additional information is set off in colored boxes. It contains a comparative chart of traditions, holy places, and scriptures; a foreword and an afterword; a glossary; and an index.

3. Brown, Julie, and Robert Brown. **How People Worship**. Milwaukee, WI: Gareth Stevens, 1992. 64p. $14.95. LC 90-23939. ISBN 0-8368-0047-8.

This useful and interesting survey begins by defining religion in general terms. Succinctly described are ancient religions; Native American, Australian Aboriginal, and other tribal religions; Buddhism and other Eastern religions; Hinduism and other Indian religions; Judaism; Christianity; Islam; and some of the newer faiths, such as Bahaism and Rastafarianism. Profusely illustrated in color and black and white, it includes a timeline, glossary, and index.

4. Children of America. **The 11th Commandment: Wisdom from Our Children**. Woodstock, VT: Jewish Lights, 1995. 48p. $16.95. LC 95-38956. ISBN 1-879045-46-X.

Asked to name an additional commandment to follow the ten Moses received from God, children from various religious backgrounds (Roman Catholic, Baptist, Jewish, Presbyterian, Unitarian, Mennonite, Methodist, and United Church of Christ) suggest a wide variety, including "love one another, no matter who," "treat men and women equally," "thou shalt not shoot people," "do sports not drugs," and other heartfelt and telling rules. These commandments are divided into five sections based upon topic: living with other people, the earth, family, ourselves, and God. Boys and girls aged three through twelve created the vivid, brightly colored illustrations.

5. Cohen, Daniel. **Cults**. Brookfield, CT: Millbrook Press, 1994. 144p. $16.40. LC 94-966. ISBN 1-56294-324-3.

These unsensationalized discussions of a wide variety of cults are straightforward and fair. Included are the Branch Davidians, Peoples Temple (Jim Jones), early American groups (Separatists, Quakers, Mormons, Shakers, Amish, and others), Lubavitcher Hasidim, Satanists, witches, Father Divine, the Moonies, and the Children of God. Brainwashing, deprogramming, and mind control are debunked, as is the supposed prevalence of such unspeakable practices as infant sacrifice. The text is factual and absorbing. After extensive research, the author finds that cults are generally short-lived and their danger exaggerated. The book contains black-and-white photographs and drawings, notes, an index, and a bibliography for further reading.

6. Forest, Heather. **Wisdom Tales from Around the World**. Little Rock, AR: August House, 1996. 156p. $17.95pa. LC 96-31141. ISBN 0-87483-479-1.

Parables and folktales from religious traditions worldwide receive broad coverage in this compendium of delightful cautionary tales from India, China, Japan, Africa, Asia, Europe, the Americas, and the Middle East. Included are examples from the Buddha's Jataka tales, the Hindu Panchatantra stories, Taoist parables, Zen Buddhist tales, the midrashic literature of Judaism, and Christian writings.

7. Ganeri, Anita. **Out of the Ark: Stories from the World's Religions**. Ill. Jackie Morris. San Diego, CA: Harcourt Brace, 1996. 96p. $18.00. LC 95-7269. ISBN 0-15-200943-4.

This is a comprehensive source of information about stories of creation, the flood, animal interactions with religious figures, and miraculous births from Buddhist, Shinto, Polynesian, Islamic, Hindu, Australian Aboriginal, Sikh, and

Judeo-Christian sources. Included are tales of Shiva, Parvati, Ganesh, the Golem, Guru Nanak, Moses and the ten plagues, Siddhartha's life, Muhammad's escape from Mecca, Jesus' crucifixion and resurrection, and much more. "Fact Files" give a short description of the history, deities, ways of worship, festivals, sacred places, and holy books of Buddhism, Christianity, Hinduism, Islam, Shintoism, and Sikhism; and a who's who section identifies the names in the book. Spirited, bright watercolors illustrate the stories appealingly.

8.   Ganeri, Anita. **Religions Explained: A Beginner's Guide to World Faiths**. A Henry Holt Reference Book. New York: Henry Holt, 1997. 69p. $18.95. LC 96-42996. ISBN 0-8050-4874-X.

This ambitious undertaking gives succinct overviews of ancient religions (Egyptian, Mesopotamian, Greek, Roman, Aztec, and Norse); "People of the Book" (Judaism, Christianity, and Islam); the religions of India (Hinduism, Jainism, Zoroastrianism, Buddhism, and Sikhism); Chinese and Japanese religions (Confucianism, Taoism, Shintoism, and Zen Buddhism); spirit religions in North and South America, Africa, and Australasia; and new religions (Rastafarianism, Bahaism, Hare Krishnaism, Mennonitism and the Amish, Mormonism, New Age movements, and the Unification Church). The crisp, readable text only touches briefly upon each religion because of the wide scope of coverage. Attractively presented, the book contains many color photographs, artwork, a glossary, and an index.

9.   Gellman, Marc, and Thomas Hartman. **How Do You Spell God? Answers to the Big Questions from Around the World**. Ill. Jos. A. Smith. New York: William Morrow, 1995. 206p. $15.00. LC 94-28770. ISBN 0-688-13041-0.

Rabbi Gellman and Monsignor Hartman review many aspects of the major religions: similarities and differences; important questions asked and answers given by each; teachers and deities; holy books, places, days, rituals, ways of training clergy, and types of architecture; and prayers and hopes for an afterlife. Instead of considering each faith in a separate section, they are compared and contrasted alongside one another. The tone is strongly ecumenical and nonexclusive. Although the subject is serious and treated with great respect, the writing is informal and often humorous and colloquial to appeal to older elementary and teenage readers, and the concepts are simplified. The book is occasionally illustrated with pleasant pen-and-ink drawings, and includes an introduction by the Dalai Lama.

10.   Hallam, Elizabeth M. **Gods and Goddesses: A Treasury of Deities and Tales from World Mythology**. New York: Macmillan, 1996. 184p. $24.00. LC 96-20795. ISBN 0-02-861421-6.

This comprehensive overview is rather arbitrarily divided into areas of dominion: supreme rule and creation; the sun; the earth, sea, and sky; the natural world; fertility; love, marriage, and motherhood; the household; arts and crafts; truth, knowledge, and justice; war and peace; and death, destruction, magic, and the underworld. Some of the deities are ancient, but many are still revered today by Native American, Polynesian, African, Japanese, Australian Aboriginal, Chinese, Hindu, and Inuit peoples. The groupings make for interesting comparisons, although the entries are necessarily succinct. Many good black-and-white and color illustrations complement the lively text, and three excellent indexes guide access to the information.

11. Kalman, Bobbie. **India: The Culture**. The Lands, Peoples, and Cultures Series. New York: Crabtree, 1990. 32p. $7.95pa. ISBN 0-86505-292-1.

Brilliant color photographs, a large format, and many short sections of information provide an appealing overall view of Indian culture, which includes Muslims, Sikhs, Buddhists, Parsees, Jains, and Christians, as well as the predominant Hindus. A condensation of each religion's beliefs is given. Festivals, religious sites, wedding ceremonies, and art are also discussed. The book has an index and a glossary.

12. Kalman, Bobbie. **Vietnam: The Culture**. The Lands, Peoples, and Cultures Series. New York: Crabtree, 1996. 32p. $14.36. LC 95-51995. ISBN 0-86505-225-5.

Because the various religions of the Vietnamese people are closely interwoven in their lives, about half of this book discusses the religious aspects of their culture. Architecture, the various beliefs (Confucianism, Christianity, Mahayana Buddhism, Taoism, Cao Dai, and Tam Giao), monks and monasteries, wedding and death customs, and Tet and other festivals are briefly described in a clear, interesting text illustrated with excellent color photographs. A glossary and index are included.

13. Langley, Myrtle. **Religion**. Eyewitness Books Series. New York: Alfred A. Knopf, 1996. 60p. $19.00. LC 96-12236. ISBN 0-679-88123-9.

The founders, tenets, and ways of worship of the Hindu, Buddhist, Taoist, Jainist, Sikh, Zoroastrian, Judaic, Christian, Islamic, primitive, and ancient Greek and Egyptian religions are discussed succinctly and illustrated lavishly. Informative captions accompany the color photographs, pictures of sculptures, drawings, and reproductions of paintings. The book includes an index.

14. Maestro, Betsy. **The Story of Religion**. Ill. Giulio Maestro. New York: Clarion/Houghton Mifflin, 1996. 48p. $14.95. LC 92-38980. ISBN 0-395-62364-2.

This extremely broad, ecumenical survey of religion and religions begins with a discussion of primitive peoples, the power of spirits, nature religions, and Egyptian and Greek deities. Segueing into Chinese Taoism and Confucianism, Hinduism, and Buddhism, the book provides more details of origins and beliefs, then progresses to the three Middle Eastern and related religions: Judaism, Christianity, and Islam. Sacred texts, festivals, and holidays are described briefly. Thumbnail sketches of Zoroastrianism, Jainism, Shintoism, and Sikhism are provided. Atheists and agnostics are also mentioned. The text stresses the similarities among the religions, as well as their differences, and concludes that many paths lead to God. The book is attractively illustrated and contains an index.

15. Matthews, Andrew. **Marduk the Mighty: And Other Stories of Creation**. Ill. Sheila Moxley. Brookfield, CT: Millbrook Press, 1997. 96p. $16.90. LC 96-41710. ISBN 0-7613-0204-2.

Creation tales from many cultures, such as Judeo-Christian, Shinto, Native American, Taoist, Hindu, Australian Aboriginal, and African, are freely interpreted, vividly written, short, and easy to read. The comparisons and contrasts among them are fascinating. The illustrations have the brilliant color and simple shapes of folk art. An index is included.

16.   McElrath, William N. **Ways We Worship**. Hauppauge, NY: Barron's Educational Series, 1997. 238p. $16.95. LC 96-39694. ISBN 0-8120-6625-1.

This rather talkative and didactic but informative discussion of Judaism, Christianity, Islam, Hinduism, Taoism, Shintoism, Buddhism, Confucianism, and Sikhism is written in a conversational style. It includes a section about primal religions throughout the world and a section about new and unusual religions. An excellent bibliography is grouped by faith, for easy use by young readers, and the glossary is extensive. Ink-and-watercolor illustrations, maps, reproductions of paintings, large type, and a varied format enhance the presentation.

17.   Meredith, Susan. **The Usborne Book of World Religions**. London: Usborne, 1995. 64p. $9.95pa. ISBN 0-7460-1750-2.

An interesting introduction discusses religion in general: its rules, scriptures, priests, ways of worship, prayer, and purpose. It also considers religion's effects on wars, persecutions, the role of women, art, architecture, and so on. Extensive information about Hinduism, Buddhism, Judaism, Christianity, Islam, and Sikhism follows, along with a few paragraphs of information each about Shintoism, Taoism, Confucianism, Jainism, Zoroastrianism, Bahaism, and Rastafarianism. The book is clearly written and generously illustrated with color photographs and artwork. It includes a world map showing the distribution of religions, a timeline, religious sayings from the major religions, a glossary, and an index.

18.   Osborne, Mary Pope. **One World, Many Religions: The Ways We Worship**. New York: Borzoi/Alfred A. Knopf, 1997. 86p. $25.00. LC 96-836. ISBN 0-679-83930-5.

In this outstanding introduction to seven major religions, the material about Judaism, Christianity, Islam, Buddhism, Hinduism, Confucianism, and Taoism is skillfully assembled and clearly expressed. The history and beliefs of each are crystallized in a respectful manner and ecumenical tone. Excellent color photographs, many of which are full page and well chosen to interest young readers; large type; maps showing the geographic distribution of the religions; and a timeline, glossary, bibliography, and index make this an admirable beginner's book for the study of comparative religion.

19.   Pilling, Ann. **Creation: Read-Aloud Stories from Many Lands**. Ill. Michael Foreman. Cambridge, MA: Candlewick Press, 1997. 96p. $19.99. LC 96-38745. ISBN 1-56402-888-7.

These entertaining tales of the beginnings of the world and its peoples include myths from the Chinese, Native American, Australian Aboriginal, and African traditions. The large ink-and-watercolor pictures are clever, creative, and bright. A bibliography is included.

20.   Sita, Lisa. **Worlds of Belief: Religion and Spirituality**. Woodbridge, CT: Blackbirch Press, 1995. 80p. $21.95. LC 94-38278. ISBN 1-56711-125-4.

This overview is unique in that it describes many more religions and religious practices than just those of the major faiths. It is divided by geographic region: the Americas; Africa; Europe and the Middle East; and Asia, Australia, and the South Pacific. Within each region, sections about community rituals and celebrations and about entering into the spiritual community include holidays and festivals, initiation rites, preparation of religious leaders, birth and death customs, and so on. Some subjects, such as the Latino Day of the Dead, the Hopi kachina spirits, the Dreamtime of the Australian Aborigines, and the Christian/African traditions of Santaria in Cuba and Vodou in Haiti, are discussed in greater depth. Altogether, this well-researched book with excellent color photographs is absorbing and ecumenical. It includes a glossary, reading list, and index.

21.   Underwood, Lynn. **Religions of the World**. Milwaukee, WI: Gareth Stevens, 1992. 64p. $14.95. LC 90-20343. ISBN 0-8368-0022-2.

An introductory section explains the development and dissemination of religion, and the difference between prophetic and mystical. Short descriptions of a wide-ranging spectrum of faiths follow. Included are ancient, tribal, Far Eastern, Indian, Jewish, Islamic, and Christian religions, as well as the more recently developed religions, such as Bahaism and Jehovah's Witnesses. The descriptions are generously illustrated with color and black-and-white photographs and artwork. A timeline, index, and glossary facilitate the use of this broad overview.

22.   Wilson, Colin. **The Atlas of Holy Places and Sacred Sites**. New York: Dorling Kindersley, 1996. 192p. $29.95. LC 96-5632. ISBN 0-7894-1051-6.

Because the text is divided into readable blocks, and superb illustrations and boxes of additional information are generously distributed on each page, what is essentially an adult reference book should appeal to younger readers. The comprehensive subject matter is divided geographically: Africa and the Middle East, Greece and the Mediterranean, the United Kingdom and Ireland, North America, Central and South America, the Pacific and Australasia, the Far East, and the East. Included are ancient and modern sites, such as the Great Zimbabwe, the Jenne Mosque, Santa Sophia, Chartres, Iona, Kilauwea, Machu Picchu, Uluru, Samarkand, and many more, all spectacularly photographed in color. Sacred sites are marked and dated in a gazetteer. The book includes notes, a glossary, a bibliography, and an index.

23.   Yolen, Jane. **Sacred Places**. Ill. David Shannon. San Diego, CA: Harcourt Brace, 1996. 40p. $16.00. LC 92-30323. ISBN 0-15-269953-8.

These evocative, unrhymed, rhythmic, deceptively simple yet gripping poems celebrate Delphi (Greek), Copan (Mayan), the Wailing Wall (Jewish), Easter Island, Stonehenge, Ganga (Hindu), Uluru (Australian Aboriginal), cathedrals, the Bo Tree (Buddhist), Mecca, Itsukushima (Shinto), and the Four Corners (generic Native American). The book begins and ends with an admonitory plea to remember and respect the holiness of a sacred place. The dramatic, full-page illustrations are monumental, massive, and mysterious. Explanatory notes are included.

Comparative Customs and Celebrations

24.   Burke, Deirdre. **Food and Fasting**. Comparing Religions Series. New York: Thomson Learning, 1993. 32p. $15.98. ISBN 1-56847-034-7.

Dietary restrictions, forbidden foods, slaughter methods, rules of preparation, blessings and graces, eating together at places of worship, food symbolism, and compulsory and voluntary fasting are discussed as they pertain to Hinduism, Islam, Judaism, Sikhism, and Christianity. The book includes color photographs, a glossary, a reading list, and an index.

25. Compton, Anita. **Marriage Customs**. Comparing Religions Series. New York: Thomson Learning, 1993. 32p. $15.98. ISBN 1-56847-033-9.

In this comparison of Hindu, Muslim, Sikh, Jewish, and Christian marriages, the main topics include vows, promises, contracts, signs, and symbols, such as the sacred fire for Hindus, the chuppah for Jews, the veil, the color of the wedding dress, and the rings. The book has good color photographs, an index, a glossary, and a reading list.

26. Kalman, Bobbie. **We Celebrate the Harvest**. Ill. Janet Wilson and Greg Ruhl. Holidays and Festivals Series. New York: Crabtree, 1993. 56p. $14.36. LC 93-27353. ISBN 0-86505-044-9.

Harvest festivals discussed include the Moon Festival of China, Sukkoth, Honensai in Japan, Pongal in India, Festa dos Tabuleiros in Portugal, Native American feasts, Harvest Home, and Thanksgiving in the United States and Canada. Recipes, stories, poems, and crafts supplement the short descriptions of the holidays. The illustrations are adequate but not outstanding. An index is appended.

27. Liptak, Karen. **Coming-of-Age: Traditions and Rituals Around the World**. Brookfield, CT: Millbrook Press, 1994. 126p. $16.40. LC 93-1414. ISBN 1-56294-243-3.

Religion and anthropology are closely interwoven in this well-researched, absorbing work that describes how young people of many cultures are initiated into the adult community. Spiritual rituals and taboos that play significant roles for Amazonia and tribal African youth, Australian Aborigines, and Native Americans of the Northwest Coastal, Sioux, Apache, and Navaho nations are discussed. Bar mitzvah and bat mitzvah, Christian confirmation, Hindu Upanaya, Buddhist Shinbyu, and Hispanic Quinceanos are detailed as well. Exploring the rich significance of each experience helps to promote cross-cultural understanding and admiration by pointing out the varieties of the rites and their meanings, thus giving readers an insight into how others live. The book has good black-and-white photographs, source notes, a glossary, a bibliography, and an index.

28. Livingston, Myra Cohn. **Festivals**. Ill. Leonard Everett Fisher. New York: Holiday House, 1996. 32p. $16.95. LC 95-31055. ISBN 0-8234-1217-2.

In a large, bright, handsome format, fourteen short poems celebrate religious and secular holidays from many cultures. Topics include the Chinese New Year, Tet Nguyen-Dan, Purim, Mardi Gras, Ramadan and Id-ul-Fitr, Diwali, the Day of the Dead, Las Posadas, and the Feast of Saint Lucy. The text of the spirited verses is placed on dramatic, double-page spreads filled with powerful shapes and brilliant colors. A table of contents, glossary, and notes are included.

29. Prior, Katherine. **Initiation Customs**. Comparing Religions Series. New York: Thomson Learning, 1993. 32p. $15.98. ISBN 1-56846-035-5.

Religious initiation is defined as being a child's entry into the responsibilities of his or her faith. It includes bar mitzvah and bat mitzvah, Roman Catholic First Communion, Upanayana for Hindu boys, Pravrajya for children training as Buddhist monks or nuns, Sikh Amrit, and Muslim study of the Koran at age seven. The details of the preparations and ceremonies are given. Attractive photographs illustrate the easy-to-read text, and the book includes a glossary, reading list, and index.

30. Prior, Katherine. **Pilgrimages and Journeys**. Comparing Religions Series. New York: Thomson Learning, 1993. 32p. $15.98. ISBN 1-56847-032-0.

The meaning of pilgrimage and how the participants travel, dress, and worship, as well as examples of holy places and their historical significance, are discussed for Hindus, Buddhists, Muslims, Sikhs, and Christians. The simply written text has good color photographs and a glossary, reading list, and index.

31. Rushton, Lucy. **Birth Customs**. Comparing Religions Series. New York: Thomson Learning, 1993. 32p. $15.98. LC 92-42174. ISBN 1-56847-030-4.

Comparisons and contrasts, not only of the ceremonies surrounding birth but also of the religious beliefs underlying them, are included for Hindus, Buddhists, Sikhs, Jews, Christians, and Muslims. Each chapter has a specific theme, such as welcoming the baby, belonging to a religious community, choosing a name, a new beginning, and so on. Good color photographs illustrate the text, and a glossary, reading list, and index are included.

32. Rushton, Lucy. **Death Customs**. Comparing Religions Series. New York: Thomson Learning, 1993. 32p. $15.98. ISBN 1-56847-031-2.

In this comparison of Christian, Jewish, Sikh, Muslim, Buddhist, and Hindu death customs and beliefs, topics include resurrection, reincarnation, nirvana, and the return to Nam and Brahman; the preparation of the body for death; funerals, burials, and cremations; mourning and remembrance; judgment; and afterlife. Color photographs illustrate a clear, interesting text. The book includes a glossary, reading list, and index.

33. Viesti, Joe, and Diane Hall. **Celebrate! in South Asia**. New York: Lothrop, Lee & Shepard, 1996. Unp. $16.00. LC 96-6315. ISBN 0-688-13774-1.

Exciting color photographs illustrate these Buddhist, Hindu, and Islamic holidays: Holi in India, Esala Perahera and Wesak in Sri Lanka, Eid-ul-Fitr in Pakistan, Paro Tsechu in Bhutan, Schwedagon Pagoda Festival in Myanmar, and Tihar in Nepal. The accompanying explanatory text is excellent, and a map is included.

34. Viesti, Joe, and Diane Hall. **Celebrate! in Southeast Asia**. New York: Lothrop, Lee & Shepard, 1996. Unp. $16.00. LC 96-6314. ISBN 0-688-13488-2.

A succinct, lucid text describes the Buddhist Songkran in Thailand; Thaipusam, the Hindu day of atonement in Malaysia; the Hindu Kesada offering given at a steaming volcano in Indonesia; a cremation ceremony in Hindu Bali; Apalit River Festival, the Catholic feast day of St. Peter and St. Paul in the Philippines; the Buddhist That Luang in Laos; and the Cambodian Chaul Chhnaim. Spectacular, large color photographs bring the festivals to life in all their brilliance and gaiety. A map is included.

35. Wilcox, Jane. **Why Do We Celebrate That?** Danbury, CT: Franklin Watts, 1996. 32p. $18.00. LC 96-419. ISBN 0-531-14393-7.

In this entertaining juxtaposition of social and religious customs of cultures ranging from Hindu, Muslim, Native American, and Chinese, to Zoroastrian, Celtic, and Aztec, the celebrations are divided into topics such as birth, coming-of-age, death, birthdays, agricultural, new year, and seasonal. A succinct paragraph, illustrated with a lighthearted cartoon, is devoted to each. This large and detailed book is replete with easy-to-assimilate information, and includes an index.

Older and Noteworthy

Older titles in the general area of religions that are worth exploring include *Caves to Cathedrals* by Carl E. Hiller (Little, Brown, 1974), *One God: The Ways We Worship Him* (Lothrop, Lee & Shepard, 1944) and *Their Search for God* (Lothrop, Lee & Shepard, 1947) by Florence Mary Fitch, *In Search of God* (Atheneum, 1979) and *In the Name of God* (Atheneum, 1980) by Marietta Moskin, *My Friends' Beliefs* by Hiley Ward (Walker, 1988), *In the Beginning: Creation Stories from Around the World* by Virginia Hamilton (Harcourt Brace, 1988), *Gods and Men: Myths and Legends from the World's Religions* by John Bailey (Oxford, 1981), *Religion* by Gilda Berger (Watts, 1983), *Beginnings: Creation Myths of the World* by Penelope Farmer (Atheneum, 1978), *American Saints and Seers* by Edward Rice (Four Winds, 1982), and *The Great Religions* by Floyd Ross (Fawcett, 1956).

Chapter Two

God

36. Appelt, Kathi. **I See the Moon**. Ill. Debra Reid Jenkins. Grand Rapids, MI: William B. Eerdmans, 1997. 24p. $15.00. LC 96-33232. ISBN 0-8028-5118-5.

A young girl dreams she is sailing alone in a tiny boat on a roughly rolling sea. The stars form a path, the wind fills the sails, the rising sun lights her way, and a dove leads her to shore. She knows that all these events are signs of God's loving care. This simple, sweet poem is resplendently illustrated in gleaming colors.

37. Boritzer, Etan. **What Is God?** Ill. Robbie Marantz. Willowdale, Ontario, Canada: Firefly Books, 1990. Unp. $5.95pa. ISBN 0-920668-88-7.

A generic God, one that pervades everything and connects all of us to one another in love, is the answer given in this gentle, caring, ecumenical exposition. It recognizes all faiths as valid, urges prayer, praises universal ethics, and mentions many great religious teachers and holy books. The text is conversational and easy to understand. Full-page, vivid, cartoon-style pictures reinforce the mood of childlike wonder about this mystery.

38. Carlstrom, Nancy White. **Does God Know How to Tie Shoes?** Ill. Lori McElrath-Eslick. Grand Rapids, MI: William B. Eerdmans, 1993. Unp. $7.50. LC 94-136880. ISBN 0-8028-5074-X.

A young girl questions her parents about God: What does he wear? How does he talk? Does he paint, sleep, sing, cry? Her parents answer her with information found in the Psalms but told at a young child's level, balancing the everyday and specific with the Bible's sweeping universality. Double-page reproductions of paintings that depict beautiful nature scenes form the backdrop for the gently comforting text.

39. Coles, Robert. **In God's House: Drawings by Children**. Grand Rapids, MI: William B. Eerdmans, 1996. Unp. $15.00. LC 95-53990. ISBN 0-8028-5126-6.

Children at risk, who are struggling to make sense of the world and seeking a better life in the next, have drawn their visions of how and where God lives. The children are aged four through twelve. Some of their ideas about God's dwellings include a gold house with two suns, where all are happy and free; clouds, enabling him to be with us always; a big castle in heaven; and the rainbow. The artists explain their drawings, and the book ends with five short, moving poems written by children. The tone throughout is sincere and spiritual.

40. Gateley, Edwina. **God Goes on Vacation**. Ill. author. Trabuco Canyon, CA: Source Books, 1994. Unp. $8.95pa. LC 94-33574. ISBN 0-940147-31-9.

God, a wavy-haired figure in athletic shoes and a daisy diadem, is tired from solving people's problems. He and his chief angel, Stardrop, an African American with corkscrew curls, head for the beach to water ski, eat ice cream, and have fun, just the way his human creations do. When he returns to heaven, he leaves a bit of his special magic in everyone's heart. Happily slapdash, color cartoons sustain the lighthearted mood.

41. Hample, Stuart, and Eric Marshall. **Children's Letters to God**. Ill. Tom Bloom. New York: Workman, 1991. Unp. $6.95. LC 90-21211. ISBN 0-89480-9997.

This collection of succinct, innocent, hilarious yet serious questions, comments, complaints, and appreciations directed to God from elementary school boys and girls is reproduced in the children's own handwriting. Their thoughts are touching and to the point. The perky illustrations, which resemble crayon work, add to the humorous effect.

42. Hebblethwaite, Margaret. **My Secret Life: A Friendship with God**. Ill. Peter Kavanagh. Wilton, CT: Morehouse, 1991. 32p. $11.95. LC 90-21550. ISBN 0-8192-1538-4.

To a young, blond-haired boy, God is like a secret, invisible friend with whom he talks freely about all his problems and interests, seeking out quiet places for his communication. He may be up in the attic or out in the garden or in bed at night. God hears, understands, and forgives everything. He always has the child's best interests at heart. Warm, lively watercolor cartoons show the boy engaged in his everyday activities.

43. McKissack, Patricia, and Fredrick McKissack. **God Makes All Things New**. Ill. Ching. Minneapolis, MN: Augsburg Fortress, 1993. Unp. $4.99pa. LC 93-70326. ISBN 0-8066-2653-4.

Life begins in spring with birds' nests and lambs, grows and changes as ducklings swim and tadpoles become frogs in summer, and then ebbs with fall and winter. Life thus begins and ends for all God's creatures, great and small, until the promised day when death will no longer exist. The watercolor pictures of winsome animals show none that are ill or dead; only a graveyard scene indicates the presence of mortality.

44. Rock, Lois. **Bible Words About Love for Children**. Ill. Claire Henley. Colorado Springs, CO: Lion, 1996. Unp. $8.99. ISBN 0-7459-3346-7.

1 Corinthians 13 is explained in easy terms for young children, emphasizing that God loves, comforts, approves, forgives, perseveres alongside, and protects them every day of their lives. These attributes are explained in anecdotes of everyday life, with a short prayer for each situation. Bright pictures show children behaving badly and being nice.

45. Sproul, R. C. **The King Without a Shadow**. Ill. Liz Bonham. Colorado Springs, CO: Chariot, 1996. Unp. $16.99. LC 95-23573. ISBN 0-7814-0257-3.

A great king who wants to lose his shadow journeys into the desert to consult a holy prophet living in a cave. He is told that the only king who has no shadow, because he is all-powerful, pure, and perfect, is God. This well-written parable for older children has vigorous, realistic pictures set in medieval times.

46. Williamson, Marianne, and Emma Williamson. **Emma and Mommy Talk to God**. Ill. Julia Neman. New York: HarperCollins, 1996. Unp. $14.95. LC 95-1697. ISBN 0-06-026464-0.

Mommy has taught Emma to pray to God every day, thank him for the beauties of nature, and ask help in times of trouble. She explains that God has created everyone on earth and that his love is in all of them. One night, Emma wakes up frightened but soon realizes that angels have gathered around her bed to comfort her. She prays for a boy at school who teases her, and he becomes happier and more considerate. The spiritual message of love and forgiveness is appropriate for all faiths that recognize a merciful supreme being. The full- and double-page illustrations are executed in an idealized realistic technique and radiate warmth and beauty.

God's Creativity As One of His Aspects

47. Bea, Holly. **Where Does God Live?** Ill. Kim Howard. Tiburon, CA: Starseed Press, 1997. Unp. $14.00. LC 96-30382. ISBN 0-915811-73-1.

This sweetly didactic story in rhyme is about Hope, an African American child who delights in the beauty and goodness of the world and wonders where God lives. Hope's wise grandmother explains that God is in all of creation, always ready to teach, strengthen, and love. This broad, nongender-specific concept is not limited to any one faith. The dynamic, decorative illustrations are primitively styled.

48. Carroll, Michael. **Lightning and Rainbows: A Child's Guide to God's Wonders in the Skies**. Ill. author. Colorado Springs, CO: ChariotVictor, 1997. Unp. $12.99. ISBN 0-78143-000-3.

This basic scientific discussion of clouds, wind, storms, and seasons has a Scripture citation for each topic and suggests that God demonstrates his power and majesty through these phenomena. The biblical-storm stories of Noah, Jonah, Jesus and his disciples on the Sea of Galilee, and Elijah rising to heaven on the whirlwind are cited. The color photographs and reproductions of paintings are magnificent.

49. Carroll, Michael. **Spinning Worlds: A Child's Guide to God's Creation in the Heavens**. Ill. author. Wheaton, IL: Victor Books, 1996. Unp. $12.99. ISBN 1-56476-571-7.

Color photographs and reproductions of meticulously detailed, large, eerie paintings of the nine planets of our solar system dramatize the clearly written text that describes them. The variety of God's creativity is stressed throughout, and a quotation from the Bible precedes each section. A glossary is included.

50. Carroll, Michael. **Volcanoes and Earthquakes: A Child's Guide to God's Power Beneath Our Feet**. Ill. author. Colorado Springs, CO: Chariot-Victor, 1997. Unp. $12.99. ISBN 1-56476-602-0.

Significant biblical mountains, such as the holy mount of the Garden of Eden, Mount Sinai, Mount Ararat, Mount Moriah, and that of the Sermon on the Mount, are discussed within simple scientific explanations of the formation and action of volcanoes, geysers, mountains, glaciers, and canyons. The section about earthquakes mentions the books of Revelation, Acts, and Matthew, and a quotation from Scripture introduces each topic. Supplementing the text are a glossary and spectacular color photographs and reproductions of paintings.

51. Hughes, Ted. **Tales of the Early World**. Ill. Andrew Davidson. New York: Farrar, Straus & Giroux, 1991. 122p. $13.95. ISBN 0-374-37377-9.

In an entertaining account by England's poet laureate, God is quite human and sweats and strains over the creation of his marvelous creatures. He has an old mother and eats sausages. Ten short, imaginative tales recount the making of Woman, mice, eels, lions, parrots, horses, earthworms, peacocks, and fleas, and the theft of the birds by an evil Black Hole. Some of the creatures are cantankerous and vain and receive their comeuppance in appropriate ways. Brilliantly written with great charm, the book is illustrated with handsome black-and-white engravings.

52. Patterson, Elizabeth Burman. **Whose Eyes Are These?** Ill. author. Nashville, TN: Tommy Nelson, 1997. 31p. $14.99. ISBN 0-8499-1464-7.

Outstanding watercolors of realistic beauty, concentrating on the eyes of a variety of creatures, show the richness of God's creation. Illustrated are a cat, frog, lion, orangutan, koala, and raccoon, along with many others. The final page is mirrored to reflect the eyes of the reader, who has also been uniquely made by God. The four-line verses accompanying the pictures are pedestrian, but they help a child reader identify the animals.

53. Rylant, Cynthia. **The Dreamer**. Ill. Barry Moser. New York: Blue Sky Press, 1993. Unp. $14.95. LC 93-19915. ISBN 0-590-47341-7.

God as a shy young artist daydreams the Creation. He sets about cutting out stars; molding Planet Earth; painting the foam-flecked waters blue and the grass and forests a soothing green; forming the whale, cow, elephant, and polar bear; and finally designing a new artist in his own image to keep him company. From this time forward, the world is filled with daydreaming artists of all races, who call the first artist "God." The poetic, simple text is illustrated with magnificent realism in watercolor.

54. Wood, Douglas. **Old Turtle**. Ill. Cheng-Khee Chee. Duluth, MN: Pfeifer-Hamilton, 1992. Unp. $17.95. LC 91-73527. ISBN 0-938586-48-3.

In this modern fable, each of God's varied creations, which include animals, rocks, winds, waters, sky, birds, trees, and fish, likens God to some lovely aspect of itself. When a loud argument ensues, an ancient turtle points out that God embodies not just one but every one of these characteristics. She also announces that God's mightiest creation, man, is about to come upon earth. Alas, in time, men forget God's truth as they quarrel, pillage, and destroy, but eventually they repent and bring smiles to the faces of Old Turtle and God. The misty, softly shaded watercolors enhance the beautifully written text.

Similes and Metaphors

55. Bohler, Carolyn Stahl. **God Is Like a Mother Hen and Much, Much More**. Ill. Dean Niklas. Louisville, KY: Presbyterian, 1996. Unp. $15.00. ISBN 1-57153-200-5.

God's qualities are described with similes: he is like a mother hen, a caring father, a smiling teacher, a best friend, a mother kissing hurts, and other everyday comparisons familiar to young children, enabling them to relate to his loving care. Supportive Scripture citations are given. The simple, colorful illustrations show anthropomorphic chickens enjoying all of God's benefits.

56. Erickson, Mary E. **What Is God Like?** Ill. Anita C. Nelson. Colorado Springs, CO: ChariotVictor, 1990. Unp. $9.99. LC 89-39729. ISBN 1-55513-273-1.

Similes for God as a potter, the rain, a shepherd, a rock, a guide, a pine tree, a king, a lamp, a gardener, and many more are drawn from the Bible. Each is introduced with a Scripture quotation, explained in simple, comforting language, and illustrated with familiar scenes from contemporary life.

57. Kroll, Virginia. **I Wanted to Know All About God**. Ill. Debra Reid Jenkins. Grand Rapids, MI: William B. Eerdmans, 1994. Unp. $15.00. LC 93-37382. ISBN 0-8028-5078-2.

The gentleness of a butterfly, the strength of the ocean, the love of a grandmother's hug, the safety and warmth of a bed at night, the artistry of a spider's web, and others of God's qualities are expressed in terms young children can understand. Large reproductions of beautiful oil paintings show happy children of many ethnic backgrounds in lush outdoor scenes.

58. McCaslin, Susan. **Thinking About God**. Ill. Dorry Clay. Mystic, CT: Twenty-Third Publications, 1994. Unp. $7.95 ISBN 0-89622-615-8.

The nondenominational concept of God as creator and spirit, blending both masculine and feminine virtues, is well expressed in a simply written dialogue between a young girl and her mother at bedtime. The two discuss God's ongoing creative work and caring love for everything and everybody, and the importance of prayer. They compare God to the wind, the sweet perfume of a flower, the ocean, and a brooding mother bird. Bright, double-page spreads with large figures show the young girl floating dreamily through starry skies as she thinks about God's various aspects.

59. Rock, Lois. **A First Look at God**. Ill. Carolyn Cox. A First Look Series. Elgin, IL: Lion, 1994. Unp. $6.99. LC 94-9715. ISBN 0-7459-2496-4.

Although oriented toward Christianity, the statements and comparisons made would be appropriate for any monotheistic religion. Similes for God as a father, mother, friend, rescuer, creator, provider, lawgiver, and ruler of the world are comforting for young children. All are expressed in understandable terms, supported by simplified quotations from the Bible, and illustrated with softly shaded watercolors.

60. Sasso, Sandy Eisenberg. **God's Paintbrush**. Ill. Annette Compton. Woodstock, VT: Jewish Lights, 1992. Unp. $15.95. LC 92-15493. ISBN 1-879045-22-2.

Large, sweeping watercolors reflect children's personal imaginings about God. A sunbeam as God's paintbrush, raindrops as God's tears, God's hands rocking the world, and God's breath in music are among the sweet and reassuring themes illustrated.

61. Sasso, Sandy Eisenberg. **In God's Name**. Ill. Phoebe Stone. Woodstock, VT: Jewish Lights, 1994. 32p. $19.95. LC 94-18262. ISBN 1-879045-26-5.

In the search for God's name, each person has a unique choice. It may be Source of Life, Creator of Light, Shepherd, Maker of Peace, Rock, Healer, Redeemer, Ancient One, Comforter, Mother, Father, or Friend. When all the people come together at a mirroring pond, they realize that although their names are good, God's truest name is One. The simple, meaningful text is illustrated with large reproductions of bright, folk-art paintings of multiethnic children and adults in mythical, mystical settings.

Pet Heavens

62. Allan, Nicholas. **Heaven**. Ill. author. New York: HarperFestival, 1996. Unp. $10.95. ISBN 0-694-00874-5.

Dill, a dog, packs to go to heaven, but his young caretaker, Lily, does not want him to leave. At the church cemetery, where they are met by dog angels, Dill describes heaven as a place where there are bones, lampposts, and smelly things for him to enjoy. He expects to go there even though he has sinned a little on earth. After his death, Lily finds a stray puppy and sees to it that he has all the special things that meant so much to Dill. Funny, cartoon-style ink-and-watercolor illustrations keep the tone lighthearted.

63. Rylant, Cynthia. **Cat Heaven**. Ill. author. New York: Blue Sky Press, 1997. Unp. $15.95. ISBN 0-590-10054-8.

Cats go to heaven, too, and have their fill of kitty toys, bowls of milk, trees to climb, dishes of sardines and salmon, caresses from affectionate angels, and close encounters with a loving God, pictured as a kindly, white-mustached senior citizen. Bright illustrations, with a winningly slapdash, childlike style, flood the double-page spreads in bursts of color.

64. Rylant, Cynthia. **Dog Heaven**. Ill. author. New York: Blue Sky/Scholastic, 1995. Unp. $14.95. LC 94-40950. ISBN 0-590-41701-0.

God knows everything dogs like best: fields in which to run and run; angel children to love them dearly; fluffy cloud beds where they have no bad dreams; biscuits shaped like cats, squirrels, and ice cream cones; and, finally, reunion with human friends in heaven. The sweet, sentimental text has big, bright, exuberant yet simple illustrations.

Older and Noteworthy

Additional recommended titles for young children, appropriate to their understanding and appreciation of God, include *Forest of Dreams* by Rosemary Wells (Dial, 1988), *Three in One* by Joanne Marxhausen (Concordia, 1973), *One Spring Day* by Shigeko Yano (Judson, 1977), *Jake and Honeybunch Go to Heaven* by Margot Zemach (Farrar, 1982), *Potter, Come Fly to the First of the Earth* by Walter Wangerin (Cook, 1985), and *What Does God Do? God Speaks to Children About His World* by Hans Wilhelm (Sweet, 1987).

Chapter Three

Prayer

65.   Fairbridge, Lynne. **We Need a Moose: A Story About Prayer**. Ill. Georgia Graham. Wheaton, IL: Victor Books, 1996. Unp. $10.99. ISBN 1-56476-565-2.

During the course of a week, because his mother is busy, tired, and cross, a young boy prays for a moose to ride, a chimp to greet him cheerfully, a camel to supply drinks, and an alligator to fill his wading pool. Though none of his requests is fulfilled, he does get a new baby brother (in what is apparently a home birth), sent from God, and feels satisfied. The whimsical, rhyming text is enlivened by well-executed, realistic artwork in bright colors.

66.   Goble, Paul. **I Sing for the Animals**. Ill. author. New York: Bradbury Press, 1991. Unp. $9.95. LC 90-19812. ISBN 0-02-737725-3.

Inspired by the respect shown by Native Americans for the natural world, this simple prayer envisions God in all creation and imagines the voices of all things on earth are engaged in constant prayer. The premise is that nature provides strength and stability in a world constantly changed by humanity. The illustrations are crisp, colorful, and bold.

67.   Marzollo, Jean. **Home Sweet Home**. Ill. Ashley Wolff. New York: HarperCollins, 1997. Unp. $14.95. LC 96-35410. ISBN 0-06-027562-6.

An endearing and loving celebration of the world asks blessings upon a variety of earth's aspects: each bee, tree, giraffe, hare, wren, turtle, snake, breath of air, moonbeam, and so on, culminating in blessings for each new birth. The sweetly rhyming, succinct text is greatly enhanced by the brilliant, double-page illustrations filled with strength and beauty.

68. Sattgast, L. J., and Jan Elkins. **Teach Me About Prayer**. Ill. Russ Flint. Portland, OR: Multnomah, 1990. Unp. $4.99. LC 90-33887. ISBN 0-88070-382-2.

A young brown-haired boy in overalls engages in a basic discussion of prayer. Pictured in expressive watercolors, he talks to God in all kinds of every-day circumstances, happy and sad, in simple words.

69. Willard, Nancy. **The Good Night Blessing Book**. New York: Blue Sky Press, 1996. Unp. $15.95. LC 95-26167. ISBN 0-590-62393-1.

Unusual montages of color photographs illustrate a simple lyric poem. They depict all types and sizes of angel sculptures, many in lovely costumes, set against backgrounds of paintings, household objects, and nature scenes. After calling for blessings upon everyday things, such as tableware, clocks, vegeta-bles, and open windows, the poem ends with a plea for bedtime blessing and protection from the dark.

General Collections

70. Batchelor, Mary. **Children's Prayers from Around the World**. Ill. Rob-ert Mills. Minneapolis, MN: Augsburg Fortress, 1995. 93p. $13.99. LC 95-8518. ISBN 0-8066-2830-8.

This extensive collection of Christian-oriented prayers gathered from a wide variety of sources is grouped into thirty-nine short sections, engaging top-ics such as home, pets, sorrow, school, play, travel, holidays, and table graces. Some prayers are traditional, but many are modern and conversational for easy comprehension and application by young children. A short Bible quotation in-troduces each section. Skillful black-and-white drawings and superb, large color photographs of children throughout the world emphasize the beauty of life and the universality of prayer. Subject and first-line indexes are included.

71. Beckett, Wendy. **A Child's Book of Prayer in Art**. New York: Dorling Kindersley, 1995. 32p. $12.95. LC 94-40362. ISBN 1-56458-875-0.

Using a series of well-reproduced paintings by Renaissance and eight-eenth- and nineteenth-century artists, Sister Wendy asks readers to study each picture in relation to the spiritual quality she has chosen it to represent. A short prayer and an explanation follow. Respect, love, family harmony, understand-ing, selflessness, and the value of learning are among the virtues portrayed. The homilies are applicable to all persons of good will in this thought-provoking, wholesome, gentle work.

72. Bernos De Gasztold, Carmen. **Prayers from the Ark**. Ill. Barry Moser. Trans. Rumer Godden. New York: Viking Press, 1992. Unp. $16.00. ISBN 0-670-84496-9.

Reproductions of powerful, realistic, somber paintings that depict the sup-plicants from this collection make this an outstanding new edition. Those pray-ing include Noah, the cock, the goat, the elephant, the ox, the dove, the dog, the pig, the donkey, the monkey, the owl, the cat, and the glowworm. Each prayer is poignant, succinct, and deeply felt.

73.   Hamma, Robert M. **Let's Say Grace: Mealtime Prayers for Family Occasions Throughout the Year**. Notre Dame, IN: Ave Maria, 1995. 120p. $6.95pa. LC 95-78470. ISBN 0-87793-555-6.

This wide-ranging work, written simply and sincerely, includes prayers for the days of the week, special family times, saints' days, Advent and Christmas, Lent and Easter, secular holidays, and some traditional table graces. Although somewhat oriented toward Roman Catholicism, it is, in general, ecumenically Christian.

74.   Harmer, Juliet. **Prayers for Children**. Ill. author. New York: Viking Press, 1990. Unp. $12.95. ISBN 0-670-83348-7.

This charming month-by-month devotional has a short inspirational or pictorial poem and a one- or two-sentence prayer framed on one page, and its accompanying illustration, which is more elaborately framed with seasonal motifs, opposite. The outdoor scenes include the seashore, the forest, farms, and orchards in all their glowing beauty. The thoughts include concern for others, appreciation of nature, gratitude for blessings, and a wish for peace.

75.   Kennedy, Pamela. **Prayers at Christmastime**. Ill. Stephanie McFetridge Brill. Nashville, TN: Ideals, 1990. Unp. $5.95. ISBN 1-57102-098-5.

Each short, gentle, childlike prayer, followed by a short, related Bible verse, concerns thoughts about Jesus, both as a baby and as ever-present help in everyday life. Softly colored pictures of young, round-faced, multiethnic children in a Christmas pageant, at home with families, praying in their bedrooms, and so forth, suit the contemplative tone of the text.

76.   Ketcham, Hank. **Dennis the Menace: Prayers and Graces**. Ill. author. Louisville, KY: Westminster/John Knox, 1993. Unp. $7.99pa. LC 92-17186. ISBN 0-664-25252-4.

Short, traditional selections include topics such as an appreciation of God's care, parents, dawn, Easter, springtime, a birthday, Christmas, July Fourth, and Thanksgiving, as well as a child's-eye interpretation of the Twenty-third Psalm. All are winningly paired with Dennis the Menace cartoons, depicting him as both lovable and mischievous, but always honest and filled with simple faith.

77.   Lincoln, Frances. **A Family Treasury of Prayers**. New York: Simon and Schuster, 1996. 93p. $16.00. LC 95-51178. ISBN 0-689-80956-5.

Reproductions of old masters' paintings, mostly from the Renaissance era, illustrate a collection of largely traditional prayers grouped by topic: praise, forgiveness, work and study, family and friends, the world's needs, troubled times, and everyday devotions. Authors include Saints Patrick, Benedict, Ignatius of Loyola, and Francis of Assisi, as well as Albert Schweitzer and Jane Austen. Artists include Raphael, Titian, Poussin, Botticelli, and Vermeer, among others. The small format sacrifices some clarity in the illustration, but the size is appropriate for a prayer book. It contains artist, painting, and first-line indexes.

78. O'Neal, Debbie Trafton. **Now I Lay Me Down to Sleep: Action Prayers, Poems, and Songs for Bedtime**. Ill. Nancy Munger. Minneapolis, MN: Augsburg Fortress, 1994. 32p. $5.99pa. LC 94-71213. ISBN 0-8066-2602-X.

Many of these simple, verse prayers include drawings of appropriate, diagrammed fingerplays for each line. Also included are the lyrics and music for seven hymns appealing to young children. Cheerful, cartoon-style pictures show multiethnic children enjoying life today, and some biblical scenes, as well.

79. O'Neal, Debbie Trafton. **Thank You for This Food: Action Prayers, Songs, and Blessings for Mealtime**. Ill. Nancy Munger. Minneapolis, MN: Augsburg Fortress, 1994. 32p. $5.99pa. LC 94-78747. ISBN 0-8066-2603-8.

Fingerplays appropriate for young children figure prominently in these prayers of thanksgiving, some original and some traditional. Seven songs with scores are included, as well as bright cartoons of button-eyed boys and girls with their families.

80. Wilkes, Paul. **My Book of Bedtime Prayers**. Ill. Sandra S. Shields. Minneapolis, MN: Augsburg Fortress, 1992. Unp. $12.95. LC 92-70386. ISBN 0-8066-2592-9.

Grateful thoughts about God's love as shown in sunshine, rain, wind, the moon and stars, flowers, food, the seasons, parents, and other aspects of life familiar to a young child are expressed as gentle, conversational prayers. Softly colored, appealing illustrations frame the prayers.

Ecumenical Collections

81. Baynes, Pauline. **Thanks Be to God: Prayers from Around the World**. Ill. author. New York: Macmillan, 1990. Unp. $13.95. LC 89-28622. ISBN 0-02-708541-4.

This collection of thirty-five well-chosen prayers from thirteen countries and cultures, all of which are suitable for any monotheistic, ethical religion, is small and lovely. Most are familiar or traditional. Prayers from England, France, Germany, Japan, Italy, Poland, and Spain are included, as well as Muslim, Hebrew, and African prayers. The sumptuous, imaginative illustrations show delicately detailed and richly colored, gemlike scenes.

82. Le Tord, Bijou. **Peace on Earth: A Book of Prayers from Around the World**. Ill. author. New York: Doubleday, 1992. 80p. $18.00. LC 91-39913. ISBN 0-385-30692-X.

This unusual collection includes Christian, Jewish, Native American, African, Japanese, Shaker, Russian, Mexican, and Bahai prayers. Some are familiar favorites, but many are new and fresh. Pale, primitively simple, delicate watercolors illustrate the prayers; title, author, and first-line indexes supplement the book.

83. Stoddard, Sandol. **Prayers, Praises, and Thanksgivings**. Ill. Rachel Isadora. New York: Dial, 1992. 152p. $18.50. LC 86-32822. ISBN 0-8037-0421-6.

In this splendid universal collection of spiritual thoughts, beautifully presented in a clear, large-print format with vivid ink-pencil-watercolor illustrations, are prayers both short and pithy and long and lovely. Their sources are

Native American, African American, Islamic, Celtic, Hindu, Jewish, Sanskrit, and Buddhist. Included are liturgies, spirituals, poems, carols, and personal comments, with a first-line index.

84. Strickland, Teresa. **One Earth, One Spirit: A Child's Book of Prayers from Many Faiths and Cultures**. San Francisco: Sierra Books, 1997. 40p. $14.95. LC 96-40387. ISBN 0-87156-978-7.

Russian Orthodox, Zen Buddhist, Native American, Hindu, and Jewish are among the traditions represented in this fresh and moving small collection. Many of the prayers are ecologically oriented. The outstanding color photographs of children and landscapes that illustrate each are tender and life-affirming. Excellent notes about each prayer and its tradition are appended.

85. Walsh, Caroline. **The Little Book of Prayers**. Ill. Inga Moore. New York: Kingfisher Books, 1993. 61p. $8.95. LC 92-30860. ISBN 1-85697-888-5.

The gentle, softly colored pictures of people and animals throughout the world movingly illustrate this group of very short prayers from a variety of sources, including India, China, Helen Keller, Saint Augustine, Mother Teresa, and Ogden Nash.

86. Yeatman, Linda. **A Child's Book of Prayers**. Ill. Tracey Williamson. New York: Stewart, Tabori, and Chang, 1992. 93p. $19.95. LC 91-37706. ISBN 0-55670-251-5.

This excellent group of 125 prayers, Psalms and other Bible quotations, hymn texts, and poems includes many traditional favorites along with less familiar material, such as "Psalm 23 for Busy People" by Toki Miyashina. Readings from the Book of Common Prayer join thoughts from Pygmy and Ghanian cultures. Divided into eleven sections, the topics cover table graces, evening and morning devotions, prayers in time of sorrow, and prayers of repentance, thanksgiving, and praise. Small, delicately executed watercolors decorate the text.

Older and Noteworthy

Other recommended books about prayer include *A Little Prayer* by Barbara Cooney (Hastings, 1967), *A Prayer for Little Things* by Eleanor Farjeon (Houghton Mifflin, 1945), *Prayer for a Child* by Rachel Field (Macmillan, 1944), *First Prayers* (Henry Z. Walck, 1952), *First Graces* (Random House, 1989), and *More Prayers* (Henry Z. Walck, 1967) by Tasha Tudor, *Prayers to Grow By* by Mary Batchelor (Christian Herald, 1977), *And God Bless Me* by Lee Bennett Hopkins (Knopf, 1982), *Tambourines! Tambourines to Glory!* by Nancy Larrick (Westminster, 1982), *Poems and Prayers for the Very Young* by Martha Alexander (Random House, 1973), *A Child's Book of Prayers* by Michael Hague (Henry Holt, 1985), *Here a Little Child I Stand* by Cynthia Mitchell (Philomel, 1985), *Prayers for Children* by Caroline Royds (Doubleday, 1989), *A Child's Prayer* by Jean Titherington (Greenwillow, 1989), and *The Golden Treasury of Prayers for Boys and Girls* by Esther Wilkin (Golden, 1975).

Chapter Four

The Bible

Reference

87.   Barton, Bruce B. **Bible Animals**. Wheaton, IL: Tyndale House, 1992. 64p. $12.99. ISBN 0-8423-1006-1.

This large and colorful presentation of a wide variety of creatures mentioned in Scripture is plentifully illustrated with bright photographs and artwork. Each topic has several paragraphs of interesting information relating to both zoology and the Bible. Included are lizards, canines, cattle and goats, sheep, horses, snakes, cats, birds, insects, and many more. The book contains an index and a Bible animal quiz.

88.   Bowsher, Julian. **Biblical Sites**. Digging Up the Past Series. Austin, TX: Raintree Steck-Vaughan, 1996. 48p. $24.26. LC 95-45266. ISBN 0-8172-4522-7.

The clear, absorbing text provides an overview of important archaeological discoveries in the area known as Palestine, from Neolithic settlements such as Ain Ghazal forward to the era of the Jewish revolt against the Roman rule in C.E. 66. Uncovered mainly in the tells, the information about Old and New Testament times adds to, and sometimes refutes, the Bible accounts. Included are many photographs and maps; an excellent timeline of archaeological events, from the founding of Jericho in 7000 B.C.E. through the discovery of a stone inscription concerning a defeat of King David, found at Tel Dan in 1993; a reading list; a glossary; an index; and a list of museums that house appropriate collections.

89.   Connolly, Peter. **The Jews in the Time of Jesus: A History**. Oxford, England: Oxford University Press, 1994. 96p. $9.95pa. ISBN 0-19-910162-0.

In this excellent source of information concerning many aspects of this period, topics include Herod the Great, Josephus, Vespasian, Titus, Pontius Pilate, Caligula, Agrippa, Claudius, Nero, the Crucifixion, the rise of the Zealots, Masada, the fall of Jerusalem, the destruction of the Temple, and the end of Judea. A wealth of additional detail is contained in family trees, relief maps, geographic information, reconstructions of buildings, and photographs with excellent captions. The book contains a Gospel timeline, a glossary, and an index.

90.   Cooper, Ilene. **The Dead Sea Scrolls**. Ill. John Thompson. New York: Morrow, 1997. 54p. $15.00. LC 96-21983. ISBN 0-688-14300-8.

This well-researched account is lucidly written and absorbing. Discussed are the discovery of the scrolls by a Bedouin shepherd, the subsequent excitement among antiquities dealers and religious scholars, further excavations at Qumran, theories as to who wrote the scrolls and why they were hidden in such a remote area, descriptions of their condition and content, and their significance to both Jewish history and Christianity. The book contains an historical timeline from 1800 B.C.E. to 1991 C.E., a glossary with lengthy descriptions of the terms, an annotated list of works consulted, and Web site information.

91.   Day, Malcolm. **The Ancient World of the Bible**. New York: Viking/Penguin Books USA, 1994. 78p. $19.99. LC 94-60486. ISBN 0-670-85607-X.

Detailed information about topics such as the location of the Garden of Eden, the construction of Noah's ark, the tabernacle of the Ark of the Covenant, idols, warfare, animals, clothing, jewelry, minerals, and more, is given in the comprehensive captions to lavish illustrations by a variety of artists. The book contains many maps. The material is grouped in categories concerning abbreviated Bible stories: the first people, Abraham's family, the Israelites in Egypt, the promised land, David's kingdom, the time of the prophets, and the exile. Altogether, this is an absorbing picture of life in biblical times, from Adam and Eve through the return from Babylon.

92.   Doney, Merle. **How the Bible Came to Us: The Story of the Book That Changed the World**. Ill. D'reen Neeves and Peter Dennis. Colorado Springs, CO: Lion, 1997. Unp. $7.99pa. LC 84-28953. ISBN 0-7324-0490-8.

This interesting Christian-oriented history of the Bible includes thumbnail descriptions of the groupings of the Old and New Testament books and their writers, timelines, a history of writing and books, biblical languages, the Dead Sea scrolls, early Bible translations, printing, later translations, Bible societies, and the outburst of translation into more and more languages today. The work of English translators is predominant but not exclusive. The large softcover format is attractive and readable, using charts, maps, information in boxes, and colorful artwork to enliven the text. The book is indexed by section.

93. Elliott, Betsy Rossen, and J. Stephen Lang. **The Illustrated Book of Bible Trivia**. Ill. S. D. Schindler. Wheaton, IL: Tyndale, 1991. 93p. $12.95. LC 90-72029. ISBN 0-8423-1613-2.

The reader's curiosity will be aroused by the questions and answers in this useful and delightful compendium of biblical information. It will lead children to further exploration of the texts cited to learn more about the who, what, where, when, and why of the happenings. Colorful, amusing, well-drawn illustrations for each query make browsing through the book even more enjoyable.

94. Graystone, Peter. **If I Had Lived in Jesus' Time**. Ill. Jacqui Thomas. Nashville, TN: Abingdon, 1995. 30p. $8.95. ISBN 0-687-00438-1.

A young boy of today dreams about children in the first century C.E. and compares and contrasts their lives with his. Housing, animals, school, transportation, shopping, games, worship, and many more topics are discussed in the simply written but informative text. Appealing, cartoon-style watercolors of scenes, both then and now, illustrate the book.

95. Green, Robert. **Herod the Great**. New York: Franklin Watts, 1996. 64p. $5.95pa. LC 95-26327. ISBN 0-531-15801-2.

Termed "the Great" because of the magnificent buildings he had constructed during his reign, Herod was the infamous king who ruled Judea at the time of Jesus' birth. Characterized by vanity, ruthlessness, and cruelty, he may have demanded the slaughter of the innocents, certainly had his wife and several sons murdered, and curried favor with Rome to the detriment of his subjects. All this is described in a briskly paced and absorbing text. The book contains color and black-and-white illustrations, a timeline, a reading list, a list of Internet sites, and an index.

96. Hepper, Nigel. **Lands of the Bible: From Plants and Creatures to Battles and Covenants**. Ill. Chris Molan and Jeffrey Burn. Nashville, TN: Thomas Nelson, 1995. Unp. $9.99. ISBN 0-7852-7908-3.

Succinct information concerning a wide variety of topics provides an interesting background to biblical times. Topics include the Tigris and Euphrates Rivers, Egypt, Israel, seasons, the wilderness, the coastline, the Jordan River, Galilee, the Dead Sea, the Highlands, Jerusalem, Masada, Qumran, Syria, Asia Minor, Macedonia, Greece, crops, animals, Tiberias, Magdala, Capernaum, and more. Photographs and artwork illustrate the book, and an index is included.

97. Jones, Graham. **How They Lived in Bible Times**. Ill. Richard and Christine Deverell. Ventura, CA: Regal Books, 1992. 48p. $12.99. LC 91-30420. ISBN 0-8307-1511-8.

Double-page pen-and-ink and watercolor cartoons highlight various biblical eras, ranging over many centuries. The lively and detailed cartoons illustrate the story of Passover, cooking and food in the time of Hezekiah, Herod feasting with the Romans, clothing styles from the time of Abraham to the time of Paul, shopping and city scenes in Jerusalem at the time of Jesus, Moses at school in Egypt, and much more.

98. Langley, Myrtle. **Bible Companion**. New York: Dorling Kindersley, 1997. 128p. $6.95. LC 96-36696. ISBN 0-7894-1495-3.

Although tiny in size, this Bible handbook contains a surprising amount of information about the Old and New Testaments, the Bible, the culture of biblical times, biblical archaeology, creation stories, Old and New Testament personalities, trade, landscapes, climate, animals, daily life, Jesus, and more. One main paragraph about each topic is supplemented by captioned photographs and artwork. The book contains timelines, a reference section, a glossary, and an index.

99. Mason, Antony. **Biblical Times (If You Were There)**. Ill. Michael Welply. New York: Simon and Schuster, 1996. 30p. $16.95. ISBN 0-689-80953-0.

Discussing the material briefly, this book encompasses early civilizations, nomads, Canaan, Phoenicians, wars, religions, Herod's Jerusalem, the Dead Sea scrolls, food, seasons, music, dress, tools, housing, and other topics. Plentifully illustrated in color with photographs, maps, and reproductions of paintings, which accompany the scant blocks of text, the book is easy to read and has a timeline and an index. Also included is a board game, "Search for the Scriptures."

100. Rock, Lois. **Discover the Bible**. Ill. Colin Smithson. Colorado Springs, CO: Lion, 1997. Unp. $14.99. ISBN 0-7459-3344-0.

This lively introduction to the Bible for young children has a smattering of Bible stories in short forms: the Garden of Eden, Noah, Joseph, the Exodus, David, Solomon, Jesus' life, some parables, Holy Week, the Resurrection, and the early church. The book includes an index.

101. Tubb, Jonathan N. **Bible Lands**. New York: Alfred A. Knopf, 1991. 64p. $15.00. LC 91-2388. ISBN 0-679-81457-4.

Voluminously illustrated with excellent color photographs, many of which show archaeological artifacts, this large, handsome work brings alive the background against which Bible events took place. Areas and topics include the Mesolithic era; the Patriarchs; Egypt; the Philistines, Canaanites, Israelites, Assyrians, Babylonians, Greeks, Romans, and Phoenicians; deities; foods; clothing; weapons; and so forth. The focus is historical and archaeological rather than religious. An index is included.

102. Walton, Fiona. **Let's Explore Inside the Bible: An Activity, Information, and Story Book**. Ill. Tony Morris and Linda Kelsey. Minneapolis, MN: Augsburg Fortress, 1994. 64p. $10.99. LC 94-070893. ISBN 0-8066-2745-X.

After an introductory section about the Bible itself, selected Old and New Testament stories about Abraham, Joshua, David, Solomon's Temple, Naboth's vineyard, the miracle at Cana, Paul on the road to Damascus, and so on, are surrounded by all kinds of supplementary information about the various biblical periods. Topics discussed include customs, clothes, houses, occupations, money, and food, among others. A great many illustrations, crafts, quizzes, recipes, garden projects, and other activities, more or less associated with each section, are included, creating a lively mix of learning and entertainment.

103.   Wansbrough, Henry. **Children's Atlas of the Bible: A Photographic Account of Journeys in the Bible, from Abraham to St. Paul**. Hauppauge, NY: Barron's Educational Series, 1997. 45p. $9.95pa. LC 97-26774. ISBN 0-7641-5050-2.

Topographic maps illustrate many aspects of Bible history, beginning with Ur and Mesopotamia and ending with Paul's journeys. The material is divided into the Bronze and Iron Ages, and the Babylonian, Persian, Hellenistic, and Roman periods, with summaries of what took place biblically during each period. The clear and readable text is suitable for elementary ages. Further illustrated with color photographs, the book includes an index and thumbnail descriptions of the books of the Old and New Testaments.

104.   Water, Mark. **The Big Book of Bible People**. Ill. Graham Round. Nashville, TN: Thomas Nelson, 1996. Unp. $9.99. LC 96-394. ISBN 0-7852-7893-1.

From Abraham to Zacchaeus, this discussion of thirty groups of personalities is arranged alphabetically. Included are Abraham and his people, Adam and Eve and their children, Amos and the minor prophets, Daniel and company, David, Jesus, the four Marys, Peter, Paul, and others. Each section has a short paragraph of identification, with Scripture references. Clever, colorful cartoons illustrate this entertaining and informative book.

Encyclopedias and Dictionaries

105.   Butcher, Debbie. **Precious Moments Children's Bible Dictionary**. Ill. Samuel J. Butcher. Grand Rapids, MI: Baker Books, 1994. Unp. $14.99. LC 94-19603. ISBN 0-8010-9736-3.

Designed for browsing by preschoolers and children learning to read, this dictionary has only a few words grouped under each letter of the alphabet. Although simplistic, the definitions, in large, easy-to-read print, are generally clear. Included are biblical words, such as *Baal*, *Holy Spirit*, and *Pharisees*, as well as everyday words, such as *donkey*, *carpenter*, and *tax*. The large, cartoon-style pictures are bright and sentimental.

106.   Hillam, Corbin. **The Biggest Bible Alphabet Book**. Ill. author. Wheaton, IL: Tyndale House, 1996. Unp. $12.99. LC 96-10602. ISBN 0-8423-0334-0.

Bible personalities from Adam, Baby Jesus, Christ, and David, through Xerxes and Zacchaeus, are represented in this large-format Christian guide for stimulating young children's interest in Bible events. Each entry has a verse identifying the subject, a short paragraph of further information, and Scripture references. Full-page cartoons encompass one or more events in the subject's life.

107.   Lucas, Daryl J. **The Baker Bible Dictionary for Kids**. Grand Rapids, MI: Baker Book House, 1997. 503p. $19.99. ISBN 0-8010-4345-X.

The Christian emphasis limits its usage, but otherwise this is an excellent tool, containing more than 2,000 words found in the Bible. Multiple definitions, particularly helpful in the case of proper names (there are three Joabs, at least six Nathans, and four Cushes, for example); thorough cross-referencing; large, clear type; Scripture citations for every definition; color highlighting of words about sin and salvation, God and Jesus, and Christian life; and a helpful introduction make the dictionary easy and pleasant to use.

108.   Water, Mark. **The Children's Encyclopedia of Bible Times**. Ill. Karen Donnelly. Grand Rapids, MI: Zondervan, 1995. 80p. $12.99. ISBN 0-310-21103-4.
A wonderful variety of facts is included in this compendium of excellent background material. Seventy-five entries embrace topics such as animals, beggars and lepers, clothing for men and women, crime and punishment, furniture, homes and housework, light and heat, soldiers, washing and toilets, and travel. The book is liberally illustrated with skillful, clever, action-filled cartoons, and contains an index.

109.   Wilson, Etta, and Sally Lloyd Jones. **Bible Encyclopedia: A First Reference Book**. Ill. Steven D. Schindler. Cincinnati, OH: Standard, 1995. Unp. $11.99. ISBN 0-7847-3442-9.
Funny, fact-filled pages of entertaining instruction about biblical times are jammed with lively color cartoons. Depicted are animals, buildings, clothes, food, jobs, school, sports, music, travel, and special days, such as Passover and the Feast of the Tabernacles.

Jerusalem

110.   Morris, Ann. **When Will the Fighting Stop? A Child's View of Jerusalem**. New York: Atheneum, 1990. Unp. $13.95. LC 88-34181. ISBN 0-689-31508-2.
Reflecting the centuries of conflict over who should rule Jerusalem, sacred to three great religions, the narrative concerns a young Jewish boy roaming the city. He mourns because his Arab friend is now forbidden to play with him, and he marvels at the multiplicity of people on the streets. He watches a Muslim at prayer and Jews swaying at the Western Wall and wishes for peace among all Jerusalem's inhabitants. Large black-and-white photographs by Lilly Rivlin illuminate the simple, affecting text.

111.   Paris, Alan. **Jerusalem 3000: Kids Discover the City of Gold**. Ill. Peter Ottavio Gandolfi. New York: Pitspopany Press, 1995. 47p. $16.95. ISBN 0-943706-59-9.
Historical highlights of various city areas include the Western Wall, the Cardo (Roman road), the Sultan's Pool, the Jaffa Gate, the Citadel, the Jewish Quarter, and Yemin Moshe. Full-page reproductions of colorful, action-filled paintings illustrate each area as it is now and as it was in the past, as well as how the city will appear 1,000 years in the future, when anticipated peace and prosperity will have transformed the world. The interesting, readable text includes a chronological summary of the invasions and conquests of Jerusalem, from David's victory at Jebus in 1004 B.C.E. through the present Israeli rule.

112.   Waldman, Neil. **The Golden City: Jerusalem's 3000 Years**. Ill. author. New York: Atheneum, 1995. Unp. $15.00. LC 95-2137. ISBN 0-689-80080-0.

This capsule history of the city includes information about David's capital and the placing of the Ark of the Covenant on Mount Moriah; Solomon's splendor; Nebuchadnezzar's destruction; the rebuilding of the Temple; Greek domination and the Maccabees; Herod, Jesus, and the Roman domination and destruction; Christianization; Arab domination; the Crusades; the reestablishment of Muslim rule; and the 1967 Six Day War, which restored Jewish control to the city. Unusual landscapes and cityscapes illustrated in watercolor and colored pencil dramatize the text. A timeline is included.

113.   Yolen, Jane. **O Jerusalem**. Ill. John Thompson. New York: Blue Sky Press, 1996. Unp. $15.95. LC 95-6013. ISBN 0-590-48426-5.

Terse, lilting, poetic meditations on the holy places of the city's three great religions are splendidly illustrated in several techniques, sometimes muted and misty, sometimes sharply realistic. King David's tomb, the Western Wall, the Dome of the Rock, and the Via Dolorosa are among the subjects, each with an explanatory note.

114.   Zanger, Walter. **Jerusalem**. The Great Cities Library Series. Woodbridge, CT: Blackbirch Press, 1991. 64p. $15.95. LC 91-10829. ISBN 1-56711-022-3.

Because three great religions are closely intertwined in Jerusalem, the history of the holy city is the setting for much of the history of Judaism, Islam, and Christianity. Divided into three sections, this interesting, clearly written overview discusses Jerusalem's geographic and architectural features; its history, from the Jebusites in 3000 B.C.E., through Kings David and Solomon, Nebuchadnezzar, Alexander the Great, the Seleucids, Herod the Great, Aelia Capitolina, the Byzantine era, the Muslims, the Crusades, the Mamelukes and Turks, the British mandate, and the recent turmoil between the Arabs and the Israelis; and its colorful variety of inhabitants. The engaging, lucid text is illustrated with photographs, and the book includes a chronology, reading list, and index.

Story Collections

115.   Aaseng, Rolf. **Augsburg Story Bible**. Ill. Annegert Fuchshuber. Minneapolis, MN: Augsburg Fortress, 1992. 271p. $24.95. LC 92-2527. ISBN 0-8066-2607-0.

A simplified and condensed New Revised Standard Version text in large, clear type encompasses thoroughly the most popular Old Testament personalities and the principal events and teachings of Jesus' life, including his death. Little about the early church is included, however. The outstanding, primitive-style illustrations are powerful, thought-provoking, and often startling.

116.   Armstrong, Carole. **Women of the Bible: With Paintings from the Great Art Museums of the World**. New York: Simon and Schuster, 1998. 45p. $18.00. LC 97-17059. ISBN 0-689-81728-2.

Full-page reproductions of Renaissance paintings by artists including Giorgione, Cranach, Filippo Lippi, Poussin, and Caravaggio grandly illustrate clear, gracefully condensed stories. Subjects include Eve, Hagar and Sarah, Rebekah, Rachel and Leah, Deborah, Delilah, Ruth and Naomi, Abigail, Bathsheba, Esther, Judith, Susanna, Elizabeth, the Virgin Mary, Herodias and Salome, Martha and Mary, and Mary Magdalene. This informative, attractive guide to outstanding Old and New Testament women has an index of artists and paintings and includes Scripture citations.

117.   Brunelli, Roberto. **A Family Treasury of Bible Stories: One for Each Week of the Year**. Ill. Mikhail Fiodorov. Trans. Lawrence Jenkens. New York: Harry N. Abrams, 1997. Unp. $19.95. LC 96-54800. ISBN 0-8109-1248-1.

A large, handsome format with elegant, expressive illustrations in glowing colors distinguishes this collection of fifty-two stories, evenly divided between the Old and New Testaments. Each has been condensed to only a few paragraphs. The Old Testament portion includes the usual favorites, such as the Creation, the flood, Joseph, and Moses. The New Testament portion is a well-integrated narrative of Jesus' life, ending with short sections about Acts and Revelation. A comparative chronological table showing biblical events and general history is included. Written in short, lively sentences (translated from the Italian), the text is based on the Douay Bible.

118.   **Children's Favorite Bible Stories**. Alexandria, VA: Time-Life Books, 1997. 256p. $19.95. LC 96-54249. ISBN 0-7835-4925-3.

Handsomely presented and readable, the collection includes the Creation, Adam and Eve, Noah, Joseph, the Nativity, the parables of the prodigal son and the good Samaritan, and material about the Resurrection. Because the stories have been retold by a number of writers and illustrated by a variety of artists, the overall quality is uneven.

119.   Costecalde, Claude-Bernard. **The Illustrated Family Bible**. Ill. Peter Dennis. New York: Dorling Kindersley, 1997. 384p. $29.95. ISBN 0-7894-1503-8.

Selected passages from the New International Version are reorganized and blended in this collection of stories. For the Old Testament, the divisions are: in the beginning, Abraham and the chosen people, from slavery to freedom, from Sinai to Canaan, Israel in the promised land, Israel ruled by kings, the kingdom divided, and praise, wisdom, and prophecy. For the New Testament, the divisions are: Jesus' early years, Jesus' early ministry, journeys to Jerusalem, last days, the birth of the church, the growth of the church, Paul's journeys, and Revelation. Summaries of the meaning and importance of each story are included. The book is lavishly illustrated with color photographs of paintings and carvings, drawings, and original artwork, which divide the text into readable blocks. Side panels give interesting, supportive factual information. Timelines, capsule biographies of biblical personalities, and an index are included.

120. Deckert, Dianne Turner. **Prayertime Bible Stories**. Elgin, IL: David C. Cook, 1992. 32p. $7.99. LC 91-35647. ISBN 0-7814-0045-7.

These sprightly and simple retellings of favorite stories using modern language all have a very short prayer related to the Scripture message and an appealing, full-page illustration. Included are the Creation, Noah's ark, David and Goliath, Joseph's sale into slavery, Jonah, the Nativity, Mary and Martha, Zacchaeus, two of Jesus' miracles, and the Resurrection.

121. Delval, Marie-Helene. **Reader's Digest Bible for Children: Stories from the Old and New Testaments**. Ill. Ulises Wensell. Westport, CT: Reader's Digest, 1995. 165p. $19.99. LC 95-7993. ISBN 0-89577-815-7.

This simple, faithful, readable work, approved by Protestant, Catholic, and Jewish clergy, has the best-known Old Testament stories. The New Testament area is a flowing narrative of Jesus' life and includes John the Baptist, the Beatitudes, and Pentecost, along with the usual events. Scripture citations are given. The large watercolors show expressive, endearing, stumpy, big-nosed people and range from dramatic to intimate, capturing the mood and content of the text.

122. dePaola, Tomie. **Tomie dePaola's Book of Bible Stories: New International Version**. Ill. author. New York: Putnam/Zondervan, 1990. 127p. $18.95. LC 88-26468. $18.95. ISBN 0-399-21690-1 (Putnam). 0-310-91235-0 (Zondervan).

This beautifully presented but limited collection includes the Creation, Adam and Eve, Cain and Abel, Noah, the tower of Babel, Abraham's sacrifice of Isaac, and Moses in the bulrushes, with the burning bush, crossing the Red Sea, and receiving the Ten Commandments. Only highlights are given of Jericho, Samson, Ruth, Jonah, Daniel, and four psalms. The New Testament section has the events of Jesus' birth, Jesus at twelve in the Temple, his baptism, two miracles, one parable, Holy Week, Pentecost, and 1 Corinthians 13:1–13. All stories are elegantly illustrated in dePaola's trademark style, which is two-dimensional, decorative, richly colored, and balanced. The figures seem frozen in time.

123. Ewing, Carol. **Brave Believers**. Ill. author. Nashville, TN: Thomas Nelson, 1991. 234p. $12.95. ISBN 0-8407-2029-7.

The text from the Contemporary English Version, telling of biblical figures who dared to act upon their faith, is clear and easy to understand. Examples are Abraham trusting God, Jacob letting God change his life, Joseph forgiving his brothers, Ruth remaining loyal, Esther risking death for her people, Mary obeying God, Peter keeping a promise, and Paul telling the world about Jesus. The principal scriptural accounts for each act of faith are drawn together, with bridging explanations between passages, to give unity to each story. Warm, lively watercolors and large type contribute to an excellent format. Scripture citations, a glossary, and notes suitable for beginning elementary readers are included.

124. Hollingsworth, Mary. **International Children's Story Bible**. Dallas, TX: Word, 1990. Unp. $9.99. LC 90-44625. ISBN 0-8499-0784-5.

This wide-ranging selection of succinct and lively, vigorously effective stories told in everyday language is delightfully illustrated, in paint, crayon, and pencil, by children throughout the world. Many of the illustrations reflect their ethnic backgrounds and thus universalize Scripture in a moving and effective way. Some material from the Epistles is included, and all the text reads well aloud.

125.   Hollingsworth, Mary. **My Little Bible**. Ill. Stephanie Britt. Dallas, TX: Word, 1991. 96p. $5.99. LC 90-26726. ISBN 0-8499-0824-8.

Forty-four stories, each taking twenty seconds to read and written in simple language, sometimes omit essentials but could spark interest for further discussion. Scripture references are cited. The illustrations are bright, appealing cartoons.

126.   Kohlenberger, John R., and Noel Wescombe. **The Amazing Book: A Bible Translation for Young Readers**. Ill. Brian Ray Davis. Portland, OR: Multnomah, 1991. 221p. $14.99. LC 91-16221. ISBN 0-88070-446-2.

Rather than retelling a large number of Bible stories, the authors choose to deal more with the theological ideas in selections from Psalms, Acts, Romans, Hebrews, 2 John, and Revelation, as well as the standard stories. Each of the seventy-two sections has introductory personal comment, definitions of words and phrases, and review questions. The tone is conservative; the text, simple and informal. The book is busily illustrated with black-and-white drawings and small cartoon animals in color, and contains a glossary of terms.

127.   Lindvall, Ella K. **Read-Aloud Bible Stories**. Vol. 3. Ill. H. Kent Puckett. Chicago: Moody, 1990. Unp. $17.99. ISBN 0-8024-7165-X.

The Creation, the flood, the Exodus, Daniel in the lions' den, and the Nativity are told using language and concepts appropriate for very young children, and pictured in ink-and-watercolor, cartoon-style scenes. The repetition, limited vocabulary, simple thought questions, and sweeping, lively illustrations will appeal to preschoolers. The first three stories are abbreviated but adequate in scope. The Nativity section, however, is awkward and misleading, skipping from the Annunciation directly to the shepherds and angels, and stating merely that Jesus came to "take away people's badness."

128.   Pilling, Ann. **Before I Go to Sleep: Bible Stories, Poems, and Prayers for Children**. Ill. Kady MacDonald Denton. New York: Crown, 1990. 93p. $15.99. LC 89-78169. ISBN 0-517-58018-7.

These abbreviated Scripture retellings are faithful to the originals and written in conversational, simplified prose. Traditional favorites include the Creation, Adam and Eve, baby Moses, Ruth, David and Goliath, the Nativity, Jesus at age twelve in the Temple, a few miracles and parables, and the events of Holy Week. Each is followed by several associated devotional poems, psalms, prayers, or other materials. The attractive, large format includes softly shaded, sweet watercolors.

129.   Rock, Lois. **Before the Stars Were Made**. Ill. Cathy Baxter. Colorado Springs, CO: Lion, 1997. Unp. $7.99pa. ISBN 0-7459-3635-0.

Bright, cheerful, folk-art-style pictures illustrate the story of the Creation and the Garden of Eden, and an account of the life of Jesus. The underlying theme is that out of darkness comes the light of God's love for the world, despite the evil practiced by mankind. The simple, poetic language is especially appropriate for young children.

130.   Schmidt, Gary D. **The Blessing of the Lord: Stories from the Old and New Testaments**. Ill. Dennis Nolan. Grand Rapids, MI: William B. Eerdmans, 1997. 152p. $25.00. LC 96-11402. ISBN 0-8028-3789-1.

The author presents creative, insightful, and moving accounts of biblical people, sometimes just peripheral characters, as they observe and react to the events in twenty-five stories. Included are Abraham's appalled servants as they see Isaac being led away to the sacrifice, the adolescent Eve pondering the forbidden fruit, the boy Samuel confused by God's call, Pharaoh gloating as his army pursues the Israelites through the Red Sea, Anna enraptured at the sight of the infant Jesus in the Temple, Peter stunned by the miracle of the full fishing nets, and a centurion shaken by the Crucifixion. With this empathetic character development, the Bible stories are enriched greatly. Handsome, realistic watercolors illustrate the smoothly written, absorbing text.

131.   Simpson, Nancy. **Face-to-Face with Women of the Bible**. Ill. Drew Ward and Nancy Ward. Colorado Springs, CO: Chariot, 1996. 238p. $15.99. ISBN 0-7814-0251-4.

Freely interpreted and informally written portions of thirty-nine Old Testament and twenty-nine New Testament stories in which women have significant roles include many who are familiar: Eve, Sarah, Delilah, Ruth, Esther, Mary, Elizabeth, Mary Magdalene, and Priscilla. Others, such as Rizpah, Jehosheba, Gomer, Rhoda, Susanna, and Phoebe, are less well known but teach equally valuable lessons. Most selections are excellent examples of bravery and dedication. Scripture citations are given throughout, and the emphasis is Christian. The big, colorful pictures are modeled after video cartoons.

132.   Stoddard, Sandol. **A Child's First Bible**. Ill. Tony Chen. New York: Dial, 1990. 96p. $14.95. ISBN 0-8037-0941-2.

Adapted from Protestant, Catholic, and Jewish traditions and texts, forty short versions of the most well-known Bible stories are written clearly and condensed effectively, but they are necessarily sketchy. The full-page illustrations in glowing colors are beautiful.

Older and Noteworthy

Reference

Other general reference titles of interest include *The Old Testament in Art* by Rena Neumann Coen (Lerner, 1970), *The New Testament in Art* by Barbara Johnson Shissler (Lerner, 1970), *Animals of the Bible* (winner of the first Caldecott Medal) by Dorothy Lathrop (Lippincott, 1937), *Animals of the Bible* by Isaac Asimov (Doubleday, 1978), *A Biblical Garden* by Carol Lerner (Morrow, 1982), *Consider the Lilies* by John Paterson (Crowell, 1986), *Life in Bible Times* by Robert Henderson (Rand McNally, 1967), *The Golden Bible Atlas* by Samuel Terrien (Golden, 1957), and *People of the Bible* by Cecil Northcott (Westminster, 1967).

Older dictionaries and encyclopedias include *The International Children's Bible Dictionary* by Lynn Waller (Sweet, 1987), *Bible Encyclopedia for Children* by Cecil Northcott (Westminster, 1964), *Young People's Bible Dictionary* by Barbara Smith (Westminster, 1967), and *Young Reader's Dictionary of the Bible* by Carolyn Wolcott (Abingdon, 1969).

Additional titles concerning Jerusalem include *Gavriel and Jamal: Two Boys of Jerusalem* by Brent Ashabranner (Dodd, 1984), *The Wailing Wall* by Leonard Everett Fisher (Macmillan, 1989), and *Jerusalem, Shining Still* by Karla Kuskin (Harper, 1987).

Story Collections

Marian's Big Book of Bible Stories by Marian M. Schoolland (William B. Eerdmans, 1947), *Egermeier's Bible Story Book* by Elsie Egermeier (Warner, 1969), and *Hurlbut's Story of the Bible* by Jesse Lyman Hurlbut (Zondervan, 1932) are the old Sunday school standbys, with extensive coverage. *A First Bible* by Helen Sewell (Henry Z. Walck, 1934), *Little Book About God* by Lauren Ford (Doubleday, 1934), *A Small Child's Bible* by Pelagie Doane (Henry Z. Walck, 1946), and *Small Rain* by Jessie Orton Jones are other gems from the past. Later worthwhile titles include *The Victor Family Story Bible* by V. Gilbert Beers (Victor, 1985), *The Story Bible* by Pearl S. Buck (Tyndale, 1976), *Amy Grant's Heart-to-Heart Bible Stories* by Amy Grant (Sweet, 1985), *Catherine Marshall's Story Bible* by Catherine Marshall (Crossroad, 1982), *The Doubleday Illustrated Children's Bible* by Sandol Stoddard (Doubleday, 1983), *The Bible* by Walter Wangerin (Rand McNally, 1981), and *Brian Wildsmith's Illustrated Bible Stories* by Brian Wildsmith (Franklin Watts, 1968).

Chapter Five

The Old Testament/ Hebrew Bible

Story Collections

General

133.   Araten, Harry. **Two by Two: Favorite Bible Stories**. Ill. author. Rockville, MD: Kar-Ben Copies, 1991. 32p. $13.95. LC 90-46841. ISBN 0-929371-53-4.

Witty, bold, cartoon-style illustrations, distinguished by heavy black lines and brilliant colors, are a delightful accompaniment to this collection. The tales of Adam and Eve, Noah, Abraham and Sarah, Isaac and Rebecca, Jacob's ladder, Joseph, Moses, Ruth, David and Goliath, Jonah, Esther, and Daniel are told very briefly in simple language.

134.   Bogot, Howard I., and Mary K. Bogot. **Seven Animal Stories for Children**. Ill. Harry Araten. New York: Pitspopany, 1997. 48p. $16.95. ISBN 0-943706-40-8.

In this collection of Jewish folktales and Bible stories with a twist, each sprightly entry teaches a lesson about human values. For example, David and a frog and spider, Solomon and a bee, Jonah and the whale, and Noah and the raven and dove all represent respect, friendship, honesty, responsibility, and good and bad attitudes. The informal, humorous text is appropriately illustrated with clever cartoons.

135.   Chaikin, Miriam. **Children's Bible Stories from Genesis to Daniel**. Ill. Yvonne Gilbert. New York: Dial, 1993. 92p. $17.99. LC 90-42588. ISBN 0-8037-0956-0.

Sensuous colored-pencil illustrations in a lush Pre-Raphaelite style decorate this attractive collection. Included are smoothly written versions of Balaam, Deborah, Saul and the Witch of Endor, Solomon and Sheba, and Isaiah, as well as the usual standards. All are short, and some are just excerpts from the larger text.

136.   Cole, Babette, and Ron Van Der Meer. **The Bible Beasties**. Ill. authors. New York: HarperCollins, 1993. Unp. $16.00. ISBN 0-551-02595-6.

Fun-filled pop-up scenes include a white-bearded God in a "Big G" T-shirt creating animals from pink clouds, ravens feeding Elijah pizza and cake, locusts munching the Egyptians' cabbages, Jonah being spewed from the whale, lions welcoming Daniel to their den, and a big fish pulling Noah's ark. Each scene has a flapped Scripture citation to direct children to the complete Bible story.

137.   dePaola, Tomie. **Tomie dePaola's Book of the Old Testament**. Ill. author. New York: Sandcastle Books, 1995. 80p. $8.95pa. LC 94-22219. ISBN 0-399-22827-6.

Selections from *Tomie dePaola's Book of Bible Stories* (Putnam/Zondervan, 1990) include concise renderings of the Creation, Adam and Eve, Cain and Abel, the flood, the tower of Babel, the sacrifice of Isaac, Moses, the fall of Jericho, Samson, Naomi and Ruth, David and Goliath, Esther, Daniel, Jonah, and several psalms. The selections are based on the New International Version and are illustrated elegantly and decoratively.

138.   Eisenberg, Ann. **Bible Heroes I Can Be**. Ill. Rosalyn Schanzer. Rockville, MD: Kar-Ben Copies, 1990. Unp. $12.95. LC 89-48188. ISBN 0-929371-10-0.

Carefully interwoven into the simple text are assurances that young children can build things, like Noah; welcome guests, like Abraham; treat animals kindly, like Rebecca; watch a baby brother, like Miriam; and so on. Charming, richly colored illustrations of the biblical personalities are flanked by smaller, modern scenes of a young girl with chestnut-colored hair.

139.   Gellman, Marc. **God's Mailbox: More Stories About Stories in the Bible**. Ill. Debbie Tilley. New York: Morrow, 1996. 92p. $15.00. LC 95-14894. ISBN 0-688-13169-7.

With a thoroughly modern vocabulary, a completely informal style, and plenty of sly humor, this collection highlights the Creation, the Garden of Eden, Jacob and the ladder of angels, the Exodus, Moses and the Ten Commandments (expanded to sixteen), and bits of moral wisdom from Leviticus and Deuteronomy. These midrashim have up-to-date dialogue and amusing anachronistic details. The easily accessible messages are clear and thoughtful, and the retention of basic characters and events prevents trivialization of Scripture. Rabbi Gellman's strong, positive points are equally valid outside the Judeo-Christian faith.

140.   Hastings, Selina. **David and Goliath: And Other Bible Stories**. New York: Dorling Kindersley, 1994. 64p. $5.95pa. ISBN 0-7894-1192-X.

Highlights from Numbers, Deuteronomy, Joshua, Judges, Ruth, 1 and 2 Samuel, 1 and 2 Kings, Jonah, Jeremiah, Daniel, Ezra, and Nehemiah give some information about Moses, Samson, Gideon, Samuel, Saul, David, Elijah, Elisha, and other major figures. The stories are truncated, but well written and attractively illustrated. Sidebars display additional background information, and indexes are included.

141.   Hastings, Selina. **The Illustrated Jewish Bible for Children**. Ill. Eric Thomas and Amy Burch. New York: Dorling Kindersley, 1994. 192p. $18.95. ISBN 0-7894-2063-5.

Profusely illustrated in color, with maps, photographs, diagrams, and artwork, this collection of Old Testament Bible stories flows smoothly from one era to another in a clear, interesting style. The material is somewhat abbreviated and includes the main portions of Genesis, Moses' life, Samson, Ruth, Samuel, Saul, David, Solomon, some of the prophets, and Daniel, among others. Introductory sections and additional information displayed in sidebars on every page add to the book's usefulness and appeal. It is descriptively indexed by personality and place, and contains a standard index as well.

142.   Hastings, Selina. **Noah's Ark and Other Bible Stories**. New York: Dorling Kindersley, 1994. 64p. $5.95pa. ISBN 0-7894-1191-1.

Selective portions of stories from Genesis and Exodus include the Creation and the Garden of Eden, Noah and the flood, the tower of Babel, Abram and Sarai, Lot, Isaac, Rebekah, Jacob, Joseph, and Moses. Attractive color photographs and artwork along with interesting supplemental information about the people and places of the period enliven the well-adapted text. An index is included.

143.   Hilliard, Susan E. **Death or Deliverance**. Decide Your Own Adventure Series. Cincinnati, OH: Standard, 1990. 144p. $3.95pa. LC 90-33965. ISBN 0-87403-728-X.

A fiery chariot takes a young boy of today back in time into the lives of Jonah, Nahum, Ezekiel, and Isaiah to discover if they prophesied accurately. Although the various segments are vividly written, the result is somewhat confusing because of the number of personalities included. Nevertheless, choosing your own next event is an interesting and thought-provoking method of retelling Bible stories.

144.   Kolatch, Alfred J. **Classic Bible Stories for Jewish Children**. Ill. Harry Araten. Middle Village, NY: Jonathan David, 1993. 68p. $14.95. LC 93-10165. ISBN 0-8246-0362-1.

By no means limited to one religion, these simple, lively retellings of classic Bible stories are abbreviated and engaging. They include the Creation, Cain and Abel, Noah, Rebecca, Joseph, Moses, Joshua, Samson, David and Goliath, Solomon's Temple, Elijah, Jonah, Ruth and Naomi, Mordecai and Haman, Shadrach and friends, and Daniel and the lions. Huge, clever illustrations in glowing colors are filled with life and character; though simple, they are artistically decorative in line and form.

145.   McCaughrean, Geraldine. **God's People: Stories from the Old Testament**. Ill. Anna C. Leplar. New York: Margaret K. McElderry Books, 1997. 120p. $19.95. LC 97-2191. ISBN 0-689-81366-X.

This collection is limited to the Christian faith because it prefigures Jesus in the stories of Abraham and Isaac, and Daniel, and at the conclusion. Thirty-two standard stories, written with verve and creativity and enhanced by lively dialogue, are fresh and engaging. Each retelling is selective in the details included but makes its point adeptly. This well-designed book includes watercolor illustrations and Scripture quotations from the King James Version.

146.   Segal, Lore. **The Story of King Saul and King David**. New York: Schocken, 1991. 123p. $20.00. LC 90-52544. ISBN 0-8052-4088-8.

This lucid new translation, appropriate for older children and adults from the Hebrew of 1 and 2 Samuel and the beginning of 1 Kings, flows smoothly and uses modern language. It is authentic, complete, and easy to read. The careers of Saul and David, with their jealousies, bloody battles, love affairs, murders, and such, are exciting; this work makes them truly accessible to the nonreligious reader, as well as to someone interested in Bible study. At the end of the book is a section that can be used as an index as well as a reference: the Scripture citations, with a summary of the events described in each, are listed in order, with page numbers. The interesting black-and-white illustrations are reproduced from the two thirteenth-century Pamplona Bibles.

147.   Steig, Jeanne. **The Old Testament Made Easy**. Ill. William Steig. New York: Farrar, Straus & Giroux, 1990. Unp. $7.95. LC 90-82137. ISBN 0-374-22583-4.

Saucy and succinct short verses satirize Adam and Eve, Cain, Noah, David, Moses, Jael and Sisera, Esther, Jezebel, and many other personalities. The typical Steig cartoon illustrations are hilarious. Occasional earthy language and nudity, such as a buxom Bathsheba bathing, limit usage to older children and adults, but the poems are funny and to the point.

148.   **Stories from the Old Testament: With Masterwork Paintings Inspired by the Stories**. New York: Simon and Schuster, 1996. 45p. $18.00. LC 95-48105. ISBN 0-689-80955-7.

A panoply of full-page, finely reproduced paintings vividly illustrates selections from the King James Version. Included are works depicting the Creation (Raphael), the Garden of Eden (Tintoretto), the fall of Adam and Eve (Cranach), Rebekah at the well (Poussin), Moses in the bulrushes (Tiepolo), Belshazzar's feast (Rembrandt), and Daniel in the lions' den (Rubens), among many others.

149.   Waddell, Martin. **Stories from the Bible: Old Testament Stories Retold**. Ill. Geoffrey Patterson. New York: Ticknor and Fields, 1993. 69p. $17.95. LC 92-36114. ISBN 0-395-66902-2.

These shortened, conversational, informal versions of the best-known portions of the biblical accounts of the Creation, Adam and Eve, Noah, Abraham, Isaac, Joseph, Moses, Joshua, Samson, David, Solomon, Daniel, and Jonah are ideal for young children. Although much detail is omitted, the basic facts are present. Big, bold, bright illustrations accompany the text.

150.   Zeldis, Yona. **God Sent a Rainbow: And Other Bible Stories**. Ill. Malcah Zeldis. Philadelphia: Jewish Publication Society, 1997. 47p. $17.95. LC 96-46241. ISBN 0-8276-0591-9.

Full-page reproductions of brilliantly colored paintings, primitively styled and overflowing with vivid images, electrify shortened, simply narrated stories of the Creation, the Garden of Eden, Noah, the tower of Babel, Abraham, Isaac, Jacob, Joseph, and Moses.

Stories About Women

151.   Bach, Alice, and J. Cheryl Exum. **Miriam's Well: Stories About Women in the Bible**. Ill. Leo Dillon and Diane Dillon. New York: Delacorte, 1991. 192p. $16.00. ISBN 0-385-30435-8.

Using rabbinic midrashic sources, as well as biblical texts, thirteen creatively and authoritatively expanded stories bring to life Sarah, Hagar, Esther, Judith, Leah and Rachel, Miriam, Hannah, Ruth, Michal, Abigail, Esther, Judith, and the two wise women who influenced King David. An interesting explanatory note follows each narrative.

152.   McDonough, Yona Zeldis. **Eve and Her Sisters: Women of the Old Testament**. Ill. Malcah Zeldis. New York: Greenwillow, 1994. 32p. $15.00. LC 93-9378. ISBN 0-688-12512-3.

These short, gracefully written accounts of Eve, Sarah, Hagar, Rebecca, Rachel and Leah, Yochebed, Miriam, Deborah, Jael, Ruth, Hannah, Abigail, the queen of Sheba, and Esther do not always tell their complete stories but highlight important aspects of their lives. The large, decorative format includes vivid, witty, folk-art illustrations full of brilliant colors, movement, and patterns.

153.   Sasso, Sandy Eisenberg. **But God Remembered: Stories of Women from Creation to the Promised Land**. Ill. Bethanne Anderson. Woodstock, VT: Jewish Lights, 1995. 32p. $16.95. LC 95-3591. ISBN 1-879045-43-5.

These imagined, midrashic embellishments of women mentioned only briefly in the Bible are illustrated with large reproductions of ethereal paintings. Included are Lilith, traditionally Adam's first wife who quarreled with him and now rules the night; Serach, Jacob's granddaughter and a skilled harpist, whom Joseph's brothers beseeched to tell their father that Joseph was alive; Bityah, the new name given by God to Pharaoh's daughter in response to her kindness to Moses; and the daughters of Zelophehad, four sisters whom Moses forced to marry within their father's tribe to keep Zelophehad's land.

Individual Stories

154.   Lashbrook, Marilyn. **"God, Please Send Fire!" Elijah and the Prophets of Baal**. Ill. Chris Sharp. Me Too! Readers Series. Dallas, TX: Roper Press, 1990. Unp. $5.95. ISBN 0-86606-440-0.

This lively, funny, modern retelling of 1 Kings 17–18 is perfectly illustrated with clever cartoons. Elijah tells King Ahab that his worship of Baal will be punished by a drought. Then, in a contest to reveal the true God, Elijah pits the Lord's power against Baal's in the matter of consuming a sacrifice with fire.

155. Lashbrook, Marilyn. **The Weak Strongman: Samson**. Ill. Chris Sharp. Me Too! Readers Series. Dallas, TX: Roper Press, 1990. Unp. $5.95. LC 90-60456. ISBN 0-86606-442-7.

Funny, colorful cartoons invigorate this informal telling of Samson's life from Judges, beginning with the angelic announcement to his mother, Mrs. Manoah, that she will give birth to a child set apart by God. The story does not overlook Samson's quick temper and predilection to fall in love with the wrong women, and stresses his self-centeredness and immaturity. The lively, didactic text is appropriate for beginning readers.

156. Marks, Jan. **The Tale of Tobias**. Ill. Rachel Merriman. Cambridge, MA: Candlewick Press, 1996. Unp. $15.99. LC 95-4812. ISBN 1-56402-692-2.

This sprightly legend from the apocryphal book of Tobit is told from the point of view of a dog who accompanies his master, Tobias, on an exciting journey to a distant city, seeking money owed to his blind father. With the help of a mysterious protector, who is actually Archangel Raphael, Tobias conquers a devil, marries a lovely girl, recovers the money, and cures his father's blindness. The illustrations show clever yet deceptively simple stick figures.

157. Paterson, Katherine. **The Angel and the Donkey**. Ill. Alexander Koshkin. New York: Clarion, 1996. 37p. $15.95. LC 94-22430. ISBN 0-395-68969-4.

Dialogue and description enliven this retelling, which adheres closely to the biblical account in Numbers, of Balaam and his ass. The watercolor, tempera, and gouache pictures in gleaming colors show richly robed and bearded Moabites, a swooping golden angel, and a long-suffering little donkey. The author's afterword discusses how the Bible was assembled from a number of sources.

158. Wolkstein, Diane. **Esther's Story**. Ill. Juan Wijngaard. New York: Morrow, 1996. Unp. $15.00. LC 94-15473. ISBN 0-688-12127-6.

In a first-person narrative of diary entries, the beautiful Esther tells of her meteoric rise to queen of Persia and of her courage and cleverness in foiling Haman's nefarious plot to destroy the Jews. Her character and early life are creatively expanded to produce a vivid text with the biblical basis intact. The book includes a short discussion of Purim and how it is celebrated, but the emphasis is on the historical and legendary foundations of the holiday. Magnificent gouache illustrations, glowing with rich colors, bring to life the people of King Ahasuerus's court.

Creation and the Garden of Eden

159. Baynes, Pauline. **Let There Be Light**. Ill. author. New York: Macmillan, 1991. Unp. $13.95. ISBN 0-02-708542-2.

This illustration of the King James Version of the seven days of the Creation is an artistic triumph. The myriad plants, animals, fish, birds, and insects are magnificently shown flooding the world in joyful swirls of color-filled movement. The stars arc and coil; the sun bursts brilliantly. The only fault is the lack of careful integration of picture and text.

160.   Beaude, Pierre-Marie. **The Book of Creation**. Ill. Georges Lemoine. Saxonville, MA: Picture Book Studio, 1991. 43p. $16.95. LC 90-35418. ISBN 0-88708-141-X.

In the oral tradition by which beliefs are passed from one generation to another, a Canaanite shepherd tending his flocks 2,500 years ago in the desert tells his son of a personal vision of the seven days of the Creation. The prose is rich with poetic images and deeply felt emotions about the natural world and the sacred duty of human beings to protect and appreciate it. Not only is this a beautiful interpretation of Scripture, but also a springboard for the study of biblical ecology. The book is illustrated with mysteriously beautiful watercolors, and includes comments by the author and the artist.

161.   Butterworth, Nick, and Mick Inkpen. **Wonderful Earth!** Ill. authors. Elgin, IL: David C. Cook, 1990. Unp. $18.99. LC 90-60360. ISBN 1-55573-736-9.

Imaginative, humorous, joyful paper art, with circles to rotate, flaps to lift, and cutouts, celebrates the wonderful variety of plants and animals God created for Planet Earth. The book ends with a plea for better stewardship of the world because human beings, though they are God's masterpieces, have devastated many of his best creations.

162.   Cassidy, Sheila. **The Creation: The Story of How God Created the World**. Ill. Emma Hunk. New York: Crossroad, 1996. Unp. $9.95. LC 95-6548. ISBN 0-8245-1506-4.

God, both male and female in this informal, freely interpreted version of the Creation, creates the world with a lump of clay and a ball of wool, with which the heavens and earth are knitted together. The world is blessed with light and greenery; the sky is filled with the stars and moon and birds; an amazing variety of animals is formed; water drenches the earth to produce rain, rivers, oceans, and sea creatures; and God laughs and loves all. Then, lonely for beings like him/herself, God knits Adam and Eve, and all look forward to a happy future. The joy and goodness of the Creation shines forth from each exuberant folk-art illustration.

163.   Greaves, Margaret. **The Naming**. Ill. Pauline Baynes. San Diego, CA: Gulliver Books, 1992. Unp. $14.95. LC 91-24144. ISBN 0-15-200534-X.

Adam, alone in the Garden of Eden at the beginning of time, names each animal pair and tells something of their characteristics. The lonely unicorn, with no companion, is consoled by the knowledge that he will live forever as life's eternal mystery. Magnificent scenes, glowing with color and portraying the animals in all their marvelous variety, perfectly complement the musical, expressive text.

164.   Hickman, Martha Whitmore. **And God Created Squash: How the World Began**. Ill. Giuliano Ferri. Morton Grove, IL: Albert Whitman, 1993. Unp. $14.95. LC 92-23654. ISBN 0-8075-0340-1.

A white-robed, white-bearded God breathes out the universe and delightedly creates all its components, culminating with a host of human beings to keep him company and to love him and one another. All the biblical elements of the Creation are accounted for and described in a charming, humorous, informal way. Folk-art watercolors exalt the variety of God's wonders.

165. Jeffs, Stephanie. **In the Beginning**. Ill. Susan Wintringham. Nashville, TN: Tamarind, 1997. Unp. $11.95. ISBN 0-687-08730-9.

This detailed account of the Creation discusses the gases of the air; the salt, minerals, and currents of the sea; rock types, such as basalt, diamond, and sandstone; plants of all appearances and uses; the solar system; and myriad birds and animals with special characteristics. Reproductions of richly colored, charming paintings accompany the melodious text.

166. Johnson, James Weldon. **The Creation**. Ill. James E. Ransome. New York: Holiday House, 1994. Unp. $15.95. LC 93-207. ISBN 0-8234-1069-2.

African Americans are the subject of brilliantly colored, powerful, double-page illustrations, which show a dignified, elderly storyteller explaining the Creation to a group of spellbound children. The text is drawn from *God's Trombones: Seven Negro Sermons in Verse* by James Weldon Johnson (Penguin Books, 1990). This moving and beautiful work is a triumph.

167. Le Tord, Bijou. **The Deep Blue Sea**. Ill. author. New York: Watts, 1990. Unp. $13.95. ISBN 0-531-05853-0.

A poetic but simple text is enhanced by softly shaded watercolors, almost primitive in their execution, which show some of the stages of the Creation. Illustrations include a lavender sky strewn with multicolored stars, a bright-green cornfield, and russet buffalo and prairie dogs on a golden plain. Man and woman are made fully clothed in modern dress and given the earth while God declares all he has made good forever.

168. Marks, Jan. **God's Story: How God Made Mankind**. Ill. David Parkins. Cambridge, MA: Candlewick Press, 1997. 179p. $17.99. LC 97-18558. ISBN 0-7636-0376-7.

This informal, entertaining account highlights familiar Old Testament stories to tell God's experiences in creating human beings, who often tend to turn away from righteous behavior and neglect their promises. The text, based upon *The Midrash Rabban*, is gracefully written and often gently humorous. The striking, emotionally shaken illustrations are outstanding.

169. Mitchell, Stephen. **The Creation**. Ill. Ori Sherman. New York: Dial, 1990. Unp. $15.95. LC 89-39726. ISBN 0-8037-0617-0.

The Hebrew text of Genesis 1:1–11 is translated and adapted into a simple form. The reproductions of unusual, dramatic, sophisticated paintings use muted colors and integrate Hebrew calligraphy.

170. Ray, Jane. **The Story of the Creation**. Ill. author. New York: Dutton, 1993. Unp. $16.00. LC 92-20862. ISBN 0-525-44946-9.

Selections from the King James Version of Genesis are illustrated with interesting, handsomely decorative detail. Striking renditions of birds, beasts, and plants fill the two-dimensional folk-art pictures. A blond-haired Eve appears fully nude.

171. Reiner, Michaela. **The Creation of the World**. Ill. author. New York: Hyperion, 1990. Unp. $13.95. ISBN 1-56282-096-6.

The text from the New International Version of Genesis is attractively illustrated with paper art in rotating circles. Darkness changes into light, water into sky, dry ground into fruitful vegetation, a sunny day into a moonlit night, the teeming ocean into a bird-filled sky, and the Garden of Eden animals into a charming Adam and Eve under the apple tree.

172. Richards, Jean. **God's Gift**. Ill. Norman Gorbaty. New York: Delacorte, 1993. Unp. $15.95. LC 92-38265. ISBN 0-385-31092-7.

After creating the world, God wants a companion, makes a man out of clay, and breathes him to life. Then God produces animals for the man to name and, finally, a companion for the man himself. Bold, exciting graphics complement the delightfully written text.

173. Waldman, Sarah. **Light: The First Seven Days**. Ill. Neil Waldman. San Diego, CA: Harcourt Brace Jovanovich, 1993. Unp. $14.95. LC 92-8767. ISBN 0-15-220870-4.

This beautifully presented, imaginative depiction of the Creation has a simple, graceful text, based on the biblical account, printed in large white letters on a black background. The full-page reproductions of acrylic paintings, facing the pages of text, gleam mysteriously with stylized, sumptuously colored, decorative detail.

174. Wangerin, Walter. **In the Beginning There Was No Sky**. Ill. Lee Stedman. Minneapolis, MN: Augsburg Fortress, 1997. 32p. $15.99. LC 97-28111. ISBN 0-8066-2839-1.

A parent reassures a crying child by telling him a personal version of the Creation: first and foremost, God plans to create a child, so he arranges the rest of the world to accommodate this human being—the sun and moon to light the child's day and night, the plants to feed him, and the animals to befriend him. God forms the child from clay and then, as the animals rejoice, brings him to life with a kiss. The gentle, sentimental text stresses love, and the sweeping, realistic illustrations are filled with the exciting variety of God's creations.

175. Wildsmith, Brian. **The Creation: A Pop-Up Book**. Ill. author. Brookfield, CT: Millbrook Press, 1996. Unp. $19.95. LC 96-7886. ISBN 0-7613-0144-5.

Creatively conceived and gorgeously realized, this paper-art representation of the first six days of the Creation has a flap on each display that lifts to reveal the appropriate biblical text. It begins with God, depicted as a cluster of men and women of all races (thus, all people are made in God's image), raising the earth triumphantly in a dizzying, deep-blue sky alive with brilliantly colored heavenly bodies. It ends with a lush, animal-filled Garden of Eden.

176. Young, Ed. **Genesis**. Ill. author. New York: HarperCollins, 1997. Unp. $16.95. LC 94-18698. ISBN 0-06-025356-8.

The essentials of the King James Version of Genesis are beautifully interpreted in sweeping illustrations with rich colors. The Creation develops from abstract forms and gradually metamorphoses into vague shapes of birds, animals, heavenly bodies, and an androgynous human being. In a moving ecological plea, the end papers list endangered and extinct species.

Daniel

177.   De Graaf, Anne. **Daniel: Prisoner with a Promise**. Ill. Jose Perez Montero. Grand Rapids, MI: William B. Eerdmans, 1990. 32p. $7.95. ISBN 0-8028-5036-7.

Translated from the Danish, this integrated narrative recounts Daniel's life, from his capture by Babylonian soldiers to his prayer at death. Reproductions of dramatic paintings illustrate the easy-to-read text.

178.   Ryan, John. **The Very Hungry Lions: A Story of Daniel**. Ill. author. Colorado Springs, CO: Lion, 1996. Unp. $5.99. ISBN 0-7459-3723-3.

An old woman tells her grandchildren about two incidents concerning Daniel that she witnessed as a child: Belshazzar's feast and Daniel in the lions' den. The lively text reads aloud well, and the action-filled cartoon illustrations are colorful and hilarious.

David

179.   Cohen, Barbara. **David**. New York: Clarion, 1995. 108p. $15.95. LC 91-8255. ISBN 0-395-58702-6.

Information from 1 and 2 Samuel is skillfully assembled and expanded into a readable, smoothly-written narrative style biography for older children. All the battles and intrigues, rape and incest, adultery, madness, vengeance, charisma, treachery, faith, and political savvy of his saga are recounted through the personal vision of the author, with plenty of dialogue. The story begins with David's anointing and ends with his death, after Solomon is safely established on the throne. The book blends archaeology, history, psychology, and politics with religion, and includes an index, reference list, and cast of characters.

180.   de Regniers, Beatrice Schenk. **David and Goliath**. Ill. Scott Cameron. New York: Orchard Books, 1996. Unp. $15.95. LC 95-22025. ISBN 0-531-09496-0.

This reprint (previously published in 1965) accentuates the classic-fairytale quality of the story: the youngest son (David) triumphs through courage and faith and wins the princess in marriage. This fresh and exciting retelling of 1 Samuel, 1 and 2 Chronicles, and Psalms is embellished just enough to create a lively narrative. The vigorous new illustrations, filled with action and strength (reproductions of luminous, textured oil paintings), add depth and drama.

181.   Fisher, Leonard Everett. **David and Goliath**. Ill. author. New York: Holiday House, 1993. Unp. $15.95. LC 92-24063. ISBN 0-8234-0997-X.

This terse but dignified retelling of the famous battle is powerfully illustrated in a variety of perspectives, unusual colors, bold lines, and vividly individualized figures, reinforcing the drama of the events.

182.   Freehof, Lillian S. **Stories of King David**. Ill. Seymour R. Kaplan. Heroes of Jerusalem Series. Philadelphia: Jewish Publication Society, 1995. 161p. $10.95pa. LC 95-20175. ISBN 0-8276-0567-6.

This reprint (previously published in 1952) integrates the folkloric material surrounding the incidents of David's life into the biblical information, creating a lively narrative. First, Adam gives David seventy years of his own life, with

God's permission, so that David can become a great warrior, a mighty king, and a composer of beautiful psalms. Much that is miraculous continues to occur: David is saved by a spider, a wasp, and a horse; led to victories by God; and cleverly evades the Angel of Death. He is portrayed as wise, pious, and strong; none of his less admirable actions are included. Black-and-white illustrations accompany the text.

Jonah

183.	Gerstein, Mordicai. **Jonah and the Two Great Fish**. Ill. author. New York: Simon and Schuster, 1997. Unp. $16.00. LC 96-31971. ISBN 0-689-81373-2.

This quintessential picture book about Jonah combines some charming legends from Jewish tradition with the basic Bible story to enhance interest, without seriously detracting from accuracy. The simple, vivid text is illustrated in an enthralling, sophisticated folk-art style, sparkling with humor, imagination, and detail.

184.	L'Engle, Madeleine. **The Journey with Jonah**. Ill. Leonard Everett Fisher. New York: Sunburst, 1991. 64p. $5.95pa. ISBN 0-374-43858-7.

In this charming short play, birds and animals observe and comment as they surround Jonah throughout his journey. He complains about his mission to hated Nineveh, tries to flee by ship, rides in the whale's belly, prophesies successfully, rages at the worm that eats the gourd vine, and finally concedes, with rather ill grace, to God's immediate and future will. Funny, literate, and to the point as a teaching tool, the play has fourteen parts appropriate for children to act out or read aloud.

185.	Patterson, Geoffrey. **Jonah and the Whale**. Ill. author. New York: Lothrop, Lee & Shepard, 1991. Unp. $14.00. LC 91-53021. ISBN 0-688-11238-2.

Imaginative, reasonably accurate, and easily readable, this version of the famous story portrays Jonah as lazy and petty rather than anti-Ninevite, and ends when the whale spits him upon the shore. The story's message of obedience to God is intact. Although the double-page watercolors have simple, almost cartoon-style figures, they are dramatic in perspective and color.

Joseph

186.	Kassirer, Sue. **Joseph and His Coat of Many Colors**. Ill. Danuta Jarecka. New York: Aladdin, 1997. Unp. $3.99pa. LC 96-20807. ISBN 0-689-81226-4.

This beginning reader with a limited but lively vocabulary tells the essence of Joseph's story but eliminates the incidents of Potiphar and his wife, the baker and the butler, some of Pharaoh's dreams, and many details of the family reunion and Joseph's forgiveness of his brothers. Unusual, sweeping illustrations combine surrealism with folk art, using brilliant color, varied perspectives, and simplified, rhythmic, sometimes awe-inspiring figures.

187.   Lewis, Lee Ann. **The Trouble with Dreams**. Scottdale, PA: Herald Press, 1991. 160p. $5.95 pa. LC 91-27503. ISBN 0-8361-3571-7.

In this fictionalized account, the spoiled and self-important Joseph, Jacob's favorite child, is heartily detested by his older half-brothers, Leah's sons. Despite his enslavement and imprisonment in Egypt, Joseph remains self-assured, however, because he is secure in the knowledge that God protects and guides him. Of course, he triumphs and forgives all in this classic story of virtue rewarded. This lively and easy-to-read narrative is a pleasant way to learn about Joseph.

188.   Williams, Marcia. **Joseph and His Magnificent Coat of Many Colors**. Ill. author. Cambridge, MA: Candlewick Press, 1990. Unp. $13.95. LC 91-71843. ISBN 1-56402-619-3.

All of Joseph's adventures are portrayed in an accurate but wonderfully humorous comic strip, providing a retelling of the story perfect for young children. Artistic, lively detail and dialogue balloons with witty talk add to the charm of the ink-and-watercolor pictures.

Moses

189.   Fisher, Leonard Everett. **Moses**. Ill. author. New York: Holiday House, 1995. Unp. $15.95. LC 94-12131. ISBN 0-8234-1149-4.

Reproductions of powerful, sometimes awesome and eerie paintings illustrate a simplified, well-written account of Moses' life. The narrative includes his rescue by Pharaoh's daughter, his escape to Midian after killing the slavemaster, his marriage to Zipporah, the burning bush, the plagues, the Exodus, the wandering in the desert, the Ten Commandments, the golden calf, and Moses' death on Mount Nebo. The book includes a genealogy of Moses, a bibliography, and a map.

190.   Gerstein, Mordicai. **The Shadow of a Flying Bird**. Ill. author. New York: Hyperion, 1994. Unp. $15.95. LC 94-7034. ISBN 0-7868-0016-X.

On Mount Nebo, Moses looks at the promised land and begs God not to end his life. He prays 515 prayers, but God shuts heaven's doors to them. God's angels cannot bring themselves to take his soul, so God himself descends to extract it with a kiss and keep it with him forever. Midrashim from the folk literature of the Kurdistani Jews, translated from a 500-year-old manuscript, are the source. Spectacular, richly inventive illustrations filled with stars, clouds, flames, and rainbows, reflect the grandeur of heaven.

191.   Kessler, Brad. **Moses in Egypt**. New York: Rabbit Ears Books, 1997. Unp. $22.00. LC 95-12493. ISBN 0-689-80226-9.

Vividly and skillfully written in a storytelling cadence, the text recounts Moses' life, from his birth and adoption by Pharaoh's daughter through his return to Egypt to plead with Pharaoh to release the Israelites. The account ends just as the Hebrew people leave the Nile Valley, immediately after the Passover. Although incomplete (Aaron is not mentioned), the narrative is gripping; and the unusual, dynamic pictures add drama and energy. A CD of the text, narrated by Danny Glover, with music by The Sounds of Blackness, is included.

192.   Levitin, Sonia. **Escape from Egypt**. Boston: Little, Brown, 1994. 267p. $16.95. LC 93-29376. ISBN 0-316-52273-2.

This fictional retelling of Exodus centers on Jesse, a young Hebrew slave in Egypt, and Jennat, a half-Egyptian, half-Syrian ward of a highborn lady. Moses soon appears, and the plagues begin. After Pharaoh finally sends away the Israelites, Jennat joins them to escape a ritual execution designed to send her to the land of the dead as a servant to her mistress's dead firstborn son. She and Jesse are attracted to each other, and eventually she begins to worship Adonai (a Hebrew name for God) and adapt to the difficult life of wandering in the desert. Thus, a love story is woven into the biblical account, and relevant scriptural passages are interspersed with the events of the story. The details are interesting and convincing.

193.   Travis, Lucille. **Tirzah**. Scottdale, PA: Herald Press, 1991. 160p. $5.95pa. LC 90-23580. ISBN 0-8361-3546-6.

Twelve-year-old Tirzah and her family, Hebrew slaves in Egypt, join Moses in the flight from Pharaoh's oppression to wander in the desert in search of the promised land. The well-written narrative includes the biblical details concerning the hardships, the complaints about Moses' leadership, the rebellion, and the idolization of the golden calf. Believable fictional characters and a little romance are blended to bring the Exodus to life.

Noah

194.   Brent, Isabelle. **Noah's Ark**. Ill. author. Boston: Little, Brown, 1992. Unp. $12.95. LC 91-35673. ISBN 0-316-10837-5.

To accompany a clear text faithful to the Revised English Bible, the artist pictures the story of the ark with the lambent colors, gleaming golds, and intensively decorative style of medieval illuminated manuscripts. The scenes have a busy, sumptuous elegance.

195.   Cousins, Lucy. **Noah's Ark**. Ill. author. Cambridge, MA: Candlewick Press, 1993. Unp. $15.99. LC 92-54589. ISBN 1-56402-213-7.

This beginning reader, perfect for children, has a simple but accurate text and witty gouache illustrations, primitive in form but sophisticated in artistic balance and the use of blocks of pure color. It begins with God's anger at the wicked, and shows Noah and his family cheerfully laboring on the ark and gathering food, the animals parading two by two, lots of rain and boundless water filled with bright fish, and the happy exit from the ark onto dry land.

196.   Gauch, Patricia Lee. **Noah**. Ill. Jonathan Green. New York: Philomel Books, 1994. Unp. $14.95. LC 92-44283. ISBN 0-399-22548-X.

Following God's direction, a black African Noah and his sons, handsome and dignified in headcloths and striped breechclouts, construct a wide, tall ark and call two of every creature into its safety during the deluge. Accompanying the simple, musical, repetitive text are reproductions of vividly colored, artistic paintings that celebrate the gorgeous variety of birds and beasts.

197.   Geisert, Arthur. **After the Flood**. Ill. author. Boston: Houghton Mifflin, 1994. 32p. $16.95. LC 93-758. ISBN 0-395-66611-2.

What happens after the ark is stranded atop Mount Ararat? Noah's family and all the animals happily burst out, haul the ark down to a fertile valley, and settle there to enjoy a life of peace and procreation. Impressive, full-page illustrations are reminiscent of Chinese landscape paintings in line and color. They show Noah and family amid a delightful multitude of birds and beasts, tilling the land, gathering the harvest, stamping grapes for wine, and so on.

198.   Greene, Carol. **Papa Noah Built an Ark**. Ill. Christopher Gray. St. Louis, MO: Concordia, 1996. Unp. $5.99. ISBN 0-570-04809-5.

This rhythmic, rhymed version of the story, to be sung to the tune of "Old MacDonald Had a Farm," will appeal to young children. The words are simple, true to the biblical events, and enlivened by refrains of the tap-tap of Noah's hammer as he builds the ark, the tee-hees of his mocking neighbors, the stomps and clomps of the entering animals, the splish-splash of the rain, and so forth. Brightly colored cartoons illustrate the story, and a musical score is included.

199.   Janisch, Heinz. **Noah's Ark**. Ill. Lisbeth Zwerger. New York: North-South Books, 1997. Unp. $16.95. ISBN 1-55858-784-5.

Unusual watercolor illustrations, with their variety of perspectives and abundance of imaginative details, give a fresh and vivid look to the story of Noah. Seahorses perch on the limbs of drowned trees; a unicorn gallops after the ark in vain; a centaur, a giant, and a satyr are among the curious onlookers watching the ark's construction; and so on. The sophisticated pictures convey both humor and a certain menace. The text is well written and accurate.

200.   Jonas, Ann. **Aardvarks, Disembark**. Ill. author. New York: Greenwillow Books, 1990. Unp. $14.95. LC 89-27225. ISBN 0-688-07206-2.

This book focuses on the glorious variety of animals aboard the ark, with pairs of exotic species filing down snowy Mount Ararat onto a grassy plain, pictured in precise, double-page watercolors. The animals descend in reverse alphabetical order. The text is sketchy, eliminating God's displeasure with humankind, the raven flights, and the rainbow. An endnote identifies the animals' habitats and which are endangered species. Humanity's stewardship of the earth and God's creativity are stressed.

201.   Lewis, J. Patrick. **The Boat of Many Rooms: The Story of Noah in Verse**. Ill. Reg Cartwright. New York: Atheneum, 1997. Unp. $16.00. LC 95-581. ISBN 0-689-80118-1.

The rhymed text, which tells the story from the building of the ark through the appearance of the rainbow, is often rhythmic and funny, but serious as well, and rather pretentious in its elevated vocabulary, which is suited to older children. The reproductions of lighthearted and cheerful folk-art oil paintings, with their winning depictions of beasts and human beings, are a complete success.

202. Ludwig, Warren. **Old Noah's Elephants**. Ill. author. New York: Putnam, 1991. Unp. $14.95. LC 90-35379. ISBN 0-399-22256-1.

Ignoring Noah's orders, the elephants have found their way into the ark's food supply and are becoming fatter by the minute. Their combined weight soon threatens to capsize the boat. Following God's advice, Noah tickles the hyena. Happily, the problem resolves itself in a fashion of sequential upsets, ending with a fleeing mouse frightening the elephants away from their feast. Witty, lively illustrations show an array of creatures prowling, leaping, perching, crawling, and standing. Noah and family are cute, short dumplings.

203. Olson, Arielle North. **Noah's Cats and the Devil's Fire**. Ill. Barry Moser. New York: Orchard Books, 1992. Unp. $14.95. LC 91-17408. ISBN 0-531-05984-7.

In this entertaining fable, the devil sneaks aboard the ark in the form of a demonic, third mouse, determined to disrupt the voyage. When Noah spies this extra mouse gnawing through the ark's hull, he sets his cats upon him. One of the cats chews him up and spits him into the sea, saving all aboard. The full-page watercolors are powerful, beautiful, and exciting.

204. Ray, Jane. **Noah's Ark**. Ill. author. New York: Dutton, 1990. Unp. $14.95. ISBN 0-525-44653-2.

The formal King James text, beginning with God's displeasure with humankind and ending with his promise never again to curse the earth, is illustrated with great charm and simplicity. Brightly colored, decorative pictures show primitively styled people, animals, and birds.

205. Reid, Barbara. **Two by Two**. Ill. author. New York: Scholastic, 1993. 30p. $4.95pa. LC 92-9013. ISBN 0-590-45869-8.

Vigorous verses in a drum-beat tempo tell Noah's story. Unusual illustrations of plasticene applied to illustration board are witty, imaginative, and exciting. The text is excellent for reading aloud, and a musical score is included.

206. Rodger, Elizabeth. **Don't Rock the Ark**. Ill. author. Mahwah, NJ: Troll, 1997. Unp. $5.95pa. ISBN 0-8167-4199-9.

This pared-down version of the ark story concentrates on the problems that result from overcrowding and the necessity for the elephants to stand perfectly still to prevent the ark from capsizing. The elephants suffer a fear of mice, an itchy flea bite, and a tickly peacock feather, but they stand firm. The cause of the flood is not mentioned. Winsome, double-page illustrations show the animal pairs and Noah devising solutions to keep the elephants calm until they reach dry land.

207. Sasso, Sandy Eisenberg. **A Prayer for the Earth: The Story of Naamah, Noah's Wife**. Ill. Bethanne Anderson. Woodstock, VT: Jewish Lights, 1996. 32p. $16.95. LC 96-42065. ISBN 1-879045-60-5.

While Noah's job is to build and provision the ark and collect the animals, Naamah's job is to gather the seeds of all the flowers and trees, from amaryllis to zinnia and acacia to ziziphus, and fruits and vegetables, from apples to zucchini. She tends them in a special garden aboard the ark and replants them upon reaching dry land. The language is colorful and poetic; the illustrations, powerful and sweeping.

208.   Walton, Rick. **Noah's Square Dance**. Ill. Thor Wickstrom. New York: Lothrop, Lee & Shepard, 1993. Unp. $15.00. LC 92-10257. ISBN 0-688-11186-6.

To lift their spirits after long days of rain, Noah and the animals stage a prancing square dance, up and down and around the ark. Suddenly, during a wild, swing-your-partner promenade, the clouds part, the rain stops, and the ark runs aground. The merry, rhymed text and the funny, lively pictures complement each other perfectly.

209.   Wildsmith, Brian. **Brian Wildsmith's Noah's Ark: The Pop-Up Book**. Ill. author. New York: HarperCollins, 1994. Unp. $16.00. ISBN 0-06-069366-5.

The biblical story is abbreviated in this book, but the basics are present. The artwork and paper engineering are spectacular, with vivid colors, clever and intricate details, and dramatic action.

Psalms

210.   Crawford, Sheryl Ann. **Psalms for a Child's Heart**. Ill. Elaine Garvin. Colorado Springs, CO: ChariotVictor, 1997. 61p. $10.99. ISBN 0-7814-3004-6.

Psalms 1, 8, 23, and 32, and excerpts from Psalms 62, 96, and 139 are freely interpreted for young children. The essential themes are intact, yet the concepts are well expressed in terms related to everyday experience. Pleasant watercolor cartoons show multiethnic children singing around a campfire, admiring the night sky, worshipping in church, and engaging in other familiar activities.

211.   Eisler, Colin. **David's Songs**. Ill. Jerry Pinkney. New York: Dial, 1992. 58p. $17.00. LC 90-25459. ISBN 0-8037-1058-5.

The psalms are examined in the context of the life of David, their creator, and arranged to highlight aspects of his personality and career. The thirty-six included are simplified but still poetic and accurate. The book has an excellent introduction and reproductions of magnificent paintings.

212.   Keane, Glen. **Parables for Little Kids**. First Adam Raccoon Series. Colorado Springs, CO: Chariot, 1995. Unp. $7.99. LC 95-42468. ISBN 0-7814-0258-1.

Excerpts from psalms 56 and 100 are warmly interpreted in stories about a little raccoon boy. When he realizes, sadly, that he cannot sing, he discovers that he can make a joyful noise by beating on a hollow log. When he is frightened by strange sounds and shapes at bedtime, his friend King Aren is there to comfort him. Lively cartoons reinforce this reassuring, simple text for preschoolers.

213.   Le Tord, Bijou. **The Little Shepherd**. Ill. author. New York: Delacorte, 1991. Unp. $13.00. LC 90-49039. ISBN 0-385-30417-X.

This modest version of Psalm 23 is true to the spirit of the original, but milder, less succinct, and more gently reassuring for very young children. Softly shaded watercolors, in a simple, primitive style, show a red-cheeked shepherd boy, his dog, and his flock in the hills of Judea, which radiate a warm tan in the daytime and a cool blue at night.

214.   Le Tord, Bijou. **Sing a New Song: A Book of Psalms**. Ill. author. Grand Rapids, MI: William B. Eerdmans, 1997. Unp. $15.00. LC 96-33231. ISBN 0-8028-5139-8.

Excerpts from fourteen psalms are combined harmoniously to form a beautiful new poem describing the attributes of God: He is like the sun and the wind, bringing blessings to the earth; free as a flying dove; and like a mountain in his love. All nature praises him. The watercolor illustrations, both childlike and subtle, shine with a warm radiance.

215.   Miner, Julia. **The Shepherd's Song: The Twenty-Third Psalm**. New York: Dial, 1993. Unp. $13.89. LC 91-31067. ISBN 0-8037-1196-4.

Pastel, double-page spreads of a shepherd family living amidst the islands of Greece beautifully illustrate the words of the psalm. The lambs are cared for tenderly by a boy and girl and their parents, while a sheepdog herds and protects them. The background includes rocky hills, stone bridges, precipitous trails, green meadows and woods, glittering cascades, and a blue-green sea. An afterword stresses the safety and harmony emphasized by the psalm's phrases, as applied to the keeping of sheep.

Solomon

216.   Freehof, Lillian S. **Stories of the Kingdom of Solomon**. Ill. Seymour R. Kaplan. Heroes of Jerusalem Series. Philadelphia: Jewish Publication Society, 1995. 175p. $10.95pa. LC 95-22098. ISBN 0-8276-0566-8.

This reprint (previously published in 1955) is a collection of well-written and charming midrashic-talmudic stories of ingenuity, sharp intelligence, and supernatural powers that read like fairytales. Solomon talks with animals and insects, flies about on a magic carpet, foils the demon Asmodeus, solves the queen of Sheba's riddles, dispenses wise judgments, and so forth. Lively black-and-white drawings illustrate the stories.

217.   MacGill-Callahan, Sheila. **When Solomon Was King**. Ill. Stephen T. Johnson. New York: Dial, 1995. Unp. $15.99. LC 93-28058. ISBN 0-8037-1589-7.

As a youth, Solomon pities a wounded lioness and cares for her and her cubs while on a hunting trip. When he becomes king and receives a "power" ring enabling him to understand the speech of animals, he becomes proud and begins hunting for pleasure, not need. He is chastised by an eagle and attacked by a lion. The old lioness he once helped saves his life. Thus, he learns to take from nature only what is necessary. Realistic, beautiful watercolors show a handsome hero.

218.   Orgel, Doris, and Ellen Schecter. **The Flower of Sheba**. Ill. Laura Kelly. A Bank Street Ready-to-Read Book. New York: Bantam, 1994. Unp. $3.50pa. LC 92-33477. ISBN 0-553-09041-0.

Hearing that King Solomon is wise beyond all others, the queen of Sheba travels to his palace to test his wisdom with three riddles. He answers the first two easily but needs the help of a small bee to solve the third. The queen is particularly impressed that the great Solomon would seek the guidance of such a tiny, modest creature, and she returns home a wiser person herself. Even with the limited vocabulary of a beginning reader, the prose is musical and imaginative. The illustrations are appropriately regal and lush, showing flowers and jewels in rich colors.

219. Renberg, Dalia Hardof. **King Solomon and the Bee**. Ill. Ruth Heller. New York: HarperCollins, 1994. Unp. $15.00. LC 92-30411. ISBN 0-06-022899-7.

This charming legend of King Solomon and the queen of Sheba, similar to the legends in the Talmud, tells of a small bee that accidentally stings the mighty king. It apologizes and promises to repay Solomon for his forgiveness. The king laughs at its audacity, but later the bee helps him in his clash of wits with the queen. Brilliant illustrations show animals, flowers, insects, and handsome Semitic people.

220. Waldman, Neil. **The Two Brothers: A Legend of Jerusalem**. Ill. author. New York: Atheneum, 1997. Unp. $17.00. LC 96-731. ISBN 0-689-31936-3.

How Solomon chose the site on which to build his magnificent temple is rooted in this traditional folktale in which two brothers show loving care for each other. Each believes that the other is more in need of the wheat they harvest; at night, each carries extra sheaves to the other's field. King Solomon observes their actions approvingly. When the brothers discover their mutual generosity, they embrace lovingly, and a spring of water miraculously appears where they stand. Thus, Solomon knows this site to be a holy place, ideal for his temple. The expressive text is illustrated with reproductions of folk-art-style acrylic paintings that flow warmly across the pages.

Older and Noteworthy

Story Collections

Other recommended collections include *Stories from the Bible* by Walter De la Mare (Faber, 1929), *Signs and Wonders* by Bernard Evslin (Four Winds, 1981), *The Book of Adam to Moses* by Lore Segal (Knopf, 1987), *In the Beginning* by Sholem Asch (Putnam, 1935), *Moses' Ark* by Alice Bach and J. Cheryl Exum (Delacorte, 1989), and *Does God Have a Big Toe?* by Marc Gellman (Harper, 1989).

Individual Stories

Additional stories about Esther include *The Story of Esther* by Ruth Brin (Lerner, 1976), *Queen Esther* by Tomie dePaola (Harper, 1986), *Esther* by Kurt Mitchell (David C. Cook, 1983), and *Esther* by Lisl Weil (Atheneum, 1980). Other Bible personalities and events are portrayed in *The Story of Job* by Beverly Brodsky (Braziller, 1986), *Joshua in the Promised Land* by Miriam Chaikin (Clarion, 1982), *The Binding of Isaac* by Barbara Cohen (Lothrop, Lee & Shepard, 1978), *The Wicked City* by Isaac Bashevis Singer (Farrar, Straus & Giroux, 1972), *The Song of the Three Holy Children* by Pauline Baynes (Henry Holt, 1986), *The Tower of Babel* by Marilyn Hirsh (Holiday, 1981), and *A Tower Too Tall* by Mildred Schell (Judson, 1979).

Some more worthwhile stories about the Creation and the Garden of Eden include *The Seven Days of Creation* by Leonard Everett Fisher (Holiday, 1981), *One Day in Paradise* by Helme Heine (Atheneum, 1986), *Genesis* by Allison Reed (Schocken, 1987), and *Adam and Eve* by Warwick Hutton (Macmillan, 1987).

Other stories about David include *David and Goliath* by Ruth Brin (Lerner, 1977), *David and Goliath* by Tomie dePaola (Winston, 1984), *David* by Lillie Patterson (Abingdon, 1985), and *David He No Fear* by Lorenz Graham (Crowell, 1970).

Further interesting stories about Jonah include *Jonah's Journey* by Danah Haiz (Lerner, 1973), *Jonah and the Great Fish* by Warwick Hutton (Atheneum, 1984), *The Book of Jonah* by Peter Spier (Doubleday, 1985), *The Story of Jonah* by Kurt Baumann (North-South, 1987), *Jonah and the Great Fish* by Clyde Robert Bulla (Crowell, 1970), and *Jonah* by Beverly Brodsky (Lippincott, 1977).

Additional excellent stories about Joseph include *I Am Joseph* by Barbara Cohen (Lothrop, 1980), *Joseph and His Brothers* (Raintree, 1982) and *Joseph the Dreamteller* (Raintree, 1983) by Catherine Storr, *Joseph and the Amazing Technicolor Dreamcoat* by Andrew Lloyd Webber (Henry Holt, 1982), *Joseph's Wardrobe* by Paul Citrin (Union of American Hebrew Congregations, 1987), and *Joseph and His Brothers* by Maud Petersham (Macmillan, 1938).

Moses as a baby is portrayed in *Moses in the Bulrushes* by Warwick Hutton (Atheneum, 1986) and *Moses, Moses* by Charles Mee (Harper, 1977). *Exodus* by Miriam Chaikin (Holiday, 1987) provides the full story of his life.

Additional outstanding tales about Noah include *Noah and the Rainbow* by Max Bollinger (Crowell, 1972), *Unicorns in the Rain* by Barbara Cohen (Atheneum, 1980), *Noah and the Ark* by Tomie dePaola (Winston, 1983), *How the Left-Behind Beasts Built Ararat* by Norma Farber (Walker, 1978), *Noah's Ark* by Margrit Haubensak-Tellenbach (Crown, 1983), *Noah and the Great Flood* by Warwick Hutton (Atheneum, 1977), *Mr. and Mrs. Noah* by Lois Lenski (Crowell, 1948), *Noah's Ark* by Lawrence T. Lorimer (Random House, 1978), *Noah* by Charles Mee (Harper and Row, 1978), *Washday on Noah's Ark* by Glen Rounds (Holiday, 1985), *Why Noah Chose the Dove* by Isaac Bashevis Singer (Farrar, Straus & Giroux, 1973), *Noah's Ark* by Peter Spier (Doubleday, 1977), *A for the Ark* by Roger Duvoisin (Lothrop, Lee & Shepherd, n.d.), and *One Wide River to Cross* by Barbara Emberley (Prentice-Hall, 1966).

The Lord Is My Shepherd by Tasha Tudor (Putnam, 1980) should also be considered.

Chapter Six

The New Testament and Jesus

Story Collections

221.   Beers, V. Gilbert, and Ronald A. Beers. **All-Time Favorite Bible Stories of the New Testament**. Ill. Daniel J. Hochstatter. Nashville, TN: Thomas Nelson, 1991. 79p. $7.95. ISBN 0-8047-9152-6.

Simple, shortened episodes from Jesus' life, from his birth through Holy Week, and incidents from Acts concerning Peter, Paul, and Stephen, are illustrated with lively watercolor cartoons. The book omits Jesus' teaching ministry, and there are no Scripture citations.

222.   Hastings, Selina. **The Birth of Jesus and Other Bible Stories**. New York: Dorling Kindersley, 1994. 64p. $5.95pa. ISBN 0-7513-5482-1.

Stories include the birth of John the Baptist; Jesus' birth, early life, baptism, and temptation; eleven of the best-known parables; the entry into Jerusalem; and the expulsion of the money lenders from the Temple. The text is competently retold in clear language, with additional helpful information about the customs and geography of the period; plentifully illustrated with color photographs and artwork; and indexed.

223.   Hastings, Selina. **The Miracles of Jesus and Other Bible Stories**. New York: Dorling Kindersley, 1994. 64p. $5.95pa. ISBN 0-7894-1194-6.

The miracles include the marriage at Cana; healing the leper, the paralyzed man, the centurion's servant, and Jairus's daughter; feeding the 5,000; calming the storm; casting out the demons from Legion; walking on water; and resurrecting Lazarus. Also included are the events of Holy Week, the Resurrection, the

Ascension, Pentecost, and several stories about Peter and Paul. The abbreviated text, accompanied by many attractive illustrations, displays additional information in sidebars.

224.   Hutchinson, Joy. **Twelve Friends: A Counting Book About Jesus' Disciples**. Ill. author. Minneapolis, MN: Augsburg Fortress, 1991. Unp. $4.99pa. LC 91-71037. ISBN 0-8066-2559-7.

Each man, such as a fisherman, a tax collector, and a doubter, is described in only a few words. For very young children, though, this book provides an excellent way to learn the disciples' names while counting them from one to twelve. Funny watercolors add appeal.

225.   **Stories from the New Testament**. New York: Simon and Schuster, 1997. 45p. $18.00. LC 96-46558. ISBN 0-689-81297-3.

Excerpts from the King James Version give an overview of Jesus' life: the Annunciation and birth events, his baptism by John, the marriage at Cana, the miracle of the full fishing nets, the raising of Jairus's daughter and Lazarus, the Last Supper, the agony in the garden, the betrayal by Judas, the Crucifixion, Mary Magdalene beholding the risen Jesus, doubting Thomas, and the road to Emmaus. John the Baptist's head on a platter and Paul on the road to Damascus are included for good measure. All are sumptuously illustrated with reproductions of dramatic paintings by Titian, Tintoretto, Rubens, Botticelli, and many other renowned artists, from the National Gallery in London. The book has an elegant typeface, Scripture citations, and an annotated index of the paintings.

Individual Stories

226.   dePaola, Tomie. **Mary: The Mother of Jesus**. Ill. author. New York: Holiday House, 1995. Unp. $16.95. LC 95-54491. ISBN 0-8234-1018-8.

Considering the paucity of information about Mary, the author has produced a well-rounded account of the Virgin's life by including appropriate legends concerning her childhood, betrothal to Joseph, and dormition, along with the biblical facts. His prose, based on the New English Bible, is dignified and expressive. The rich colors, balanced design, and medieval setting of the illustrations have a timeless quality perfect for the subject.

227.   Figley, Marty Rhodes. **The Story of Zacchaeus**. Ill. Cat Bowman Smith. Grand Rapids, MI: William B. Eerdmans, 1995. Unp. $15.00. LC 94-46174. ISBN 0-8028-5092-8.

The biblical account is expanded into a simply told but entertaining tale for young children. Zacchaeus is a short, fat, friendless, rich cheat whom Jesus transforms into a generous man, beloved by babies, dogs, and everyone else in his village. The bright, saucy cartoons are full of fun and action.

228.   Napoli, Donna Jo. **Song of the Magdalene**. New York: Scholastic, 1996. 240p. $15.95. LC 96-7066. ISBN 0-590-93705-7.

Mary Magdalene is portrayed as Miriam, a spirited and independent young girl who suffers from epilepsy, which is considered to be a sign of demonic possession. She falls in love with a young man crippled by cerebral palsy, also an outcast, and becomes pregnant. Tragically, the man dies, and Miriam miscarries their child after being raped. Disgraced and desolate, she seeks the new healer, Joshua, and joins in his work. This is an imaginatively conceived and movingly expressed story for young adults of a caring and loving woman who is cruelly rejected by society.

Mary and Martha

229.   Figley, Marty Rhodes. **Mary and Martha**. Ill. Cat Bowman Smith. Grand Rapids, MI: William B. Eerdmans, 1995. Unp. $15.00. LC 95-5151. ISBN 0-8028-5079-0.

In this sweet and lively version of the story from the Gospel of Luke, Martha is a whirlwind housekeeper and Mary a dreamy intellectual. After Jesus' kindly admonition that Mary's choice to sit and listen is superior to Martha's busyness, both sisters change. Funny, bright, cartoon-style pictures suit the informal, easy-to-read text.

230.   Simon, Mary Manz. **Sit Down! Mary and Martha**. Ill. Dennis Jones. Hear Me Read Series. St. Louis, MO: Concordia, 1991. 24p. $2.39pa. ISBN 0-570-04701-3.

Even with only a nineteen-word vocabulary, this beginning reader has a lively account of the story of Mary and Martha. Mary will not stop her work long enough to listen to Jesus, and she criticizes Martha for shirking household duties. The illustrations are lively, colorful cartoons.

Paul

231.   De Graaf, Anne. **Paul: A Change of Heart**. Ill. Jose Perez Montero. Outstanding Men of the Bible Series. Grand Rapids, MI: William B. Eerdmans, 1990. 32p. $7.95. ISBN 0-8028-5034-0.

Paul's life, beginning with the stoning of Stephen and ending with his confinement in Rome, is chronicled in an easy-to-read style, with plenty of dialogue to give drama and interest. Colorful, realistic, action-filled pictures add excitement to the narrative.

232.   Hostetler, Marian. **We Knew Paul**. Scottdale, PA: Herald Press, 1992. 128p. $5.95pa. LC 92-10562. ISBN 0-8361-3589-X.

With material drawn from Acts, John, 1 and 2 Timothy, Philippians, Romans, 1 Corinthians, Galatians, and Ephesians, various incidents in Paul's life are described imaginatively in letters to Luke from young people who encountered him. Incidents include his persecution of Jesus' followers, his recovery after being struck down on the road to Damascus, and his release from the jail collapsed by the earthquake, among other events. All the writers are touched by Paul's message in some way, and many are converted to Christianity.

233.   Lashbrook, Marilyn. **The Great Shake-up: Miracles in Philippi**. Ill. Chris Sharp. Me Too! Readers Series. Dallas, TX: Roper Press, 1991. Unp. $5.95. ISBN 0-86606-445-1.

This is a lively, beginning-reader version of the story from Acts 6 in which Paul and Silas are imprisoned for casting an evil spirit from the slave girl and then miraculously freed from their chains during the night. As a result, they are able to convert the jailer and his family to Christianity. Funny ink-and-watercolor cartoons enliven the text.

234.   Williams, Michael E. **The Turnabout Paul Storybook**. Ill. Cheryl Mendenhall. Nashville, TN: Abingdon Press, 1995. 39p. $7.95pa. ISBN 0-687-00793-3.

This interesting narrative details the known incidents of Paul's life and includes his experiences with Lydia, with Priscilla and Aquila, in the shipwreck, in prison, and in Rome and Athens. Full-page cartoons show a bearded, balding man with his robes flying about him, moving with speed and enthusiasm.

Peter

235.   De Graaf, Anne. **Peter: The Fisher of Men**. Ill. Jose Perez Montero. Outstanding Men of the Bible Series. Grand Rapids, MI: William B. Eerdmans, 1990. 32p. $7.95. ISBN 0-8028-5033-2.

Drawn from the Gospels, Acts, and tradition, Peter's story begins with Jesus walking on the water, then reverts to his first meeting with Jesus and the miracle of the full fishing nets. Also included are the events of Holy Week, the Resurrection, and Pentecost. His devotion to Jesus and his maturation into a fearless evangelist are stressed. Action-filled, realistic pictures illustrate the lively narrative.

236.   Smouse, Phil A. **Pete, Feet, and Fish to Eat**. Ill. author. Uhrichsville, OH: Barbour, 1994. 32p. $9.95. ISBN 1-55748-556-9.

Excerpts from Peter's life, told in breezy, rollicking rhyme, include his miraculous release from prison, the time when Jesus filled his fishing nets to overflowing, the time when Jesus washed his feet at the Last Supper, and his three-time denial of Jesus before the Crucifixion. The full-page illustrations are funny cartoons. The point of all the accounts is that despite Peter's weaknesses and mistakes, Jesus loved and forgave him.

Stories of Jesus

237.   Berry, James. **Celebration Song**. Ill. Louise Brierley. New York: Simon and Schuster, 1994. Unp. $14.00. ISBN 0-671-89446-3.

Jesus' first birthday is celebrated in poetry. All kinds of animals, fish, and birds dance with joy as his mother tells him the story of his "born-day," when shepherds and astrologers came to worship him. In the end, however, she wonders what will happen when he grows up, when her mothering is finished. The story is pictured in a land of palm trees and seashores. Mary is a serene black woman with tender, dreaming eyes. The wise men arrive at the tiny hut/stable in rowboats. The poetry is simple, flowing, mystical, and suffused with a warm radiance.

238.   Bomer, John M. **A Child's Life of Jesus**. Ill. Lizzi Napoli. Notre Dame, IN: Ave Maria Press, 1990. 40p. $8.94. LC 89-81355. ISBN 0-87793-415-0.

Out of print until recently (originally published as *La Vie de Jesus.* Paris: Pomme d'Api, Editions du Centurion, 1971), this English translation from the French is Gospel-based. It extends from the Nativity through Pentecost, with a simplified, episodic text briefly highlighting the significant events of Jesus' life and teaching. The semi-abstract watercolors brim with expressive life.

239.   Carlson, Melody. **Benjamin's Box**. Ill. Jack Stockman. Sisters, OR: Questar, 1997. 31p. $9.99. ISBN 1-57673-139-1.

A young boy in Jerusalem fills his wooden box with remembrances of Jesus and Holy Week: a tuft of hair from the donkey that carried Jesus into Jerusalem, a broken cup from the Passover dinner, a twig from the Garden of Gethsemane, a thorn from Jesus' crown, a nail from Golgotha, and a piece of the burial cloth. Altogether, the items comprise the treasure of Jesus himself and his redemptive sacrifice. With idealized, full-page pictures and a framed text, the format is handsome.

240.   Doney, Merle. **Jesus: The Man Who Changed History**. Colorado Springs, CO: Lion, 1997. Unp. $7.99pa. LC 87-22857. ISBN 0-7459-2099-3.

This clear and thoughtful biography separates biblical facts from mere traditions and fills in the historical background well, explaining the condition of the Middle East and the Jewish people at the time. The calling of the disciples, the Sermon on the Mount, some of the parables and miracles, the events of Holy Week, the Resurrection, and other known events are drawn together smoothly into an absorbing narrative. Maps, diagrams, cartoons, quizzes, drawings, boxed summaries of information, color photographs, and stills from the film *Jesus of Nazareth* add to the interest and information of the text, which is indexed by section.

241.   Griffin, William. **Jesus for Children**. Mystic, CT: Twenty-Third Publications, 1994. 134p. $9.95pa. ISBN 0-89622-610-7.

This revised and expanded edition (published in 1985 by Harper and Row) presents sixty-one stories from the Gospels in abbreviated forms. The language is modern and vivid, excellent for reading aloud, and the basic meanings are retained. The book has Scripture and lectionary indexes.

242.   Handel, George Frideric. **The Messiah: The Wordbook for the Oratorio**. Ill. Barry Moser. New York: HarperCollins, 1992. Unp. $20.00. LC 91-21661. ISBN 0-06-021779-0.

This handsomely printed libretto has Scripture citations for each portion and full-page reproductions of dramatic paintings. The portrayals of Jesus during Holy Week are particularly moving. The scholarly introduction, the Christian symbolism, and the forcefulness of the illustrations direct this work to older children and adults.

243. **Jesus of Nazareth: A Life of Christ Through Pictures**. New York: Simon and Schuster, 1994. 38p. $16.00. LC 93-35867. ISBN 0-671-88651-7.

Reproductions of vibrant, beautiful paintings from the National Gallery of Art in Washington, D.C., illustrate excerpts from the King James Version. The topics include the Nativity, the baptism, the temptation in the wilderness, the calling of Peter and Andrew, the marriage at Cana, the events of Holy Week, and the Ascension. The European artists, from the fourteenth through seventeenth centuries, include Botticelli, Lippi, David, El Greco, and Veneziano, among others.

244. L'Engle, Madeleine. **The Glorious Impossible**. New York: Simon and Schuster, 1990. Unp. $19.95. LC 89-6104. ISBN 0-671-68690-9.

Stunningly illustrated with color reproductions of twenty-four frescoes by Giotto, found in the Scrovegni Chapel in Padua, this book reiterates the miraculous theme that "with God, nothing is impossible." The text is a series of wise and joyous meditations on Jesus' life, from the Annunciation to the Ascension, as well as the Pentecost, stressing the events of his birth and Holy Week rather than the details of his ministry.

245. Le Tord, Bijou. **The River and the Rain: The Lord's Prayer**. Ill. author. New York: Delacorte, 1994. Unp. $15.95. LC 93-20730. ISBN 0-385-32034-5.

This charming, simplified adaptation of the Lord's Prayer is paired with delicate, primitive, pale watercolors that tell the story of humanity's destruction of the rainforests with fire, bulldozer, and chainsaw. The adaptation serves as a reminder that our stewardship of the earth is at risk.

246. Rock, Lois. **The Gentle Carpenter**. Ill. Cathy Baxter. Colorado Springs, CO: Lion, 1997. Unp. $7.99. ISBN 0-7459-3636-9.

This pared-down version of Jesus' life is ideal as an introduction for young children. His birth, his visit to the Temple at age twelve, examples of his teachings and miracles, his death and resurrection, and the spread of the Gospel of love are briefly discussed and brightly illustrated in a sweet, folk-art manner.

247. Thomas, Mack. **Through the Eyes of Jesus**. Ill. Hilber Nelson. Sisters, OR: Gold'n'Honey Books, 1995. 62p. $14.99. LC 95-40220. ISBN 0-88070-803-4.

This imaginary autobiography of Jesus includes his baptism, temptation in the desert, miracles, transfiguration, and Holy Week. His parents have told him early in his life about his divine origin, and all the events emphasize this assurance. Vivid and creative, the text has large, bold illustrations with irregular, forceful lines.

Miracles

248. Billington, Rachel. **The First Miracles**. Ill. Barbara Brown. Grand Rapids, MI: William B. Eerdmans, 1990. Unp. $12.95. ISBN 0-8028-3687-9.

A chronological account of Jesus' miracles, beginning with that of his birth and ending with the healing of the servant's cut-off ear, is illustrated with reproductions of traditional, realistic paintings. The straightforward text draws the incidents together with dignified simplicity and without unnecessary elaboration.

249.   Caswell, Helen. **Loaves and Fishes**. Ill. author. Nashville, TN: Abingdon Press, 1993. Unp. $11.95. LC 93-25308. ISBN 0-687-22526-4.

Thomas, a young brown-haired boy, leaves home carrying five small barley loaves. He hooks two fish and is cooking them when he sees a crowd of people on the beach. Jesus arrives in a boat, and Thomas listens to him. At suppertime, Thomas offers his little bounty of food to share with the people. Softly colored pictures enhance this well-told story.

250.   Lashbrook, Marilyn. **Nothing to Fear: Jesus Walks on Water**. Ill. Chris Sharp. Me Too! Readers Series. Dallas, TX: Roper Press, 1991. Unp. $5.95. LC 96-61060. ISBN 0-86606-443-5.

Funny and appealing watercolor-and-ink cartoons reinforce a lively rendition, in a beginning-reader vocabulary, of Jesus calming the storm and walking on the water. The Scripture sources are cited.

251.   Thomas, Suzanne. **Read-It-Again Bible Stories: The Miracles of Jesus**. Ill. Michael Fleishman. Elgin, IL: David C. Cook, 1991. 62p. $9.95. LC 91-12039. ISBN 1-55513-410-6.

Clever, rollicking verses narrate how Jesus turns water into wine, heals the man lowered from the roof, tells the man at the Bethesda Pool to take up his bed and walk, feeds the 5,000, and fills the disciples' fishing nets. The lighthearted tone and funny cartoon illustrations do not detract from the spiritual messages but instead make them more properly joyful.

Parables

252.   Caswell, Helen. **Parable of the Lost Coin**. Ill. author. Growing in Faith Library Series. Nashville, TN: Abingdon Press, 1993. Unp. $5.95pa. LC 92-33875. ISBN 0-687-30026-6.

In this modern version of Luke 15:8–10, Maria, a young Hispanic girl, takes her handmade pots by donkey to an outdoor market and sells them for ten coins. When she arrives home, she has only nine. She and her gray tiger cat sweep and shake out everything in the house, discovering the coin at last in a crack in the floor. Delighted, Maria has a party to celebrate, just as God and the angels celebrate the return of a lost soul. Warm, full-page watercolors suit the happy mood.

253.   Caswell, Helen. **Parable of the Mustard Seed**. Ill. author. Growing in Faith Library Series. Nashville, TN: Abingdon Press, 1992. Unp. $5.95pa. LC 92-15160. ISBN 0-687-30025-8.

In this modern version of Matthew 13:31–32, a young African American boy picks a tiny seed from a field of mustard plants, places it into a pot in a sunny window, waters it, and watches it grow into a big, yellow, flowering plant, just like the ones in the field. He knows that faith in God is like the mustard seed, tiny at first and then large and beautiful. Each simple line of text faces a charming, framed illustration, painted with softly rounded forms, sunny yellow, and sky blue.

254.   Doney, Merle. **The 99th Sheep**. Ill. Taffy Davies. Wheaton, IL: Tyndale House, 1991. Unp. $8.95. LC 90-72028. ISBN 0-8423-4740-2.

Illustrated with lively cartoons, the parable of the lost sheep (Luke 15:1-7) is told in a bright, informal style with lively dialogue. The sheep complain about tired feet, the crowding in the fold, and that stupid Daisy, who always strays. The story is well shaped with entertaining details, and the essential message is retained.

255.   Keane, Glen. **Adam Raccoon and the King's Big Dinner**. Ill. author. Elgin, IL: David C. Cook, 1991. Unp. $7.99. LC 90-23327. ISBN 1-55513-362-2.

In this freely interpreted version of the parable of the Great Supper (Luke 14:15–24) illustrated with jolly cartoons, Adam Raccoon is sent out by the Lion King with invitations to a grand dinner, but chooses to give them only to animals who seem important. He ignores the very old turtle, the very young birds, and the unappealing skunk. All the important animals are too busy to come, and so he is sent out again to invite the less elevated animals to the feast. They come gladly. Discussion questions reinforce the parable's message.

256.   Lane, Christopher A. **King Leonard's Great Grape Harvest**. Ill. Sharon Dahl. Wheaton, IL: Victor Books, 1991. Unp. $7.99. ISBN 0-89693-268-0.

The parable of the workers in the vineyard (Matthew 10:1–16) is retold as the action of King Leonard the Lion in Kidderminster Kingdom. Leonard hires different groups of animals throughout the day to pick his grapes before they spoil. He pays them all the same wage, regardless of the amount of time they work, causing some resentment. Although somewhat overwritten, the story makes its point successfully. Its appeal is increased by the large, action-filled illustrations.

257.   Lane, Christopher A. **Kingdom Parables: Favorite Bible Parables for Children**. Ill. Sharon Dahl. Wheaton, IL: Victor Books, 1994. 188p. $15.99. ISBN 1-56476-275-0.

This is a revised collection of individually published Kidderminster Kingdom tales. The parables include Sir Humphrey's honeystands (the unforgiving servant, Matthew 18:21–35), Nicholas and his neighbors (the good Samaritan, Luke 10:25–37), King Leonard's celebration (the great banquet, Luke 14:15–24), Cornelius T. Mouse and Sons (the prodigal son, Luke 15:11–32), Mrs. Beaver and the wolf at the door (the importunate widow, Luke 18:1–7), and King Leonard's great grape harvest (the workers in the vineyard, Matthew 20:1–16). Each is retold creatively, using anthropomorphic animals and different plots, but the messages are the same as in Jesus' parables, which are included with the Scripture citations at the end of each story. The illustrations are large and handsome.

258.   Lane, Christopher A. **Mrs. Beaver and the Wolf at the Door**. Ill. Sharon Dahl. Wheaton, IL: Victor Books, 1991. Unp. $7.99. ISBN 0-89693-269-9.

The parable of the importunate widow (Luke 18:1–7) who wore down the indifferent judge with her pleas for justice is retold with animal characters. The widowed Mrs. Beaver, threatened with eviction from her home by an unscrupulous wolf and his weasel henchman, pesters a stuffy elk judge until he declares the eviction illegal. Large, dynamic pictures add interest to the somewhat overly detailed narrative.

259.   Laughlin, Charlotte. **Where's the Lost Sheep?** Ill. Charles Reasoner. Dallas, TX: Zondervan, 1992. Unp. $9.99. ISBN 0-8499-0919-8.

Lift-the-flap-style, brightly colored, lively cartoons appealingly illustrate the shepherd's search for the missing lamb (Luke 15:1–7) in many amusing places. The expressed theme is that of Jesus as the good shepherd who keeps us safe.

260.   St. John, Patricia. **Stories That Jesus Told: The Parables Retold for Children**. Ill. Tony Morris. Ridgefield, CT: Morehouse, 1995. 57p. $16.95. LC 95-7421. ISBN 0-8192-1644-5.

Eighteen well-known parables, such as the wise and foolish virgins, the sower and the seeds, the prodigal son, and the lost sheep, have explanatory introductions relating the events to everyday experiences, an easy-to-read form of the story, and conclusions as to how the teachings apply. The illustrations are realistic and attractive.

261.   Strong, Dina. **The Vineyard and the Wedding: Stories of God's Kingdom**. Ill. Allan Eitzen. Storyteller Series. Denver, CO: Living the Good News, 1996. 32p. $18.95pa. ISBN 1-889108-09-X.

In a huge paperback format suitable for storytelling to groups of young children, four parables from the Gospel of Matthew dealing with the kingdom of God are retold in extremely simple versions. Included are the wise and foolish virgins, the king's feast, the workers in the vineyard, and the two sons whose father asks them to pick grapes. Explanations of the parables' meanings are not given. The brightly colored illustrations are set in various nonbiblical locales, which resemble medieval Europe, modern Italy, and an exotic eastern country where the men wear turbans.

Holy Week, Easter, and the Resurrection

262.   Heyer, Carol. **The Easter Story**. Ill. author. Nashville, TN: Ideals, 1990. Unp. $11.95. LC 89-49056. ISBN 0-8249-8439-0.

This condensed account of Holy Week eliminates the role of Judas Iscariot completely but otherwise covers the main events, ending when Jesus appears to Mary Magdalene in the garden. The purpose of the book is to explain Easter as the Christian celebration of Jesus' resurrection. The somber, full-page, realistic illustrations never show Jesus' face.

263.   Kennedy, Pamela. **An Easter Celebration: Traditions and Customs from Around the World**. Nashville, TN: Ideals, 1990. 32p. $10.95. LC 90-21722. ISBN 0-8249-8506-0.

An absorbing text discusses the pre-Christian background of spring festivals and goddesses; the symbolism of new birth and rebirth found in flowers, eggs, rabbits, and lambs; the customs celebrating Holy Week; Passover; and two Easter legends. A variety of photographs, prints, and reproductions of paintings and stained-glass windows illustrates this pleasant, instructive introduction to the Christian meaning of Easter. It is suitable for all faiths and ages.

264. Spellman, Susan. **A Small Treasury of Easter Poems and Prayers**. Honesdale, PA: Boyds Mills Press, 1997. 32p. $8.95. LC 96-79428. ISBN 1-56397-647-1.

The first section of the book contains secular poems about spring and the Easter bunny. The second section contains gently religious poetry about flowers, blessings, Jesus' love for children, Easter Sunday at church, and so on. Interspersed are Bible quotations about the entry into Jerusalem (Palm Sunday), the morning of the Resurrection, and John 11:25–26. The poetic ideas are easily grasped; the imagery, pleasant and positive. The colored-pencil illustrations are undistinguished.

265. Wildsmith, Brian. **The Easter Story**. Ill. author. New York: Alfred A. Knopf, 1993. Unp. $15.00. LC 93-25097. ISBN 0-679-84727-8.

A little donkey accompanies Jesus through the events of Holy Week and witnesses his resurrection and ascension. The book's huge, panoramic illustrations, full of action and detail, in sumptuous colors of jewels and gold, depict the walled, arched, and domed Jerusalem of the Crusades, and splendidly costumed angels, soldiers, followers of Jesus, and curious onlookers. The simple text is sketchy but adequate.

Older and Noteworthy

Other books related to Jesus' life and teachings include *The 99 Plus One* by Gerard A. Pottebaum (Augsburg, 1971), *The Bronze Bow* by Elizabeth Speare (Houghton Mifflin, 1961), *The Story of Jesus* by Norman J. Bull (Abingdon, 1982), *The Story of Jesus* by Christopher Rawson (Usborne, 1981), *My First Book About Jesus* by Walter Wangerin (Rand McNally, 1983), *Dance in the Desert* by Madeleine L'Engle (Farrar, Straus & Giroux, 1969), *Easter* by Jan Pienkowski (Knopf, 1989), *Easter* by Gail Gibbons (Holiday, 1989), *Mary of Nazareth* by Cecil Bodker (R & S Books, 1989), *Petook* by Caryll Houselander (Holiday, 1988), and *He Is Risen* by Elizabeth Winthrop (Holiday, 1985).

Chapter Seven

The Nativity Story and Christmas

266. Branley, Franklyn M. **The Christmas Sky**. Rev. ed. Ill. Stephen Fierser. New York: Thomas Y. Crowell, 1990. 48p. $14.95. LC 89-71210. ISBN 0-690-04770-3.

Bold new illustrations in unusual colors, depicting sturdy figures, billowing clouds, and a streaming comet, adorn the revised edition of this excellent study of the Star of Bethlehem. Was it a meteor, comet, supernova, conjunction of planets, or miracle? While discussing the various possibilities, the author, a distinguished astronomer and science writer for children, traces the biblical events in their historical setting.

267. Cooney, Barbara. **The Story of Christmas**. Ill. Loretta Krupinski. New York: HarperCollins, 1995. Unp. $14.95. LC 94-18687. ISBN 0-06-023433-4.

This newly illustrated reprint of *Christmas* (Crowell Holiday Books, 1967), written and illustrated by Barbara Cooney, opens with the story of Jesus' birth. It continues with a discussion of the pre-Christian and pagan midwinter festivals and merry customs that were amalgamated into the Christian celebration. Joyous Christmas traditions throughout the world are stressed, as well as the Nativity story, with its surrounding legends of worshiping and gift giving, speaking animals, the three kings, and so forth. Brightly colored, decorative colored-pencil and gouache pictures illustrate the book.

268. Hague, Michael. **Michael Hague's Family Christmas Treasury**. Ill. author. New York: Henry Holt, 1995. 118p. $19.95. LC 95-6068. ISBN 0-8050-1011-4.

Three sections discuss the story, spirit, and celebration of the Christmas. This attractive book contains Gospel excerpts from Luke and Matthew, King James Version; traditional carols; poetry by Christina Rosetti, e e cummings, and

Eleanor Farjeon; and familiar stories by O. Henry, Truman Capote, Willa Cather, Charles Dickens, and others. The illustrations are mixed-media pictures in various sizes and artistic techniques, from vividly realistic to winsome.

269. Kennedy, Pamela. **A Christmas Celebration: Traditions and Customs from Around the World**. Nashville, TN: Ideals, 1992. 32p. $12.00. LC 92-6135. ISBN 0-8249-8551-6.

Although the underlying theme is Christmas as the celebration of Jesus' birth, this book includes discussion of pre-Christian festivals that have expanded and enriched the event over the centuries, such as Saturnalia and Yuletide, which are times of gift giving and reconciliation. Symbols, legends, and ways of celebration are also part of the widespread coverage. Attractively arranged photographs, drawings, and reproductions of paintings illustrate the factual text, and the book is indexed.

270. Lankford, Mary D. **Christmas Around the World**. Ill. Karen Dugan. New York: William Morrow, 1995. 48p. $16.00. LC 93-38566. ISBN 0-688-12166-7.

Christmas customs in twelve countries are described. Nations such as Australia, Canada, Greece, Sweden, and Alaska, vary in their degree of religious emphasis, but in Ethiopia, Guatemala, and Mexico, the spiritual aspects predominate. The book is crammed with information about Christmas in each area; and crafts, a pronunciation guide, a bibliography, and an index are included. The text emphasizes the celebratory joy of the holiday, with bright, busy illustrations of smiling people.

271. Rollins, Charlemae. **Christmas Gif': An Anthology of Christmas Poems, Songs, and Stories Written by and About African-Americans**. Ill. Ashley Bryan. New York: William Morrow, 1993. LC 92-18976. ISBN 0-688-11667-1.

This reprint of the American classic (first published in 1963) has a new introduction and illustrations comprised of striking and powerful linoleum block prints in black and white. Poems, stories, spirituals, and memoirs of African Americans, such as Countee Cullen, Booker T. Washington, Langston Hughes, and Zora Neale Hurston, are included, all infused with a memorable Christmas message. The writing tones vary from funny to bittersweet, poignant, heartbreaking, wry, devout, and didactic.

272. Wilner, Isabel. **B Is for Bethlehem: A Christmas Alphabet**. Ill. Elisa Kleven. New York: Dutton, 1990. Unp. $14.99. LC 89-49481. ISBN 0-525-44622-2.

Simple rhymed couplets for each letter begin with *A* for *Augustus* (Caesar, that is), who decreed the census, through *Zeeland*, *Zurich*, and *Zanzibar*, where people will be lighting candles on Christmas Eve. All the personages, events, and places are cleverly and exuberantly illustrated with mixed-media folk art using brilliant colors, scintillating patterns, and star-spangled backgrounds.

273.   Yolen, Jane. **Hark! A Christmas Sampler**. Ill. Tomie dePaola. New York: Putnam, 1991. 128p. $19.95. LC 90-42865. ISBN 0-399-21853-X.

This big, beautiful, outstanding volume contains original poems and stories; adapted legends; traditional and new carols with lyrics and music; a history of the development of the holiday and its plants, foods, animals, music, and gift giving; and a Nativity play about the shepherds. Brilliant, beautifully balanced, elegantly decorative artwork, both witty and meditative, provides a sumptuous complement to the text. The emphasis is on the Christ Child.

Versions of the Nativity Story
Using Traditional Bible Texts

274.   Chorao, Kay. **The Christmas Story**. New York: Holiday House, 1996. Unp. $15.95. LC 96-5066. ISBN 0-8234-1251-2.

The simplified text, adapted from the King James Version of Luke 2:1–21 and Matthew 2:1–12, retains the dignity and flow of the original Christmas story. The events between the Annunciation and the journey to Bethlehem are omitted, but the flight to Egypt is included. Drawing upon the techniques of the Renaissance masters Murillo, Veronese, and Gerard Houthorst, the full-page illustrations are sweet, serene, and graceful, with beautifully embellished initial capital letters. Jesus is a robust infant and toddler, the Holy Family is traditionally fair-skinned, and Joseph has a grizzled beard.

275.   **The First Christmas**. New York: Simon and Schuster, 1992. 29p. $16.00. LC 92-11580. ISBN 0-671-79364-0.

Excerpts from Isaiah and the Gospels of Matthew and Luke are printed in a clear and elegant typeface and triumphantly illustrated with rich, golden beauty. Artists include Fra Filippo Lippi, Carlo Crivelli, Giorgione, Botticelli, and David, and all illustrations are reproductions of artwork from the National Gallery in London. The book includes notes about each painter.

276.   Hogrogrian, Nonny. **The First Christmas**. Ill. author. New York: Greenwillow, 1995. 32p. $15.00. LC 94-19367. ISBN 0-688-13579-X.

Quotations from the King James Version of Matthew and Luke, with some simple, bridging narrative, cover the Annunciation, Joseph's reassuring dream, the marriage of Mary and Joseph, Jesus' birth, and the visit of the wise men. Large reproductions of oil paintings, with skillfully individualized characters and an aura of warmth, reflect the awe surrounding these events.

277.   Muhlberger, Richard. **The Christmas Story: Told Through Paintings**. San Diego, CA: Harcourt Brace Jovanovich, 1990. 40p. $16.95. LC 90-4774. ISBN 0-15-200426-2.

Glowing with reds and golds, superb reproductions of paintings by Flemish and Italian Renaissance masters and owned by New York's Metropolitan Museum of Art illustrate the King James Version of the Nativity, from Zacharias and Elisabeth through the flight to Egypt. A fascinating commentary about religious symbolism and artistic techniques accompanies each reproduction.

278.   Ray, Jane. **The Story of Christmas: Words from the Gospels of Matthew and Luke**. Ill. author. New York: Dutton, 1991. Unp. $15.95. LC 91-11357. ISBN 0-525-44768-7.

Sweeping green sheep meadows below star-studded skies, angels wearing gorgeously decorated robes and swooping down from heaven, and an open-sided stable filled with adoring animals are some of the spectacular scenes illustrating the traditional King James text from the Gospels of Matthew and Luke. The decorative folk art gleams with jewel tones and gold. The Virgin, with her hair in a thick braid, is a being of tenderness and serenity as she cuddles and nurses her infant.

279.   Sanderson, Ruth. **The Nativity: From the Gospels of Matthew and Luke**. Ill. author. Boston: Little, Brown, 1993. Unp. $15.95. LC 92-9071. ISBN 0-316-77064-7.

The text, taken from the Revised Standard Version, includes the Annunciation, the journey to Bethlehem, the visit of the magi, the slaughter of the innocents, the flight to Egypt, and the return to Nazareth. In a beautiful format, each page of text and each illustration is framed with tendrils, flowers, birds, stars, butterflies, and vignettes of landscapes. The reproductions of Renaissance-influenced paintings show Mary as a blue-robed maiden, Joseph as a graybeard, and Jesus as an ivory-skinned infant, all with gold haloes.

280.   **Visions of Christmas**. New York: Simon and Schuster, 1997. Unp. $18.00. LC 96-31506. ISBN 0-689-81359-7.

The traditional King James text from Matthew, Luke, and Isaiah, beautifully printed, is illustrated with finely executed, richly colored reproductions of Renaissance triptychs from various European museums and the Cloisters, and from the Metropolitan Museum of Art in New York. Most of the triptychs fold out to reveal the three panels. The book includes an index of paintings, with explanatory notes.

281.   Wijngaard, Juan. **The Nativity**. Ill. author. New York: Lothrop, Lee & Shepard, 1990. 29p. $13.95. LC 90-53095. ISBN 0-688-09870-3.

The traditional passages from Luke, Matthew, and Isaiah are presented in an exceptionally handsome format. Reproductions of formal, muted, but effectively dramatic and realistic paintings, suffused with a spiritual beauty, illustrate the text.

Retellings of the Nativity Story

282.   Alavedra, Joan. **They Followed a Bright Star**. Ill. Ulises Wensell. New York: Putnam, 1994. Unp. $15.95. LC 93-6065. ISBN 0-399-22706-7.

In a thoughtful, simply dramatized text, the shepherds, summoned by the herald angels, are wending their way to the stable when they pass four people involved in preparing the way for Jesus' later ministry, as they have been instructed to do by the angels. Thus, they cannot leave their duties to join in the rejoicing at the stable. Large, sweeping pictures show peasants toiling through the snowy night to the glowing stable, lit by the fire-raining star.

283.   Allan, Nicholas. **Jesus' Christmas Party**. Ill. author. New York: Random House, 1992. Unp. $9.99. LC 91-17092. ISBN 0-679-82688-2.

The benighted innkeeper is being awakened constantly: first by Mary and Joseph, to whom he gives blankets and directs to the stable; then by Joseph, asking for a smaller blanket, please; then by a brilliant star shining in his eyes; then by shepherds; then by kings; and, lastly, by a loud chorus of angels. Out of patience, he storms out to the stable and is thrilled by what he finds. Winsome ink-and-watercolor cartoons illustrate this lively and humorous tale.

284.   Carlstrom, Nancy White. **I Am Christmas**. Ill. Lori McElrath-Eslick. Grand Rapids, MI: William B. Eerdmans, 1995. Unp. $17.00. LC 94-47931. ISBN 0-8028-5075-8.

This is a moving, poetic account of the journey to Bethlehem and the birth of the holy infant. Interwoven are images of Jesus as the way, the vine, the cup, bread, a lily, Emmanuel, light, a shepherd, a door, the truth, the life, the morning star, the word, a gift, the beginning, and the end. Reproductions of dramatic oil paintings, filled with disquieting, sweeping forms, illustrate the story powerfully. The book includes Scripture references.

285.   Carlstrom, Nancy White. **Ten Christmas Sheep**. Ill. Cynthia Fisher. Grand Rapids, MI: William B. Eerdmans, 1996. Unp. $13.00. ISBN 0-8028-5137-1.

This cheerful pop-up book about a Nativity pageant is dominated by ten multiethnic children in sheep suits. They bleat, giggle, wiggle, and nap as the Holy Family, kings, shepherds, and angels watch benignly. Appealing, lively sketches illustrate a short, descriptive poem.

286.   Ganeri, Anita. **The Story of Christmas: A Nativity Tale for Children**. New York: Dorling Kindersley, 1995. 29p. $12.95. LC 94-44796. ISBN 0-7894-0146-0.

Young children dressed in simple but effective costumes act out the Nativity, from the Annunciation through the flight to Egypt, in a series of excellent, appealing color photographs with simple, painted backdrops. Live donkeys, goats, calves, lambs, chickens, and camels are added to the scenes. The multiethnic angels and shepherds are especially charming. The story is told clearly in short sentences, making this large-format book well suited for preschoolers, kindergarteners, and beginning readers.

287.   Goffin, Josse. **The Christmas Story**. Ill. author. New York: Ticknor and Fields, 1994. Unp. $8.95. LC 94-4134. ISBN 0-395-70929-6.

This charming, simple, condensed version of the Christmas story is told in rhyme. Mary and Joseph come to the Bethlehem stable where Jesus is born, welcomed by the barn animals, visited by shepherds and sheep, and worshipped by kings. Appealing, childlike artwork with warm pastel shades helps young children understand the basic facts.

288.   Goffin, Josse. **Silent Christmas**. Ill. author. Honesdale, PA: Boyds Mills Press, 1991. Unp. $14.95. LC 90-83430. ISBN 1-878093-08-8.

This sweet, wordless picture book, with simple but expressive and warmly colored cartoons, begins with a blond-haired Mary in a peasant dress receiving a dove-borne letter for the Annunciation. Pregnant, she journeys by donkey to Bethlehem. Included are the appearance of the Christmas star and the worship of the shepherds and kings, while approving animals stand by the manger.

289.   Graham, Lorenz. **Every Man Heart Lay Down**. Ill. Colleen Browning. Honesdale, PA: Boyds Mills Press, 1993. Unp. $15.95. LC 92-72829. ISBN 1-56397-184-4.

This welcome reprinting (the work was first copyrighted in 1946 and first printed with these illustrations in 1970) tells about the Nativity, with poignant freshness, in the lilting cadences of a Liberian storyteller. God is vexed with the world and ready to "break the world and lose the people" when his small "pi-can" boy begs his father to let him go down to earth and teach the people, even knowing that he will suffer and die as a consequence. The book is splendidly illustrated with stylized, compelling African art.

290.   Heyer, Carol. **The Christmas Story**. Ill. author. Nashville, TN: Ideals, 1991. Unp. $11.95. LC 91-9101. ISBN 0-8249-8512-5.

This clear and accurate retelling of the Nativity uses simple language and skillfully connects Jesus' birth with Christmas celebrations. The book ends with a summary of Jesus' life and importance to Christians. The full-page pictures in vivid colors illustrate the story with dramatic realism.

291.   Johnson, Pamela. **The Story of the First Christmas**. Ill. author. New York: HarperCollins, 1991. 24p. $2.95pa. LC 90-23154. ISBN 0-694-00364-6.

Warmly shaded watercolors illustrate this matter-of-fact retelling of the Nativity portions of the Gospels. The pictures show a variety of Semitic people in authentic earthly settings and a bevy of robust feminine angels in the starry heavens, glorifying God with upraised arms.

292.   MacMath, Fiona. **The Coming of the King**. Ill. Francesca Pelizzoli. Nashville, TN: Oliver-Nelson, 1991. Unp. $9.95. ISBN 0-8407-9607-2.

The clear, dignified text begins with an introductory section that likens the coming of Jesus to the lighting of an eternal flame. Next are succinct versions of the stories of Zacharias and Elizabeth, Mary and Gabriel, Mary's visit to Elizabeth while she is pregnant with John the Baptist, Joseph's reconciliation to Mary's pregnancy, the Nativity, Simeon and Anna at the Temple, the visit of the magi, the flight to Egypt, the slaughter of the innocents, and the return of the Holy Family to Nazareth, all supported by quotations from the New King James Version. Large, stylized, dramatic illustrations with luminous colors show lots of blue eyes and blond hair in the manner of Renaissance paintings.

293.   McFadzean, Anita. **One Special Star**. Ill. Kate Jaspers. New York: Simon and Schuster, 1990. Unp. $3.95pa. ISBN 0-671-74024-5.

In a simple way, this cheerfully rhymed counting book tells and shows the events of Jesus' birth. There are ten stars twinkling above Bethlehem, nine startled shepherds, eight trembling sheep, seven shimmering angels, six sleepy donkeys, five friendly calves, four fleecy lambs, three royal gifts, two smiling parents, one precious baby, and one shining star.

294. Pfister, Marcus. **The Christmas Star**. Ill. author. New York: North-South Books, 1993. Unp. $17.95. LC 93-15143. ISBN 1-55858-203-7.

Eye-catching, gleaming silver accents the stars, palace roofs, crowns, and gifts in the misty watercolors of this attractive book. Freely and gracefully interpreted, this version of the Nativity story opens with the shepherds, switches to the three kings, adds a parade of wild animals, and culminates in a peaceful and loving gathering at the stable.

295. Strong, Dina. **Many Miles to Bethlehem**. Ill. Jenny Williams. Story-Teller Series. Denver, CO: Living the Good News, 1996. 32p. $18.95pa. ISBN 1-889108-10-3.

This huge picture book, providing easy viewing for story hours, has three sections: "Mary of Galilee"—sprightly verses about a cheerful, bright-eyed young woman going about her daily chores; "Many Miles to Bethlehem"—Mary and Joseph's journey over rough terrain and Jesus' birth in the stable cave, told in simple prose; and "One Baby Sleeping"—a cumulative account of the animals, shepherds, and angelic choirs surrounding the birth. Lively watercolors are filled with action and detail.

296. Teasdale, Sarah. **Christmas Carol**. Ill. Dale Gottlieb. New York: Henry Holt, 1993. Unp. $14.95. ISBN 0-8050-2695-9.

Merry, bright, gouache illustrations in a bold, primitive style portray multiethnic shepherds, kings, and wise men striding toward the Nativity stable while smiling angels hover. The simple, melodious poem is charming in its imagery.

Christmas Stories

297. Anaya, Rudolfo. **The Farolitos of Christmas**. Ill. Edward Gonzales. New York: Hyperion, 1995. Unp. $14.95. LC 94-48073. ISBN 0-7868-0060-7.

In northern New Mexico during World War II, Luz's grandfather, who makes luminaria from wood each year, is too ill to go outdoors. Luz fears that the shepherds in the Christmas Eve procession to the church will pass by their house if it has no lights. She conceives a new idea: candles in paper bags, weighted by sand. She sets out dozens, and a new farolito tradition is born. Crowning the celebration, her papa comes home from the war, and her grandfather recovers, thanks to the Santo Nino. Reproductions of expressive, realistic paintings illustrate this sweet story, and a glossary of Spanish terms is included.

298. Ciavonne, Jean. **Carlos, Light the Farolito**. Ill. Donna Clair. New York: Clarion, 1995. 28p. $14.95. LC 94-24510. ISBN 0-395-66759-3.

Young Carlos and his family are preparing to celebrate La Noche Buena, but his grandfather, who always sings the part of the innkeeper when the pilgrims in the Las Posadas procession reach his home, has been delayed. Carlos must take his place. The gentle text and bold, bright acrylic illustrations capture the festivity and the sacredness of this lovely Hispanic tradition. The book includes an explanatory note.

299. Collington, Peter. **A Small Miracle**. Ill. author. New York: Alfred A. Knopf, 1997. Unp. $18.00. LC 96-53916. ISBN 0-679-88725-3.

This exquisitely executed, wordless picture book celebrates Christian love at Christmas in the story of a poor elderly woman who lives in a caravan and plays the accordion as a street musician to earn money for food. On the brink of exhaustion, somehow she summons the strength to fight a thief who has stolen her few coins and vandalized the church where the Nativity creche is arranged. She restores lovingly the figures to their proper places and then collapses in the snow. The Holy Family, shepherds, and kings come alive and minister to her graciously.

300. Dellinger, Annetta. **The Jesus Tree**. Ill. Susan Stoehr Morris. St. Louis, MO: Concordia, 1991. Unp. $8.99. ISBN 0-570-04191-0.

In a traditional, middle-class home, two young girls and their parents explore the symbolism of the ornaments, shown in pictures of cozy, sentimental scenes, as they decorate their Christmas tree. The lights represent Jesus as the light of the world; each snowflake is different, just as each person in the world is unique; the candy canes are like shepherds' crooks; the multicolored, round globes are the world and its peoples of many colors; the star represents the Star of Bethlehem; and so on. Their exploration leads to a discussion of Jesus as God's gift to the world.

301. dePaola, Tomie. **Country Angel Christmas**. Ill. author. New York: Putnam, 1995. Unp. $16.95. LC 94-37433. ISBN 0-399-23002-5.

This charming story, mixing St. Nicholas and angels, is illustrated with winsome, pink-winged children and animals in dynamic, decorative patterns. Santa is in a red plaid lumber jacket and tam. The plot deals with the competition between the multiethnic, country child-angels and the bigger, more powerful archangels and heavenly choir angels to create the best Christmas for heaven. The country angels prepare a simple but festive celebration and surprise and delight all by pulling the Star of Bethlehem across the sky like a giant balloon. As a result, they are placed first in the procession to the Nativity stable.

302. Dixon, Ann. **Merry Birthday, Nora Noel**. Ill. Mark Graham. Grand Rapids, MI: William B. Eerdmans, 1996. Unp. $15.00. LC 96-30392. ISBN 0-8028-5105-3.

As a father lights the five Advent candles, one for each of the five weeks preceding Christmas Day, he tells his youngest daughter about her development and birth, accompanying his discourse with meditations about the birth and meaning of Jesus. The poetic text is beautifully illustrated with radiant, dreamy, idealized family scenes.

303. Hoffman, Mary. **An Angel Just Like Me**. Ill. Cornelius Van Wright and Ying-Hwa Hu. New York: Dial, 1997. Unp. $14.99. LC 97-1428. ISBN 0-8037-2265-6.

Tyler, a young African American boy, asks some penetrating questions about how the Nativity is depicted traditionally: Why are there no black angels? Why does the baby Jesus not look Jewish? His parents have no explanations, but an artist friend creates an angel carved in Tyler's likeness. After his Hispanic, Asian, and other friends see it, they clamor for their own special angels. Idealized, realistic watercolors offer charm and radiance to this straightforward, sympathetic story.

304.   Lussert, Anneliese. **The Christmas Visitor.** Ill. Loek Koopmans. New York: North-South Books, 1995. Unp. $15.95. LC 95-1642. ISBN 1-55858-449-8.

In this moral tale, a wealthy, arrogant man hears that a king will visit his town and orders his crippled wife to put candles in every window and cook a fine meal. Instead, a poor, hungry man asks for shelter. The rich man rejects him, but his wife, feeling pity, clothes and feeds the stranger. When she is cured, the husband realizes that he has rejected the awaited king and rushes out into the snow to follow him, sharing his own clothing with people along the way who are suffering from the cold. He is rewarded by finding the Nativity stable, shimmering in the forest. Large pictures show the characters in Renaissance dress in a dimly lit, chilly house and cold, blue, snowy woods.

305.   McKissack, Patricia, and Fredrick McKissack. **From Heaven Above: The Story of Christmas Proclaimed by the Angels.** Ill. Barbara Knutson. Minneapolis, MN: Augsburg Fortress, 1992. Unp. $4.95pa. LC 92-70385. ISBN 0-8066-2609-7.

Six very short stories, each introduced by a quotation from the Gospels concerning angelic communication, teach lessons about forgiveness, trust, kindness, courage, and overcoming fear. The stories stress relationships between grandparents and grandchildren. Multiethnic American families are shown in softly colored illustrations.

306.   Paterson, Katherine. **A Midnight Clear: Stories for the Christmas Season.** New York: Lodestar, 1995. 212p. $16.00. LC 95-12590. ISBN 0-525-67529-9.

These didactic short stories emphasize how, often surprisingly, the holiness of Christmas penetrates ordinary lives. Subjects include a boy who befriends a sprightly homeless woman, an old Chinese Christian who forms a strong bond with a young communist teacher, an elderly African American man who nurtures a young girl grudgingly tolerated by his white employer, and holiday love reawakened in the heart of a jaded father by the music of Mozart. The messages of love are simple and obvious.

307.   Watts, Bernadette. **The Christmas Bird.** Ill. author. New York: North-South Books, 1996. Unp. $15.95. ISBN 1-55858-603-2.

In the tradition of stories about a modest but loving gift offered to the infant Jesus, the Nativity scene is transported to a snowy, mountainous, northern European village. Young Katya, seeing the Christmas star and hearing of the birth nearby of a baby king, gathers three gifts to take to him: a cat, which runs away; bread, which is fed to hungry animals; and a whistle, which is spoiled when it falls into the snow. When she arrives, however, the laughing baby touches the mute whistle, transforming it into a live, singing bird. Large, charming, folk-art pictures illustrate the story.

308.   Wilkon, Jozef, and Hermann Moers. **Lullaby for a Newborn King.** Ill. Jozef Wilkon. New York: North-South Books, 1991. Unp. $14.95. LC 91-11684. ISBN 1-55858-123-5.

The familiar theme of a humble person having no gift for the baby Jesus, save his own talent, is pleasantly presented in an imaginative story. Simon and the other poor shepherds are frightened by the blazing light of the Bethlehem star, but their village wise man tells them to bring gifts to the new baby, to whom the star will lead them. Young Simon has nothing to take but his flute. His gift of a lullaby to soothe the crying infant, however, pleases everyone gathered in the stable. Sweeping, double-page illustrations in which the star flames gold, orange, rose, and purple show the simple, appealing peasants and their animals wide-eyed with awe.

309. Wojciechowski, Susan. **The Christmas Miracle of Jonathan Toomey**. Ill. P. J. Lynch. Cambridge, MA: Candlewick Press, 1995. Unp. $17.99. LC 94-48917. ISBN 1-56402-320-6.

A satisfying Christmas miracle occurs when a skilled woodcarver, misanthropic and bitter because of the loss of his wife and child, is redeemed by the task of creating a Nativity set for a widow and her young son. The boy's gentle reminders of the significance of each creche figure inspire the carver to work late each night to make them perfect. Large, realistic watercolors, dramatic and varied in their use of perspective and light, reflect perfectly the mood of the text.

Animals Gathered About the Manger

310. Coatsworth, Elizabeth. **Song of the Camels: A Christmas Poem**. Ill. Anna Vojtech. New York: North-South Books, 1997. Unp. $15.95. ISBN 1-55858-811-6.

This reprint of Coatsworth's affecting, artistic work (first published in 1935) celebrates the camels of the three magi. Far from their desert home, the camels carry their masters majestically to the Bethlehem stable, wait patiently as the magi kneel to worship, and then drift away, casting shadows of portending glory and danger at the feet of the baby. Reproductions of unusual, powerful oil paintings, suffused with the mystery of the holy event, show the camels wending their way through the deepening night to reach the radiance of the rough stone shelter where Mary and Joseph cherish their infant.

311. Duncan, Beverly K. **Christmas in the Stable**. Ill. author. San Diego, CA: Harcourt Brace Jovanovich, 1990. 32p. $14.95. LC 88-37953. ISBN 0-15-217758-2.

Nineteen charming and varied poems portray the Nativity through the eyes of all kinds of creatures, from camels and donkeys through mice and bees. The text is beautifully set on gracefully patterned floral backgrounds symbolic of Christmas and winter, and accompanied by delicate watercolor pictures.

312. Farber, Norma. **When It Snowed That Night**. Ill. Petra Mathers. New York: HarperCollins, 1993. Unp. $16.00. LC 92-27414. ISBN 0-06-021707-3.

In a wreath of Christmas poems, a stork, ladybug, camel, sloth, turtle, giraffe, dove, spider, cricket, lamb, and hog sing their protective and loving songs to the infant Jesus. After the kings have departed, the three queens come hurriedly, knowing that Mary will understand that they need to return to their homes. The poems vary in form, meter, and rhyme to suit each subject. The folk-art illustrations are bright and bold.

313.   Jewell, Nancy. **Christmas Lullaby**. Ill. Stefano Vitale. New York: Clarion, 1994. Unp. $14.95. LC 93-38786. ISBN 0-395-66586-8.

This artistic, simple poem about the loving gifts presented by various birds and animals to the infant Jesus has a smooth and soothing rhythm. It mentions the spider's blanket of silk, the lamb's pillow of fleece, the donkey's bed of hay, and so on, climaxing with a lullaby of purrs from the cat and her kittens. The figures parading to the stable are depicted with humor and verve in reproductions of glowing oil paintings.

314.   Kajpust, Melissa. **A Dozen Silk Diapers**. Ill. Veselina Tomova. New York: Hyperion, 1993. 32p. $13.95. LC 92-41937. ISBN 1-56282-456-2.

A kindly mother spider and her forty children, living in a stable outside Bethlehem, observe the birth of Jesus. Although one spiderlet has been warned that human beings are afraid of spiders and may hurt them, he is determined to see the baby and falls into the manger. Mary gently lifts him out, and the grateful spiders spin a dozen beautiful silk diapers to add to the infant's gifts. Charming folk-art watercolors gleam with jewel-like colors and depict the spiders with humanoid faces.

315.   Kennedy, X. J. **The Beasts of Bethlehem**. Ill. Michael McCurdy. New York: Macmillan, 1992. 39p. $13.95. LC 91-38417. ISBN 0-689-50561-2.

Short, insightful, poignant poems express the thoughts of the cow, owl, horse, camel, sheep, mouse, cat, snail, hen, hawk, ant, hummingbird, bat, mosquito, gnat, worm, ox, beetle, and donkey as they gather about the manger. Some are self-absorbed or bewildered, but most are deeply sensitive to the importance of Jesus' birth. The powerful, handsome pictures are prints of colored woodcuts.

316.   McClure, Gillian. **The Christmas Donkey**. Ill. author. New York: Farrar, Straus & Giroux, 1993. Unp. $5.95pa. ISBN 0-374-41191-3.

A fractious little donkey, who boasts that he will one day carry a king, is rejected by several rich buyers and eventually finds himself carrying Mary to Bethlehem. Although he is scornful of his modest burden at first, he becomes protective and heroic, escaping many dangers along the way and taking pride in his role as her steed. He is the first to kneel in worship after the Christ Child is born. The detailed, bright illustrations have a medieval flavor.

317.   Mills, Claudia. **One Small Lost Sheep**. Ill. Walter Lyon Krudop. New York: Farrar, Straus & Giroux, 1997. Unp. $16.00. LC 96-18609. ISBN 0-374-35649-1.

With misty, contemplative illustrations, this sweet story tells of a lame lamb, beloved of a young shepherd boy but lost somewhere in the hills of Bethlehem. Distraught and exhausted by his fruitless search for her, the boy sleeps through the songs of the herald angels but wakes in time to join the procession to the Nativity stable. He finds loving animals there, his lamb among them, warming the baby with their breath.

318. Westfall, Robert. **The Witness**. Ill. Sophy Williams. New York: Dutton, 1994. Unp. $14.99. ISBN 0-525-45331-8.

An Egyptian cat, pampered and revered as the spirit of Bastet-Ra, is stolen from her home to be used as a ratter. She escapes from her captor and creeps into the stable, where she cuddles close to Mary. After Jesus is born, the cat, ebullient with purrs, crouches in worship. The magi, who recognize the cat's pedigree, say that even Bastet-Ra has come to give homage, describing her, to Mary's relief, as a gentle fertility spirit. Sensuous, richly colored, impressionist illustrations accompany the vividly written, creative, ecumenical text.

Legends

319. dePaola, Tomie. **The Legend of the Poinsettia**. Ill. author. New York: Putnam, 1994. Unp. $15.95. LC 93-87720. ISBN 0-399-21692-8.

Lucida, who lives high in the mountains of Mexico, is helping her mother weave a new blanket for the infant Jesus, to be used in the annual Christmas procession. When her mother becomes ill, Lucida tries to finish the blanket but tangles the threads terribly. Despondent that she has no gift for the Christ Child, she hides outside the church. A mysterious old woman finds Lucida and tells her that all gifts, even the bunch of weeds she carries, are acceptable, if given lovingly. The woman's weed bouquet blossoms with huge, flaming-red stars, and the poinsettia is miraculously born. The illustrations are elegant and tender.

320. Greene, Ellin. **The Legend of the Christmas Rose**. Ill. Charles Mikolaycak. New York: Holiday House, 1990. Unp. $15.95. LC 89-77511. ISBN 0-8234-0821-3.

An outlaw family living in the deep forest is privileged to experience a special miracle each Christmas when spring, with its warmth, flowers, and baby animals, comes briefly to celebrate the Savior's birth. In exchange for the promise of a pardon from the bishop, they show an elderly abbot and a hardheaded lay brother from a nearby monastery where this beautiful event takes place. The abbot dies in a state of joy, and the brother learns tolerance and faith. This lovely story, with magnificent illustrations, was originally adapted by Selma Lagerlof from a Swedish folktale.

321. Holder, Mig. **The Fourth Wise Man**. Ill. Tony Morris. Minneapolis, MN: Augsburg Fortress, 1993. 30p. $9.99. LC 94-74224. ISBN 0-8066-2713-1.

Handsomely illustrated with realistic watercolors, this is a lively retelling of the legend made famous by Henry Van Dyke. A fourth king, Artaban, who travels by himself in search of Jesus, sells all he owns to buy rich gifts for the infant. During his long journey, though, he sells his treasures, one by one, to help those in need. Distraught that he has nothing left for the Christ Child, he is reassured by a wise woman that, with every sacrifice he has made, he has truly served the king he seeks.

322. Mora, Pat, and Charles Ramirez Berg. **The Gift of the Poinsettia**. Ill. David Leckon. Houston, TX: Pinata Books, 1995. Unp. $14.95. LC 94-37233. ISBN 1-55885-137-2.

Carlos and his elderly aunt are so poor that they have no gift, except for a lowly plant from the field, to bring to the infant Jesus on Christmas Eve. When

Carlos weeps on his small plant, though, its leaves turn scarlet and beautiful from the magic of his love. The Las Posadas customs in Mexico, with singing children who go from door to door for eight nights before Christmas Eve, bearing statues and repeating the journey of Mary and Joseph as they seek an inn, are described. Colorful, full-page scenes of the festivities illustrate the bilingual English and Spanish text. The book includes the musical scores and lyrics of the special Posadas songs.

Carols and Songs

323.   Blumen, Karen L. **The Friendly Beasts**. Ill. John J. Blumen. Minneapolis, MN: Augsburg Fortress, 1997. Unp. $7.00pa. LC 97-28193. ISBN 0-8066-3330-1.

This augmented version of the well-known song adds five additional verses to Robert Davis's original lyrics, which have been slightly altered. The donkey, cow, cat, dove, spider, sheep, dog, camels, and mice sing of their gifts to the baby Jesus as they gather about the manger. The double-page pictures show winsome animals with large, bright eyes gazing in wonder and love. The musical score is included.

324.   Brebeuf, John de. **The Huron Carol**. Ill. Frances Tyrrell. New York: Dutton, 1990. Unp. $15.00. LC 91-35965. ISBN 0-525-44909-4.

This beautiful Christmas song, which relates the Nativity to the spiritual beliefs of the Huron nation, was written by a French missionary. In it, God (Gitchi Manitou) sends Native American maiden choirs to hunters, and three chiefs bear gifts of fox and beaver pelts to the newborn king. The baby brings beauty, peace, and joy to all the world. The book includes the musical score, with lyrics in English and French, and one verse in the old Huron, and an explanatory note. Stunning illustrations of Native Americans in deerskins and furs, against blue-and-white winter backgrounds of birches, birds, stars, animals, and snowflakes, are a perfect complement.

325.   Chamberlain, Sarah. **The Friendly Beasts**. Ill. author. New York: Dutton, 1991. Unp. $13.95. LC 91-2115. ISBN 0-525-44773-3.

Warm blues, browns, and golds and simple, crisply outlined figures illustrate this well-known song about the animals' gifts to the baby Jesus in the Nativity stable.

326.   Delacre, Lulu. **Las Navidades: Popular Christmas Songs from Latin America**. Ill. author. New York: Scholastic, 1990. 32p. $12.95. LC 89-28375. ISBN 0-540-43548-5.

Twelve joyful songs, with lyrics in Spanish and English, are illustrated with large reproductions of tropically colored paintings, depicting Puerto Rican families celebrating the holidays, from Christmas through Epiphany. Explanatory notes discuss various customs, and the book includes simple arrangements of the music.

327. Downes, Belinda. **Silent Night**. Ill. author. New York: Alfred A. Knopf, 1995. Unp. $18.00. LC 94-39435. ISBN 0-679-86959-X.

Many traditional carols are scored for voice and piano and outstandingly illustrated with full-page pictures of fabrics embroidered in gold and vibrantly colored threads. In a folk-art style blending naiveté and sophistication, the illustrations show simple figures against sumptuous backgrounds: the Virgin and child surrounded by oval insets of singing angels; joyful bellringers in the arched windows of a church; ships with full, white sails on a cobalt sea; and more. Each illustration is an exceptional expression of the carol it represents.

328. Forrester, Maureen. **Joy to the World**. Ill. Frances Tyrrell. New York: Dutton, 1993. 31p. $14.99. LC 93-2894. ISBN 0-525-45169-2.

This assortment of old favorites and lesser-known carols has historical notes for each carol and musical scores for voice and piano. The illustrations do not relate to the carols but to modern, wintry, Christmastime activities and events in the city, including Christmas pageants, snow shoveling, skating, a bell choir, and snow angels, all beautifully executed in a realistic technique. Children of all races are shown experiencing the joys of the season.

329. Granfield, Linda. **Silent Night: The Song from Heaven**. Ill. Nelly Hofer and Ernst Hofer. Plattsburgh, NY: Tundra Books of Northern New York, 1997. Unp. $15.95. ISBN 0-88776-395-2.

The preparation of the Christmas creche in the Church of St. Nicola, Oberndorf, Austria, on the Christmas Eve during which the new carol "Silent Night" was first sung, is the central theme of this story. It is beautifully illustrated with elaborate cut-paper scenes of the Nativity in golds against black backgrounds. The informative end material discusses the history of the carol: its conception by Father Mohr and Franz Gruber in 1818, the growth of its popularity in the nineteenth century, the incident during World War I in 1914 in the trenches on Christmas Eve, when the battle stopped briefly as the German soldiers sang "Stille Nacht," and the various artists who have performed it. The first two stanzas' lyrics are included in German and English.

330. Guback, Georgia. **The Carolers**. Ill. author. New York: Greenwillow, 1992. Unp. $14.00. LC 90-41756. ISBN 0-688-09772-3.

Joyful, triumphant folk art shows winsome children dressed in vividly colored, intricately patterned garments, trudging merrily through the snow while singing eleven old favorites. Sometimes the children are shown beside appropriate biblical scenes and sometimes outside the windows of cozy homes where families are busily enjoying Christmas activities. The number of carolers grows as more and more children and adults from the various houses join them. The book includes lyrics and simple versions of the music.

331. **Hark! The Herald Angels Sing**. New York: Simon and Schuster, 1993. 45p. $17.00. LC 93-9144. ISBN 0-671-87146-3.

Eighteen beloved carols, arranged for voice and keyboard instruments, are gorgeously illustrated with full-page color reproductions of appropriate paintings, mostly Renaissance, from the National Gallery in London. Breughel, Fra Angelico, and Botticelli are among the artists represented. Excellent notes accompany an index of paintings.

332. Hodges, Margaret. **Silent Night: The Song and Its Story**. Ill. Tim Ludwig. Grand Rapids, MI: William B. Eerdmans, 1997. Unp. $16.00. LC 97-16408. ISBN 0-8028-5138-X.

An engagingly embellished account of the hasty composition by Franz Gruber and Father Mohr of "Silent Night" takes place in a realistic setting of Christmas Eve in Oberndorf. The book includes material about the carol's subsequent growth in popularity and significance from 1818 through the present day. Large reproductions of lush, evocative paintings illustrate the text. The musical score is included.

333. McCullough, L. E. **Plays of the Songs of Christmas**. Young Actors Series. Lyme, NH: Smith and Kraus, 1996. 132p. $19.95. LC 96-22834. ISBN 1-57525-062-4.

Stage plans, musical scores, and suggestions for sets, props, special effects, and period costumes accompany short plays, both humorous and serious, based upon religious and secular songs and carols. The interesting and unusual settings include southern New Mexico in 1701, for "Let Us Go, O Shepherds"; Provence in 1676, for "Bring a Torch, Jeanette, Isabella"; fourth-century Sicily, with Nicholas of Myra, for "O Thou Joyful Day"; and Appalachia in 1898, with feuding families, for "Go Tell It on the Mountain." Each play has engaging dialogue and a moral, which is reinforced by the lyrics of the song.

334. Richardson, Jean. **Stephen's Feast**. Ill. Alice Englander. Boston: Little, Brown, 1991. Unp. $15.95. LC 91-6392. ISBN 0-316-74435-2.

In this story based upon the carol "Good King Wenceslas," a diminutive, reluctant page must follow the king on his mission of mercy. Resentfully, he toils through the deep snow to reach a hut, dragging a sledge loaded with expensive gifts. Once he sees how the poor family is living, though, he is motivated to share a treasure of his own with a boy his age. Splendid illustrations with vivid reds, golds, and blues contrast the snowflake-spangled, chilly winter night with the sudden glow of the hut, once the king's gifts are bestowed. The lyrics of the carol are printed in handsome calligraphy on the endpapers.

335. Wallner, John. **Good King Wenceslas**. Ill. author. New York: Philomel, 1990. Unp. $14.95. LC 89-26640. ISBN 0-399-21620-0.

This dazzlingly illustrated version of the carol "Good King Wenceslas" shows a handsome, youthful, medieval king in his crenellated castle, then slogging through a howling blizzard to bring food and warmth to a peasant family in a half-ruined hut. A coldly blazing winter moon in lowering skies contrasts bleakly with the busy warmth of the castle, making the king's journey of love seem even more arduous. The musical score is included.

336. Wheeler, Judy. **The First Noel**. Ill. author. Nashville, TN: Ideals, 1992. Unp. $13.95. LC 92-14438. ISBN 0-8249-8565-6.

Each verse of the carol is illustrated with an elegant, luminous watercolor of shepherds, kings on camels, or the Nativity stable. The book includes the musical score (for the melody only) and an historical note.

337.   Yolen, Jane. **Sing Noel**. Ill. Nancy Sippel Carpenter. Honesdale, PA: Boyds Mills Press, 1996. 96p. $17.95. LC 95-80779. ISBN 1-56397-420-7.

Thirty-four carols and songs, most of them familiar, are scored for piano and guitar and beautifully presented on double-page spreads. The warmly colored pictures, radiating cheer and vitality, depict charming angels, children, and animals in an attractive, ethereal style, using watercolor and colored pencil. Each carol or song includes an introduction describing its origin, and the book contains a table of contents and index.

Older and Noteworthy

Other worthy books about Christmas in general include *Christmas Time* by Gail Gibbons (Holiday, 1982), *Merry Christmas* by Patricia Bunning Stevens (Macmillan, 1979), and *Merry Christmas* by Robina Beckles Willson (Philomel, 1983).

Versions of the Nativity Story Using Traditional Bible Texts

Other exceptional versions include *The Nativity* by Julie Vivas (Harcourt Brace Jovanovich, 1988), *The Christ Child As Told by Matthew and Luke* by Maude Petersham (Doubleday, 1931), *Christmas* by Jan Pienkowski (Knopf, 1984), *The Story of the Three Wise Kings* by Tomie dePaola (Putnam, 1983), and *A Child Is Born* by Elizabeth Winthrop (Holiday, 1983).

Retellings of the Nativity Story

Additional recommended retellings include *The Christmas Pageant* by Tomie dePaola (Winston, 1978), *Spirit Child* by John Bierhorst (Morrow, 1984), and *The Story of Christmas* by Felix Hoffman (Atheneum, 1975).

Christmas Stories

Other memorable Christmas stories include *Christmas in the Stable* by Astrid Lindgren (Coward-McCann, 1962), *The Shepherd* by Helga Aichinger (Crowell, 1966), *Amahl and the Night Visitors* by Gian-Carlo Menotti (McGraw Hill, 1952), *A Charlie Brown Christmas* by Charles Schulz (Random House, 1977), *Why the Chimes Rang* by Raymond MacDonald Alden (Bobbs Merrill, 1906), *The Best Christmas Pageant Ever* by Barbara Robinson (Harper and Row, 1972), *King Island Christmas* by Jean Rogers (Greenwillow, 1985), and *A Northern Nativity* by William Kurelek (Tundra, 1976).

Additional stories about animals include *Poor Gabriella* by Victoria Forrester (Atheneum, 1986), *The Donkey's Dream* by Barbara Helen Berger (Philomel, 1985), *Christmas in the Barn* by Margaret Wise Brown (Crowell, 1952), *Christmas Eve* by Edith Thacher Hurd (Harper and Row, 1962), *The Animals' Christmas* by Anne Thaxter Eaton (Viking, 1944), *A Wreath of Christmas*

Legends by Phyllis McGinley (Macmillan, 1967), and *How the Hibernators Came to Bethlehem* by Norma Farber (Walker, 1980).

More recommended legends include *The Clown of God* by Tomie de-Paola (Harcourt, 1978), *Baboushka and the Three Kings* by Ruth Robbins (Parnassus, 1960), *The Little Juggler* by Barbara Cooney (Hastings, 1961), *The Legend of Old Befana* by Tomie dePaola (Harcourt, 1980), and *Babushka* by Charles Mikolaycak (Holiday, 1984).

Carols and Songs

Other noteworthy books of carols and songs include *The Christmas Carol Sampler* by Margaret Cusack (Harcourt, 1983), *The Friendly Beasts* by Tomie dePaola (Putnam, 1981), *Din, Dan, Don, It's Christmas* by Janine Domanska (Greenwillow, 1975), *Silent Night* by Susan Jeffers (Doubleday, 1984), *The Little Drummer Boy* by Ezra Jack Keats (Collier, 1972), and *A Christmas Panorama* by Virginia Parsons (Doubleday, 1977).

Chapter Eight

Christianity

General Works

338.   Drane, John. **Christians: Through the Ages—Around the World**. Elgin, IL: Lion, 1994. 22p. $13.95. ISBN 0-7456-2516-2.
        Written by an enthusiastic Christian in an evangelical tone, this discussion emphasizes Jesus' life; the spread of Christianity; the four branches of the church (Pentecostal, as well as Protestant, Roman Catholic, and Eastern Orthodox); worship; ceremonies and festivals; and extensive sections on how to be a good Christian today. The easy-to-read format has short blocks of text accompanied by color photographs, maps, charts, and artwork, as well as interesting sidebars of information about topics such as the mission field and the design of churches. An index and Bible references are included.

339.   Logan, John. **Christianity**. World Religions Series. New York: Thomson Learning, 1995. 48p. $16.98. LC 95-8282. ISBN 1-56847-374-5.
        This unbiased and crisply written, succinct survey includes a short biography of Jesus, a timeline and a world map for the spread of Christianity, and facts about the three main divisions of the church, the Bible, family life, worship, clergy, sacraments, and festivals. The book is readable, well designed, and plentifully illustrated with good color photographs. It contains a glossary, index, and list of books and movies.

340.   Penney, Sue. **Christianity**. Discovering Religions Series. Austin, TX: Raintree Steck-Vaughan, 1997. 48p. $16.98. LC 96-3730. ISBN 0-8172-4396-8.
        This overview of the Christian faith is divided into many sections, for clarity and eye appeal. Section topics include the characteristics of the Roman Catholic, Orthodox, and Protestant churches, church buildings and furnishings, ways of worship, the Bible and Jesus' life and ministry, the early church, saints,

holidays, and ceremonies. Words that may be unfamiliar to middle elementary readers are defined in boxes. Good color photographs; a straightforward and clearly written text; accurate, basic information; and an index combine to make this a useful work.

341.   Thompson, Jan. **Christian Festivals**. Celebrate Series. Crystal Lake, IL: Heinemann Library, 1997. 48p. $13.95. LC 96-52605. ISBN 0-431-06961-1.

This attractively presented survey of the major holidays has a conversational text and excellent color photographs in varied shapes. Holidays include Advent, St. Lucia's Day, Christingle, Christmas, Epiphany, Lent, Holy Week and Easter, Sunday, Ascension and Pentecost, harvest festivals, All Saints' Day, and the Day of the Dead. The book contains a calendar of the Christian year, a glossary, a reading list, and an index.

Christian Life

342.   Boddy, Marlys. **ABC Book of Feelings**. Ill. Joe Boddy. St. Louis, MO: Concordia, 1991. Unp. $7.95. LC 56-1649. ISBN 0-570-04190-2.

From *afraid* through *zany*, colorful anthropomorphic mice-children experience a wide but normal range of emotions as they perform human activities in big, bright illustrations. The emphasis is on the importance and universality of emotions, and how God accepts, supports, and forgives, if necessary, all kinds of feelings.

343.   Graham, Ruth Bell. **One Wintry Night: The Christmas Story**. Ill. Richard Jesse Watson. Grand Rapids, MI: Baker Book House, 1994. 72p. $25.00. LC 91-48107. ISBN 0-8010-3848-0.

Although the story takes place shortly before Christmas, it is actually a recital of God's work in the world, as told to a young mountain boy by a kindly woman who is sheltering him in her cabin during a blizzard. She begins with the first sin of Adam and Eve; briefly mentions Noah, the Exodus, Abraham, and David; and then discusses the Annunciation, Nativity, Crucifixion, and Resurrection. The unifying theme is sin both past and present and God's final redemption of humankind through Jesus. The well-written narrative is elevated by spectacular, excitingly varied, effective, realistic pictures, often lush with beautiful detail.

344.   Hunkin, Oliver. **Dangerous Journey**. Ill. Alan Parry. Grand Rapids, MI: William B. Eerdmans, 1990. 125p. $22.00. ISBN 0-8028-3619-4.

John Bunyan's *Pilgrim's Progress* is retold in rather formal but comprehensible prose and lavishly illustrated with meticulously executed, dramatic, full- and double-page pictures. The monsters and dissolute, evil human beings are especially well executed. The large, artistic format and allegorical content make this a coffee-table book for older children and adults, rather than a picture book.

345.   Lucado, Max. **Just in Case You Ever Wonder**. Ill. Toni Goffe. Dallas, TX: Word, 1992. Unp. $14.99. LC 92-25059. ISBN 0-84990978-3.

The Christian assurance of life after death is given to a young child, who is told from infancy that she is God's special creation, and that God and her parents will always love and protect her as she grows up. Ultimately, they will all meet again in heaven, where they will remain together forever. Large, comforting pictures of a happy childhood reinforce the encouraging message.

346.   Marxhausen, Joanne. **Some of My Best Friends Are Trees**. Ill. Benjamin Marxhausen. St. Louis, MO: Concordia, 1990. Unp. $7.95. LC 56-1640. ISBN 0-570-04182-1.

The life experience of trees is said to reflect all the virtues of friendship: sharing, giving, hoping, enduring, and trusting. In turn, this points to the ways in which human beings relate to God. Simple, bold, cut-paper graphics help express these basic truths.

347.   Parks, Rosa. **Dear Mrs. Parks: A Dialogue with Today's Youth**. New York: Lee and Low Books, 1996. 112p. $16.95. LC 96-18389. ISBN 1-880000-45-8.

The redoubtable woman who refused to give up her seat on a Montgomery, Alabama, bus and changed the course of history responds to letters from young people throughout the world with words of faith, morality, encouragement, and inspiration. She expects them to continue the fight for freedom and equality, to prize education, and to look to God in all things. Her tone is that of a firm but kindly teacher who believes in the capabilities of future generations.

348.   Sattgast, L. J., and Jan Elkins. **Teach Me About the Holy Spirit**. Ill. Russ Flint. Portland, OR: Multnomah, 1990. Unp. $4.99. LC 90-35422. ISBN 0-88070-384-9.

Flora and Flossie, identical twins in pink dresses, do not act alike: Flora wants to obey God, and Flossie wants to do as she pleases. Flora demonstrates the fruits of the spirit—love, joy, peace, patience, kindness, goodness, faithfulness, gentleness, and self-control—in her everyday life, but Flossie sulks, teases, grabs, cries, and pushes. Flossie is never happy, though, and soon begins to do as Flora does. Charming ink-and-watercolor pictures reinforce the message.

349.   Simcox, Helen Earle. **For All the World**. Ill. author. Minneapolis, MN: Augsburg Fortress, 1994. Unp. $15.99. LC 94-70619. ISBN 0-8066-2712-3.

The simple, meaningful text points out that although Jesus was born to Mary in Bethlehem, God could have chosen anywhere: Japan, Alaska, Lithuania, or Africa. The Virgin and child could have been of any race, because God loves all the people in the world. Appealing, artistic pictures show multiethnic madonnas and infants to emphasize the message.

350.   Wilde, Oscar. **The Happy Prince**. Ill. Jane Ray. New York: Dutton, 1994. Unp. $15.99. ISBN 0-525-45367-9.

A broken lead heart and a dead swallow are brought to God by one of his angels as the two most precious things in the city. The heart belonged to the statue of the Happy Prince, who, with the help of the loyal and loving swallow, distributed his gold and jeweled decorations to the poor. When the statue began to appear shabby, it was pulled down, and the swallow died from the cold, but God proclaimed that they would live forever in the Garden of Paradise. Compassion, charity, and love underlie the tender storytelling, abridged for easy reading and splendidly illustrated in lustrous colors.

Special Problems

351. Coleman, William L. **Straight Answers: For Kids About Life, God, and Growing Up**. Ill. Michael Baze. Elgin, IL: David C. Cook, 1992. 127p. $9.99. LC 91-41504. ISBN 1-55513-336-3.

Answers to many problems children have with family, friends, drugs, school, sexuality, death, illness, and God are given in an informal question-and-answer format. The replies are short and sometimes simplistic, but generally helpful.

352. Coleman, William L. **What You Should Know About a Parent Who Drinks Too Much**. Minneapolis, MN: Augsburg Fortress, 1992. 92p. $5.95pa. LC 92-18314. ISBN 0-8066-2610-0.

This simple, heartfelt counseling comes from one who understands the devastated feelings of betrayal, fear, disappointment, loneliness, and so on, experienced by the children of alcoholics. His advice to them is to believe in themselves, be assured that God cares about them deeply, and try to forgive, but he recognizes that there are no magical cures.

353. Coleman, William L. **What You Should Know About Getting Along with a New Parent**. Minneapolis, MN: Augsburg Fortress, 1992. 92p. $5.95pa. LC 92-18335. ISBN 0-8066-26119.

Sensible thoughts about coping with the emotions engendered by suddenly becoming part of a blended family are grouped into short, easy-to-read sections. The author stresses cooperation, communication, a positive attitude, and trust in God.

354. Courtney, Anne. **Corey's Dad Drinks Too Much**. Ill. Melodye Rosales. Wheaton, IL: Tyndale House, 1991. 46p. $3.95pa. LC 91-65135. ISBN 0-8423-0223-9.

This simple explanation of what life is like in a family with an alcoholic father and why alcoholism should be seen as a disease offers no easy answers for the sadness. God's supportive role in helping family members cope is stressed. The realistic black-and-white drawings are expressive and accurate.

Story Collections

355. Beers, V. Gilbert. **The Toddlers Bedtime Story Book**. Colorado Springs, CO: Victor Books, 1993. 351p. $14.99. ISBN 1-56476-181-9.

A series of short, simple stories dealing with ethical and religious matters in everyday situations includes topics such as honesty, cleanliness, generosity, good manners, consideration, and bravery. Thanksgiving for God's creativity and special gifts is stressed. Questions to test comprehension and aid discussion follow each story. The book contains a special index to the values represented.

356. Erickson, Mary E. **I Can Make God Glad!** Ill. Len Ebert. Elgin, IL: Chariot Books, 1994. Unp. $10.99. LC 93-33070. ISBN 0-7814-0102-X.

Gently didactic short stories, set in places such as Korea, the Philippines, Bolivia, Thailand, and Russia, as well as the United States, stress qualities of generosity, obedience, honesty, forgiveness, and other universal virtues. Each is introduced by a quotation from the Bible and completed with a simple prayer. Pleasant, full-page pictures show children in their native settings.

357.   Stelten, Gene. **Home for the Holidays**. Atlanta, GA: Peachtree, 1995. 148p. $13.95. LC 95-16366. ISBN 1-56145-114-2.

This collection of stories for older children and adults is divided into topics: there's no place like home, the gift of one's self, giving thanks, traditions, the power of example, and considering yourself at home. Authors include sports figures, politicians, executives, and professional writers. Many stress Christian values, testimonials, charity, and good deeds. The messages are effective, obvious, and to the point.

Series Books

358.   Johnson, Lois Walfrid. **Adventures of the Northwoods** series. Minneapolis, MN: Bethany House. $5.99pa.

This appealing, ongoing mystery series is set at the turn of the century and features lively twelve- and thirteen-year-olds. Kate, her stepbrother Anders, and their friend Erik find themselves involved in solving thefts, arson, kidnapping, and vandalism in rural northwestern Wisconsin. Easy to read, suspenseful, and wholesome, the books have well-researched historical figures intermingled with the characters and vivid settings. Belief in God's help is a normal part of the devout Scandinavian family life depicted.

Titles include:

358.1.   **The Creeping Shadows**. 1990. 160p. LC 90-49143. ISBN 1-55661-102-1.

358.2.   **The Disappearing Stranger**. 1990. 142p. LC 90-2. ISBN 1-55661-100-5.

358.3.   **Disaster on Windy Hill**. 1994. 170p. LC 94-25694. ISBN 1-55661-242-7.

358.4.   **Grandpa's Stolen Treasure**. 1992. 159p. LC 92-30093. ISBN 1-55661-239-7.

358.5.   **The Hidden Message**. 1990. 144p. LC 89-78390. ISBN 1-55661-101-3.

358.6.   **The Mysterious Hideaway**. 1992. 158p. LC 92-13903. ISBN 1-55661-238-9.

358.7.   **Mystery of the Missing Map**. 1994. 158p. LC 93-43770. ISBN 1-55661-241-9.

358.8.   **The Runaway Clown**. 1993. 160p. LC 93-1496. ISBN 1-55661-240-0.

358.9.   **Trouble at Wild River**. 1991. 160p. LC 91-26802. ISBN 1-55661-144-7.

358.10.   **The Vanishing Footprints**. 1991. 158p. LC 91-15042. ISBN 1-55661-103-X.

359. Johnson, Lois Walfrid. **The Riverboat Adventure** series. Minneapolis, MN: Bethany House. $5.99pa.

A connected narrative traces the involvement of twelve-year-old Libby Norstad, along with her father, a riverboat captain, and his cabin boy, in the rescue of a young male slave and, eventually, his mother and siblings. Exciting flights from slave catchers and Underground Railroad stations, along with vivid scenes of steamboat life in the 1850s, are described in a brisk, suspenseful narrative with an interesting historical background. The Christian faith is a normal part of the main characters' lives.

Titles include:

359.1. **Escape into the Night**. 1995. 176p. LC 95-18990. ISBN 1-55661-351-2.

359.2. **Midnight Rescue**. 1996. 175p. LC 96-45763. ISBN 1-55661-353-9.

359.3. **Race for Freedom**. 1996. 188p. LC 96-4433. ISBN 1-55661-352-0.

360. Snelling, Lauraine. **High Hurdles** series. Minneapolis, MN: Bethany House. $5.99pa.

Plenty of suspense and action for horse-loving girls is in this series starring thirteen-year-old DJ Randall, who adores riding, caring for, and drawing pictures of horses. The plots center around the problem of a difficult person who must be encouraged with kindness to change, but the focus is on the heroine and her riding experiences.

Titles include:

360.1. **DJ's Challenge**. 1995. 160p. LC 95-9624. ISBN 1-55661-506-X.

360.2. **Olympic Dreams**. 1995. 155p. LC 95-483. ISBN 1-55661-505-1.

360.3. **Out of the Blue**. 1996. 173p. ISBN 1-55661-508-6.

360.4. **Setting the Pace**. 1996. 173p. LC 95-43932. ISBN 1-55661-507-8.

Many Christian publishing houses produce reams of series books, some with much stronger Christian emphases, and some of much poorer quality than those mentioned above, but all sell well in the Christian bookstores.

Hymns and Songs

361. Alexander, Cecil Frances. **All Things Bright and Beautiful**. Ill. Carol Heyer. Nashville, TN: Ideals, 1992. Unp. $11.95. LC 91-28428. ISBN 0-8249-8544-3.

Beautiful, double-page spreads of nature scenes, illustrated with felt-tip pen, are bold and lively accompaniments to the text of the well-loved hymn. Sea creatures, flowers, rabbits, raccoons, butterflies, swans, wolves, hummingbirds, and children are among the subjects of God's creation depicted. No music is included.

362. Blumen, Karen L. **One More River**. Ill. John J. Blumen. Minneapolis, MN: Augsburg Fortress, 1995. Unp. $6.99pa. LC 95-21209. ISBN 0-8066-2759-X.

From one by one to ten by ten, the animals enter Noah's ark in this jolly spiritual. The full-page illustrations are clever and delightful, showing everything from a fat elephant couple picnicking on caraway buns, to a wide-hipped hippo stuck in the on-ramp door, to a burly bear marching up to the ramp with his pot of honey. The musical score is included.

363. Brown, Judith Gwyn. **Bless All Creatures Here Below: A Celebration for the Blessing of the Animals**. Ill. author. Ridgefield, CT: Morehouse, 1996. Unp. $15.95. LC 96-23109. ISBN 0-8192-1665-8.

This new and original hymn rejoices in all God's creatures, including mythical dragons and unicorns, Noah's menagerie, and the Nativity stable animals, as well as dogs, fish, squirrels, cats, butterflies, and more, and asks God to bless them all. Appealing watercolors show multiethnic children, some with their pets and some costumed as animals, with floats and balloons, parading through the church, then picnicking on the church lawn after the blessing.

364. Dellinger, Annetta. **Ann Elizabeth Signs with Love**. Ill. Michael Hackett. St. Louis, MO: Concordia, 1991. 30p. $8.95. LC 90-38171. ISBN 0-570-04192-9.

A lively deaf child shows how to sign the children's hymn "Jesus Loves Me." As each word is demonstrated, large color pictures portray scenes of modern multiethnic children at school, play, and church, and biblical children happily interacting with Jesus.

365. Farjeon, Eleanor. **Morning Has Broken**. Ill. Tim Ludwig. Grand Rapids, MI: William B. Eerdmans, 1996. 32p. $15.00. LC 96-935. ISBN 0-8028-5124-4.

Written for children and inspired by Psalm 118:24 ("this is the day the Lord hath made; we shall rejoice and be glad in it"), the hymn celebrates the morning, the blackbird, the rain, the dew on the grass, and the wet garden as having the same fresh beauty as when God first created them. Big illustrations show a boy and his grandfather leaving their house on a sunny, sparkling morning to enjoy a day in the park, with its lush grass, bright flowers, and glittering fountain. The music is included.

366. Gill, Madelaine, and Grey Pliska. **Praise for the Singing: Songs for Children**. Ill. Madelaine Gill. Boston: Little, Brown, 1993. 32p. $18.95. LC 91-750562. ISBN 0-316-52627-4.

Hymns and spiritual music from African American, Shaker, American folk, and Jewish traditions are grouped into four sections: joy and celebration, peace and freedom, hope and faith, love and thanksgiving. The excellent variety of familiar and new selections ranges from "Michael, Row the Boat Ashore" to "Dona Nobis Pacem," and "We Shall Overcome" to "Dayenu." The musical scores are elegantly and clearly presented and imaginatively illustrated.

367. Higginsen, Vy. **This Is My Song! A Collection of Gospel Music for the Family**. Ill. Brenda Joysmith. New York: Crown, 1995. 96p. $25.00. LC 93-34303. ISBN 0-517-59492-7.

This large, handsome book contains the hand-set musical scores of thirty gospel favorites and spirituals. Also included are an informative introduction about the history and meaning of gospel, and photographs and short biographies of twelve significant performers, from Thomas A. Dorsey, the "Father of Gospel," to Whitney Houston. Each hymn is annotated to expand its message and background. Reproductions of idealized, artistic paintings, depicting African Americans joyfully singing and worshipping at church, add immensely to the reverent and positive nature of the music. A first-line index is included.

368. Johnson, James Weldon. **Lift Ev'ry Voice and Sing**. Ill. Jan Spivey Gilchrist. New York: Scholastic, 1995. Unp. $14.95. LC 92-32283. ISBN 0-590-469-82-7.

Double-page, mixed-media illustrations filled with dramatic power accompany the lyrics, printed in elegant calligraphy, of what is considered the African American national anthem. The stirring song exhorts African American people to remember their bitter past, but encourages them to celebrate their progress toward freedom, face the future with faith and hope, and remain true to God and loyal to America. The score is included.

369. Langstaff, John. **Climbing Jacob's Ladder: Heroes of the Bible in African-American Spirituals**. Ill. Ashley Bryan. New York: Macmillan, 1991. Unp. $13.95. LC 90-27297. ISBN 0-689-50494-2.

Noah, Abraham, Jacob, Moses, Joshua, David, Ezekiel, Daniel, and Jonah are celebrated in familiar spirituals with music arranged for piano and guitar accompaniment. The illustrations, with their power and warmth, are reminiscent of African art forms and show black versions of the Bible stories. Short explanations of the spirituals are included.

370. Scott, Lesbia. **I Sing a Song of the Saints of God**. Ill. Judith Gwyn Brown. Ridgefield, CT: Morehouse, 1991. Unp. $6.95pa. LC 91-10393. ISBN 0-8192-1618-6.

In this reprint (first published in 1929) with illustrations from a 1981 edition, notes about each saint and the musical score are included. The sweet children's hymn praises St. Luke, the doctor; St. Margaret, a queen; St. Joan, a shepherdess; St. Martin of Tours, a soldier; and more; and proclaims that saints abound everywhere because all the people who love to do Jesus' will are saints. Winsome and exuberant pictures of a children's church pageant, with robed choristers and boys and girls acting out scenes from the saints' lives, are a perfect complement.

371. Staines, Bill. **All God's Critters Got a Place in the Choir**. Ill. Margot Zemach. New York: Puffin Unicorn, 1993. Unp. $4.99pa. LC 88-31696. ISBN 0-14-054838-6.

A lively folk melody acclaims the goodness of all animal creation, as dogs, cats, bees, crickets, donkeys, hippos, foxes, and many other creatures add their voices to the chorus in a song praising life everywhere. The sprightly lyrics are illustrated with genial watercolors filled with noisy, cheerful birds and beasts. The score is included.

Angels

372.   Bartone, Elisa. **The Angel Who Forgot**. Ill. Paul Cline. New York: Green Tiger Press, 1992. Unp. $10.00. LC 91-34233. ISBN 0-671-76037-8.

A young boy lies ill and wishes for an angel to come to cure him, but the angel who arrives is powerless, because he has lost all his memories. A dragonfly sent by God reveals to the boy's mother the secret of the angel's amnesia, she retrieves his box of memories from the depths of a lake, and her son is cured. The slight narrative is distinguished by lovely, dreamy watercolors.

373.   Cowen-Fletcher, Jane. **Baby Angels**. Ill. author. Cambridge, MA: Candlewick Press, 1996. Unp. $15.99. LC 95-19911. ISBN 1-56402-666-3.

A rambunctious toddler is guarded by a group of multiethnic, plump, diapered angels as she climbs out of her crib and slips outdoors. Immediately, they summon her parents to keep her safe. Having guardian angels is a comforting thought for the very young children who are addressed by this gentle story in rhyme. Idealized pastel illustrations accompany the text.

374.   Downes, Belinda. **Every Little Angel's Handbook**. Ill. author. New York: Dial, 1997. Unp. $14.99. LC 96-50158. ISBN 0-8037-2264-8.

This is a delightful and fanciful portrayal of child-angels under the tutelage of role-model angels. The little angels are shown learning star repair, snowflake construction, angel-cake baking, singing in the heavenly choir, flying, weather production, how to guard people, the use of Cupid's arrows, and the production of special effects. The book is exquisitely and exuberantly illustrated with reproductions of hand-embroidered scenes in vibrant colors.

375.   Falda, Dominique. **The Angel and the Child: An Incidental Incident in Twelve Scenes**. Ill. author. New York: North-South Books, 1995. LC 95-13134. ISBN 1-55858-488-9.

A little, cartoon-style angel flies down to earth to plant a tree. The only one to notice him is a small child, who promises to keep the tree watered. The message is that most people are too jaded or busy to appreciate beauty or to see angels. The unusual illustrations add photographed objects to the free-form, brightly colored scenes of the tree and the city.

376.   Haidle, Helen. **Angels in Action**. Ill. David Haidle. Nashville, TN: Thomas Nelson, 1996. 48p. $12.99. ISBN 0-7852-7576-2.

A thorough exposition of angels stresses their role as God's messengers and is suitably illustrated with softly shaded watercolors. Supported by citations from the Old and New Testaments, the book answers questions about who angels are, who sees them, their power of miraculous intervention, their ability to protect human beings, their divinity, and many other aspects of angels.

377.   Lucado, Max. **Alabaster's Song: Christmas Through the Eyes of an Angel**. Ill. Michael Garland. Dallas, TX: Word, 1996. Unp. $14.99. LC 96-14749. ISBN 0-8499-1307-1.

A six-year-old boy is fascinated by the angel atop the Christmas tree, and has conversations with him, which are only one-sided until the boy asks, "What was it like in Bethlehem?" Then the angel appears life-sized beside his bed, answers enthusiastically, and sings a heavenly melody, which only children can hear. As the boy matures, he can no longer hear the angel, but years later, his young son hears the angel's song in the same manner. Reproductions of skillfully executed, realistic paintings capture the sweetness of the story.

378.   McKelvey, Douglas Kaine. **The Angel Knew Papa and the Dog**. New York: Philomel, 1996. 96p. $13.95. ISBN 0-399-23042-4.

This unusual, vivid, and well-written novel for older elementary children describes how seven-year-old Evangeline is trapped by quickly rising flood waters during a severe winter storm. An angel looms outside the door of her cabin, and its radiant presence gives her so much courage that she is ready to walk through the valley of the shadow of death, if necessary. Fortunately, however, she is rescued by a woman in a boat, who has found her through some miraculous coincidences.

379.   Nolfo-Wheeler, Amy. **All God's Creatures Go to Heaven**. Ill. N. A. Noel. Indianapolis, IN: Noel Studio, 1996. Unp. $19.95. LC 96-68622. ISBN 0-9652531-0-4.

In heaven, child-angels are entrusted with the care of animals and birds who have died, because children and pets are among God's greatest blessings: they are innocent, honest, and true. Jacob, a newly arrived six-year-old boy, receives a fluffy rabbit. Gorgeously illustrated with full-page reproductions of idealized paintings, this heaven is a happy, beautiful place for all God's creatures.

380.   Tazewell, Charles. **The Littlest Angel**. Ill. Paul Micich. Nashville, TN: Ideals, 1991. Unp. $14.95. LC 91-2442. ISBN 0-8249-8516-8.

This is a stunning new production of the classic story (previously published in 1939) about a four-year-old boy who reluctantly enters heaven and becomes the despair of his fellow angels because of his exuberance and clumsiness. The book has tender, multiethnic angelic figures, beautifully rendered, inhabiting a heaven of clouds and stars painted in vivid purples, blues, and golds. The touching story tells of how the child redeems himself in God's eyes by timidly offering his most precious possession, his box of boyhood treasures, to the infant Jesus.

381.   Willard, Nancy, and Jane Yolen. **Among Angels**. Ill. S. Saelig Gallagher. New York: Harcourt Brace, 1995. 55p. $20.00. LC 93-42103. ISBN 0-15-100195-2.

Although all the poems are in some way related to angels, they vary widely. The inspirations include the herb Angelica, the angel in charge of poison ivy and snail darters, snow angels, the Nativity shepherds, Lucifer, the type font Celeste, and St. Andrews golf links. Humor, melody, and vivid imagery abound. The occasional illustrations are reproductions of mysterious paintings.

382.   Woody, Marilyn J. **A Child's Book of Angels: Stories from the Bible About God's Special Messengers**. Elgin, IL: Chariot Books, 1992. 32p. $10.99. LC 92-12862. ISBN 1-55513-756-3.

Fourteen references to angels in the Old and New Testaments are cited, each accompanied by a short explanation of its application to everyday life, as well as a short prayer. The book is appropriate for young children. Each reference is illustrated by a different artist.

383.   Yolen, Jane. **Good Griselle**. Ill. David Christiana. New York: Harcourt Brace, 1994. Unp. $14.95. LC 93-11691. ISBN 0-15-231701-5.

A cheerful, caring widow is tested by the stone angels and gargoyles of the cathedral on Christmas Eve. The gargoyles send her a hideous, rough, smelly, mean child, whom she cherishes and protects until she dies of old age. Love conquers all, the angels win their bet, and the child becomes a stone angel. The illustrations are swirling, eerie watercolors.

Older and Noteworthy

General Works

Other useful titles include *Young Reader's Book of Christian Symbolism* by Michael Daves (Abingdon, 1967), *Thank God for Circles* by Joanne Marxhausen (Concordia, 1973), *Christianity* by Irene Cumming Kleeberg (Watts, 1976), *Signs of God's Love* by Jeanne S. Fogle (Geneva, 1984), *Leading Little Ones to God* by Marian Schoolland (William B. Eerdmans, 1981), *And the Beagles and the Bunnies Shall Lie Down Together* by Charles Schulz (Henry Holt, 1984), and *C. S. Lewis, His Letters to Children* by C. S. Lewis (Macmillan, 1985).

Christian Life

Worthy young adult novels with Christian themes include *Daffodils in the Snow* by LouAnn Gaeddert (Dutton, 1984), *Is That You, Miss Blue?* by M. E. Kerr (Harper, 1976), and *Christy* (Avon, 1978) and *Julie* (McGraw, 1984) by Catherine Marshall. *If Jesus Came to My House* by Joan Gale Thomas (Lothrop, 1951) is a sweet classic, and *Heidi* by Johanna Spyri (Grosset, 1925) has a strong Christian flavor. Also recommended is *The Shoemaker's Dream* (Judson, 1982), adapted by Mildred Schell from a story by Leo Tolstoy.

Hymns and Songs

Other recommended books with hymns and songs include *I'm Going to Sing* (Atheneum, 1982) and *Walk Together Children* (Atheneum, 1974) by Ashley Bryan, *Children, Go Where I Send Thee* by Kathryn Shoemaker (Winston, 1980), and *Songs of Praise* by Kathleen Krull (Harcourt Brace, 1988).

Chapter Nine

Christian Denominations and Churches

384.   Moore, Ruth Nulton. **Distant Thunder**. Scottdale, PA: Herald Press, 1991. 160p. $6.95pa. LC 91-10845. ISBN 0-8361-3557-1.

Although firmly opposed to war, the Moravian community in Bethlehem, Pennsylvania, rallies to care for the wounded and dying rebel soldiers in a makeshift hospital during the Revolutionary War. Fifteen-year-old Kate and her cousin, caring for all in need, also rescue and hide a young Hessian soldier in this fast-paced, upbeat novel with a well-authenticated historical background.

385.   Sevastiades, Philemon D. **I Am Eastern Orthodox**. New York: Power-Kids Press, 1996. 24p. $13.95. LC 96-1508. ISBN 0-8239-2377-0.

Simple sentences briefly describe the Orthodox beliefs, ways of worship, baptism, and marriage customs, as told by a child communicant in Chicago. The faith is strongly traditional. Full-page color photographs, a glossary, and an index are included.

386.   Williams, Jean Kinney. **The Christian Scientists**. The American Religious Experience Series. New York: Franklin Watts, 1997. 111p. $15.00. LC 96-9878. ISBN 0-531-11309-4.

Because Mary Baker Eddy and the Christian Science faith are inextricably entwined, this book serves as her biography as well as a religious history and statement of Christian Science tenets. Examples of verified healings are also included. Seriously reasoned thought and a background in religion are necessary to understand this faith, in which matter is considered the opposite of spirit, Jesus is not divine, and sin and disease are conquered by prayer alone. The author presents the concepts as simply as possible. Thoroughly researched and illustrated with helpful black-and-white photographs and reproductions, the book contains source notes, a reading list, an index, and a list of Web sites for the Church of Christ, Scientist.

387.   Williams, Jean Kinney. **The Mormons**. The American Religious Experience Series. New York: Franklin Watts, 1996. 112p. $15.00. LC 96-33829. ISBN 0-531-11276-4.
    From Joseph Smith's revelation of God and Jesus in 1820, through Utah's problems in achieving statehood, this is an evenhanded and thorough history of the Mormon Church. Topics of discussion include the angel Moroni and the golden plates containing the Book of Mormon, Smith's persecution by enemies within and without the church, his assassination, Brigham Young's leadership and doctrine of plural marriage, the establishment of the Mormon bastion at Salt Lake City, and the ongoing controversies concerning polygamy, community living dominated by the church, and exclusivity. The book includes black-and-white photographs and artwork, a reading list, source notes, a list of Web sites, and an index.

African American Churches

388.   Grimes, Nikki. **Come Sunday**. Ill. Michael Bryant. Grand Rapids, MI: William B. Eerdmans, 1996. Unp. $7.50. LC 95-33067. ISBN 0-8028-5108-8.
    In this exuberant, poetic tribute to a day of worship, a young girl dressed in her best goes to the Paradise Baptist Church, where the ladies wear beautiful hats and white gloves, and the music rocks your soul. A baptism, the altar call, the offering, the visiting preacher, and the church supper are all seen from the child's point of view and celebrated with enthusiasm. The big reproductions of bold paintings depict the congregation with spirit and warmth.

389.   Saint James, Synthia. **Sunday**. Ill. author. Morton Grove, IL: Albert Whitman, 1996. Unp. $15.95. LC 95-52934. ISBN 0-8075-7658-1.
    A city-dwelling family celebrates the Sabbath with worship and togetherness in this joyful evocation of pancake breakfasts, church services, and supper at Grandma's. The minimal text is triumphantly illustrated with simple figures dramatized by blocks of vibrant color.

390.   Thomas, Joyce Carol. **When the Nightingale Sings**. New York: HarperCollins, 1992. 149p. $13.89. LC 92-6045. ISBN 0-06-020294-7.
    In this poetically written young adult novel, fourteen-year-old Marigold is, Cinderella-style, belittled and exploited by her foster mother and her talentless twin stepsisters. Marigold's blessings are a glorious singing voice and a talent for composing gospel music. The ball, in this case, is the Great Gospel Convention, where Marigold's true worth is recognized, and where she wins the love of a handsome choir director. This sweet story of virtue rewarded has an unreal, fairytale quality.

391. Woodtor, Dee Parmer. **Big Meeting**. Ill. Dolores Johnson. New York: Atheneum, 1996. Unp. $16.00. LC 95-15299. ISBN 0-689-31933-9.

The southern tradition of Homecoming Weekend, at the Bethel A.M.E. Church in Oakey Streak, is celebrated joyously in text and illustration. All dress in their best for the services and then stream outdoors to greet friends and relatives, gathered from all over, to enjoy sumptuous home cooking. Prints of softly muted, summery etchings and aquatints show all the events with warmth and vitality.

Amish and Mennonite

392. Ayres, Katherine. **Family Tree**. New York: Delacorte, 1996. 165p. $15.95. LC 95-53820. ISBN 0-385-32227-5.

In this well-written, satisfying story, a twelve-year-old girl in Ohio is assigned to research her family tree for a sixth-grade class project and discovers that her father is Amish and was expelled from his Old Order Pennsylvania community when he married an "English" outsider. Shunned by his own family and rejected by his wife's prejudiced parents, he has chosen to raise his daughter alone and away from all her relatives after the death of her mother. Strong Amish values of simplicity, self-reliance, and faith are portrayed.

393. Bial, Raymond. **Amish Home**. Boston: Houghton Mifflin, 1993. 40p. $15.95. LC 92-4406. ISBN 0-395-59504-5.

This clear and simple explication of Amish history and way of life centers on their plain but comfortable and industrious agrarian communities, stressing their cherished separation from much of the worldliness of their "English" neighbors to maintain their traditional values. Worship, food, family solidarity, education, and dress are discussed, and beautiful, artistic color photographs illustrate the book. A reading list is included.

394. Faber, Doris. **The Amish**. Ill. Michael E. Erkel. New York: Doubleday, 1991. 45p. $12.95. LC 84-7829. ISBN 0-385-26130-6.

This sympathetic, in-depth study of the Amish deals with their history, culture, and current problems, including the controversy concerning school attendance. The strength of their beliefs, their diligence, their simple lifestyle, and their sterling stewardship of the land are stressed in the clearly written text. Big, two-dimensional watercolor illustrations of plain-faced Plain People of the past and present supplement the text.

395. Kenna, Kathleen. **A People Apart**. Boston: Houghton Mifflin, 1995. 64p. $17.95. LC 94-18545. ISBN 0-395-67344-5.

This is an outstanding account of life among the Old Order Mennonites, a group of sects who believe in living separately and simply on their family farms, unpolluted by American society. Facts about their religious observances, education, gender roles, and community closeness fill a book written with warmth and admiration. The artistic black-and-white photographs are sympathetic to and appreciative of the Mennonites, and a bibliography is included.

396.   Mitchell, Barbara. **Down Buttermilk Lane**. Ill. John Dandford. New York: Lothrop, Lee & Shepard, 1993. Unp. $15.00. LC 90-46876. ISBN 0-688-10114-3.

Outstanding, double-page pictures show a charming Amish family enjoying an outing in their buggy, against a background of rural autumn splendor. A warm, golden glow permeates the scenes of daily life: the opulent farms, Zimmerman's general store overflowing with foods and clothing, and a hearty meal at Dawdi and Mammi's house. The text, filled with pleasant details and Pennsylvania Dutch expressions, is equally celebratory of plenty and simple contentment.

397.   Polacco, Patricia. **Just Plain Fancy**. Ill. author. New York: Bantam, 1990. Unp. $14.95. LC 89-27856. ISBN 0-553-05884-3.

Two young Amish girls, longing for something to pleasure them, rescue an unusual speckled egg fallen from a delivery truck. It produces an unusual chick, which they call "Fancy." After they overhear their elders gravely declaring that the penalty for being fancy in the Amish community is shunning, the girls become frightened and try to hide their special bird. When he escapes and spreads his gorgeous tail, the weeping children are gently reassured that peacocks are just one of God's beautiful creations, and are commended for raising him so well. The warmth and simplicity of the Amish community and its rural life are lovingly portrayed in dynamic, double-page spreads of daily events on the farm, showing people with apple-cheeked, expressive faces.

398.   Williams, Jean Kinney. **The Amish**. The American Religious Experience Series. New York: Franklin Watts, 1996. 112p. $15.00. LC 96-33830. ISBN 0-531-11275-6.

This excellent, thorough overview of Amish history and way of life begins with the Anabaptist movement and its stricter interpretation (espoused by Jakob Ammann), which became the Amish faith, and continues with the emigration to America and settlements in the United States and Canada. It discusses how communities vary in their degree of their separateness and use of modern conveniences, as well as Amish worship, schools, gender roles, family closeness, marriage customs, dress, shunning, houses and furnishings, problems with the government, and difficulties in accommodating to changing times and shrinking areas of farmland. Written in a clear and interesting style, the book has black-and-white photographs, notes, lists of supplementary reading and Internet sites, and an index.

Fundamentalist

399.   Lasky, Kathryn. **Memoirs of a Bookbat**. San Diego, CA: Harcourt Brace, 1994. 215p. $10.95. LC 93-36402. ISBN 0-15-215727-1.

In this young adult novel with a mission, fourteen-year-old Harper Jessup, an avid reader and freethinker, is appalled when her parents become involved with Family Action for Christian Education (FACE) and Families Involved in Saving Traditional Values (FIST), conservative religious organizations that oppose humanism, government hirelings in charge of their children's upbringing, and books they identify as being subversive (e.g., *Are You There, God? It's Me, Margaret* by Judy Blume). Despite this numbing family pressure, Harper has the courage to be herself and, finally, to run away to seek sanctuary with her grandmother. The characters are stereotypical, but the style is brisk and easy to read.

400. Nolan, Han. **Send Me Down a Miracle**. San Diego, CA: Harcourt Brace, 1996. 250p. $6.00pa. LC 95-38169. ISBN 0-15-200979-5.

A Bohemian artist decides to conduct a sensory deprivation experiment in a small, conservative Alabama town. Her claims of having seen three visions of Jesus sitting in one of her chairs send the church congregation into an uproar. Fourteen-year-old Christy's fire-and-brimstone preacher father, who has indirectly caused a suicide, driven away his wife with his insistence that his ways are the only right ways, and controlled his daughters rigidly, rejects all possibilities of a miracle until she finally teaches him that God is love and forgiveness, not rules. This fast-paced, absorbing story for young adults has skillful characterization and an engaging coming-of-age plot.

401. Rodowsky, Colby. **Lucy Peale**. Aerial Fiction Series. New York: Sunburst Books, 1994. 167p. $3.95pa. ISBN 0-374-44659-8.

Seventeen-year-old, completely naive Lucy, is the product of a Fundamentalist preacher and his browbeaten wife. Looking for some color and excitement in their lives, she and her sister slip away to Ocean City and meet some unscrupulous boys. Lucy is raped and becomes pregnant. Rather than face the public confession of her scarlet sin, which her father demands, she runs away, meets an exceptional young man, and lives happily ever after. The sweet romance emphasizes the value of real love as opposed to the legalistic hypocrisy of her father's so-called Christianity.

402. Schaeffer, Frank. **Portofino**. New York: Macmillan, 1992. 248p. $15.00. LC 92-9334. ISBN 0-02-607051-0.

In this funny coming-of-age story, Calvin Becker and his family vacation in Portofino. They are members of a Presbyterian splinter sect of born-again, Bible-believing Reformed Christians who live in Switzerland to minister to the Roman Catholics there (because the Beckers believe that Roman Catholics worship the Virgin Mary instead of Jesus). Dad is a fiery, saved, working-class preacher whose congregation is his family; Mom is a repressed, sugar-sweet lady; and Calvin is a normal, curious, adventurous boy of the 1960s. The characterization is sharp, but the satire is always good-humored.

403. Tolan, Stephanie. **Save Halloween!** New York: William Morrow, 1993. 168p. $14.00. LC 93-10635. ISBN 0-688-12168-3.

The eleven-year-old daughter of the minister of a very conservative small church becomes actively involved in the sixth-grade Halloween pageant, against the wishes of her family, who believe that Satan dominates the celebration. After researching the holiday carefully and praying earnestly, she does not agree with them and leads the opposition to a movement intended to shut down Halloween completely. This lively school story does not attack the conservative Christian point of view but maintains that no one group should be allowed to determine what is right behavior.

Roman Catholic

404. Cormier, Robert. **Other Bells for Us to Ring**. Ill. Deborah Kogan Ray. New York: Delacorte, 1990. 136p. $13.95. LC 90-3326. ISBN 0-385-30245-2.

Kathleen Mary O'Hara, an imaginative, lively, outspoken, eleven-year-old girl, full of hope and energy, dazzles Unitarian Darcy Webster with her fascinating Catholic ways, even to the point of splashing Darcy with holy water and declaring her a Catholic for eternity. Darcy half-believes her and worries about eating meat on Friday, not going to confession, and entering church without wearing a hat. A loving friendship develops, and Kathleen Mary promises never to desert her, even after death. A miracle happens to prove that love is, indeed, eternal. The moving and unusual story is set in Massachusetts during World War II.

405. Sevastiades, Philemon D. **I Am Roman Catholic**. Religions of the World Series. New York: PowerKids Press, 1996. 24p. $13.95. LC 96-3288. ISBN 0-8239-2376-2.

Victor, a boy in Los Angeles, discusses Jesus, the Pope, the Trinity, Christmas and Easter, the Mass, confession, First Communion, confirmation, and baptism. Each topic has one page of short sentences in large type. Colorful, full-page photographs, a glossary, and an index are included.

406. Stivender, Ed. **Still Catholic After All These Fears**. Little Rock, AR: August House, 1995. 222p. $11.95. LC 94-49236. ISBN 0-87483-403-1.

Twelve stories about a boy growing up in Philadelphia parochial schools in the 1950s are funny, touching, and typical of the Irish Catholic experience. Beginning with his third-grade confirmation preparation, under the firm guidance of Sister Patrick Mary, and ending with his acceptance at St. Joseph's College, the author chronicles some of his favorite experiences, especially as he maintains his reputation as class clown. However, in this perfect blend of doctrine and storytelling, all these boyhood shenanigans never threaten his sincere religious devotion.

Liturgy and Doctrine

407. Biffi, Inos. **The Apostles' Creed**. Ill. Franco Vignazia. Grand Rapids, MI: William B. Eerdmans, 1993. 45p. $10.00. LC 93-39151. ISBN 0-8028-3756-5.

A clear and grave explication of each phrase of the creed is illustrated with artistic simplicity and vigor in brilliant color. Many of the ideas are transferable to other Christian faiths.

408. Biffi, Inos. **An Introduction to the Liturgical Year**. Ill. Franco Vignazia. Grand Rapids, MI: William B. Eerdmans, 1995. 97p. $17.00. LC 94-40623. ISBN 0-8028-5103-7.

The entire life of Christ is celebrated during the liturgical year. Advent and Christmas explore the character and meaning of Jesus; the Christmas season includes Saints Stephen and John, the Holy Innocents, and Thomas à Becket, as well as the Holy Family; Lent and Easter commemorate Jesus in the wilderness, his various roles, and Holy Week events and the Resurrection; and so on. The dramatic illustrations have swirling lines and vivid colors.

409.   Biffi, Inos. **Prayer**. Ill. Franco Vignazia. Grand Rapids, MI: William B. Eerdmans, 1993. 46p. $10.00. LC 93-41090. ISBN 0-8028-3759-X.

This discussion of prayer as part of humanity's experience in communicating with the creator includes prayers of Old Testament figures, such as Abel, Noah, Elijah, Job, Jonah, Hannah, and David; Jesus' prayers; the Lord's Prayer explained; liturgical prayer; and personal prayer. The illustrations are handsome, bright, and stylized.

410.   Biffi, Inos. **The Sacraments**. Ill. Franco Vignazia. Grand Rapids, MI: William B. Eerdmans, 1994. 29p. $10.00. LC 93-39150. ISBN 0-8028-3757-3.

The sacraments of Baptism, Confirmation, the Eucharist, Reconciliation, the Anointing of the Sick, Holy Orders, and Matrimony are explained clearly and understandably. Striking color illustrations show solemn, large-eyed, robed people.

411.   Biffi, Inos. **The Ten Commandments**. Ill. Franco Vignazia. Grand Rapids, MI: William B. Eerdmans, 1993. 29p. $10.00. LC 93-39147. ISBN 0-8028-3758-1.

Many examples from Jesus' life are included in this interpretation according to Catholic doctrine. Expressive, animated illustrations with glowing colors enliven the didactic tone of the text.

412.   Dyches, Richard W., and Thomas Mustachio. **A Child's First Catholic Dictionary**. Ill. Ansgar Holmberg. Notre Dame, IN: Ave Maria, 1994. 112p. $14.95. LC 94-71885. ISBN 0-87793-525-4.

Simple definitions of terms such as *absolution, Blessed Mother, catechist, diocese, Eucharist, feast day, genuflect, hell, incarnation, Jew, lectionary, miracle,* and so on, along with discussion of a few biblical personalities, such as Abraham, Moses, Peter, and Paul, are illustrated with bright and lively cartoons. In addition to being a help to young Catholic children, this book could serve as a friendly introduction to Catholic principles for those of other persuasions.

413.   Ramshaw, Gail. **Sunday Morning**. Ill. Judy Jarrett. Chicago: Liturgy Training, 1993. Unp. $15.95. ISBN 1-56854-005-1.

This useful introduction to the elements of the worship service includes the readings from the Old and New Testaments, the Eucharist, the offering, and so forth. Each is supported by a short example from Scripture. Primitively styled, mixed-media illustrations depicting people of all races, both biblical and modern, brim with action and detail.

Celebrations

414.   Bertrand, Diane Gonzales. **Sweet Fifteen**. Houston, TX: Arte Publico Press, 1995. 296p. $7.95pa. LC 94-32656. ISBN 1-55885-133-X.

Quinceanera, a coming-of-age ceremony for fifteen-year-old girls in Mexico, is the event around which this wholesome, pleasant romance takes place. The young woman, wearing an elaborate white dress, is presented at a mass in church before her family and friends as a symbol of God's goodness and everlasting love. The central part of this well-written and uplifting story deals with the preparations for the event and how the relationships within the family are redefined.

415. Chambers, Catherine. **All Saints, All Souls, and Halloween**. A World of Holidays Series. Austin, TX: Raintree Steck-Vaughan, 1997. 31p. $14.98. LC 96-34334. ISBN 0-8172-4606-1.

The short discussions of the histories and celebrations of Celtic Samhain, Halloween on October 31, All Saints' Day on November 1, and All Souls' Day on November 2 explain how each holiday honors the dead. The large-print text is illustrated liberally with color photographs, many of religious celebrations. A glossary, index, and reading list are included.

416. Lasky, Kathryn. **Days of the Dead**. New York: Hyperion, 1994. 48p. $5.95pa. LC 93-47957. ISBN 0-7868-0022-4.

Magnificently photographed in brilliant color, the Days of the Dead holidays (October 31–November 2) are shown as they are celebrated by a family in rural Mexico. The spirits of the departed relatives are welcomed back with a family altar heaped with food and lit by candles, and their graves are tended and decorated. Children dress up as scary creatures and demand treats. The text is warm and poetic. Other Days of the Dead celebrations are described briefly at the end of the book, and a glossary is included.

417. Talbert, Marc. **A Sunburned Prayer**. New York: Simon and Schuster, 1995. 108p. $14.00. LC 94-38682. ISBN 0-689-80125-4.

In this beautifully written novel about an eleven-year-old Mexican American boy, Eloy hopes that holy soil from the Santuario de Chimayo gathered on a Good Friday pilgrimage to the sanctuary will cure his grandmother's cancer. After a seventeen-mile trek during which he suffers from heat, thirst, and painful fatigue, he reaches his goal. The realistic, vividly descriptive characterization, writing style, and evaluation of the boy's sacrifice make this book outstanding.

418. Van Laan, Nancy. **La Boda: A Mexican Wedding Celebration**. Ill. Andrea Arroyo. Boston: Little, Brown, 1996. Unp. $15.95. LC 94-39169. ISBN 0-316-89626-8.

When Luisa and Alfredo marry, the ceremony combines the Roman Catholic faith and the celebratory customs of the Zapotec people of Oaxaca, Mexico. Many Spanish words are part of the simple text, in which a young girl and her grandmother observe the special wedding preparations in the village, attend the ceremony, and join in the exuberant rejoicing afterward. The cheerful, cartoon-style illustrations are brightly colored.

419. Viesti, Joe, and Diane Hall. **Celebrate! In Central America**. New York: Lothrop, Lee & Shepard, 1997. Unp. $16.00. LC 96-6716. ISBN 0-688-15161-2.

Big, brilliant color photographs show the exuberant Catholic/mestizo festivals, which integrate Spanish and Native American traditions. Pictured are the Day of the Dead in Guatemala, Mardi Gras carnivals in Belize and Panama, Holy Week in El Salvador, the feast day of St. Joseph in Honduras, and the celebration of the Virgin of Masaya in Nicaragua. The lively, informative text describes the holidays and their celebrants.

Shaker

420. Bial, Raymond. **Shaker Home**. Boston: Houghton Mifflin, 1994. 40p. $15.95. LC 93-17917. ISBN 0-395-64047-4.

Artistic color photographs emphasize the graceful simplicity of Shaker architecture and design, while the clearly written, appreciative text describes the history and beliefs of the oldest communal society in America. The United Society of Believers in Christ's Second Appearing was founded by Mother Ann Lee in 1774, and it continues to remain industrious, inventive, devout, celibate, immaculate, and separated from the world.

421. Bolick, Nancy O'Keefe, and Sallie G. Randolph. **Shaker Inventions**. Ill. Melissa Francisco. New York: Walker, 1990. 96p. $13.85. LC 89-70618. ISBN 0-8027-6933-0.

The ingenuity of Shaker inventions, the simple elegance of their furniture and architecture, and the beauty of their herb and medicinal gardens arise from their religious beliefs, which stress wasting nothing, to maximize time for prayer and worship, and have a practical purpose for everything. The purity of celibacy, the community of sharing, and the separation from the influence of the outside world all undergird their faith, and are expressed in the organization, cleanliness, and efficiency represented throughout the book. The descriptions of labor-saving devices, from washing machines to apple peelers, are fascinating.

422. Turner, Ann. **Shaker Hearts**. Ill. Wendell Minor. New York: Harper-Collins, 1997. Unp. $14.95. LC 95-45087. ISBN 0-06-025369-X.

Reproductions of acrylic paintings reflect the beauty, dignity, and harmony of the brothers and sisters as they ply their daily tasks in the field, kitchen, herb garden, barn, weaving room, and woodworking shop. A lovely, spare, poetic text is a paean to their simple goodness and high precepts. A fact-filled introduction describes the utopian, orderly, peaceful, and celibate faith.

Older and Noteworthy

The Perfect Life by Doris Faber (Farrar, Straus & Giroux, 1974) is also useful.

The Quakers are no longer the popular subjects they once were, evidently, but much excellent older material deals with the Society of Friends, including *The Witch of Blackbird Pond* by Elizabeth George Speare (Dell, 1958), *The Quiet Rebels* by Margaret H. Bacon (Basic, 1969), *Thee, Hannah* (Doubleday, 1940) and *Henner's Lydia* (Doubleday, 1946) by Marguerite De Angeli, and *The Friendly Persuasion* (Harcourt, 1940) and *Except for Me and Thee* (Harcourt, 1949) by Jessamyn West.

A Gentle War by Lawrence Fellows (Macmillan, 1979) deals with the Salvation Army.

Commendable young adult fiction concerning the clergy includes *The Saving of P.S.* by Robbie Branscum (Dell, 1977), *One-Eyed Cat* by Paula Fox (Bradbury, 1984), *What I Really Think of You* by M. E. Kerr (Harper, 1982), *Secrets* by L. T. Lorimer (Henry Holt, 1981), *A String of Chances* by Phyllis Reynolds

Naylor (Atheneum, 1982), *Edgar Allen* by John Neufeld (Phillips, 1968), *I Will Call It Georgie's Blues* by Suzanne Newton (Viking, 1983), *Seems Like This Road Goes on Forever* by Jean Van Leeuwen (Dial, 1979), and *Callie's Way* by Ruth Wallace-Brodeur (Atheneum, 1984).

Amish and Mennonite

Other recommended books about the Amish are *Plain Girl* by Virginia Sorenson (Harcourt, 1955), *Amish People* by Carolyn Meyer (Atheneum, 1976), *Beyond the Divide* by Kathryn Lasky (Macmillan, 1981), *Which Way Courage* by Eiveen Weiman (Atheneum, 1981), and *Growing Up Amish* by Richard Ammon (Macmillan, 1989).

Chapter Ten

Christian Church History and Biography

423. Mullett, Michael A. **The Reformation**. History Through Sources Series. Crystal Lake, IL: Rigby Interactive Library, 1996. 48p. $13.95. LC 95-36151. ISBN 1-57572-011-6.

This interesting discussion of the Reformation and the Counter Reformation begins with the corruption in the Catholic Church. Following are sections about Martin Luther and Menno Simons and the Anabaptists; the spread of the Reformation to Scandinavia and Switzerland; John Calvin; Henry VIII as head of the church in England; religious tolerance in France; and William of Orange in the Netherlands. The Counter Reformation examines the sack of Rome, Ignatius Loyola, Francis Xavier, the Council of Trent, missionary activities, the Index, and the Inquisition. Primary and secondary information sources are frequently quoted. Color photographs and reproductions, a timeline, a glossary, and an index are included.

424. Wilson, Elizabeth B. **Bibles and Bestiaries: A Guide to Illuminated Manuscripts**. New York: Pierpont Morgan Library/Farrar, Straus & Giroux, 1994. 64p. $25.00. LC 94-6687. ISBN 0-374-30685-0.

The art of illumination is reviewed from the beginning of the Middle Ages, when small groups of monks living in isolation began copying and decorating sacred texts, through the sixteenth century, when richly adorned manuscripts were still being created, even after the invention of printing. The absorbing, scholarly, readable text discusses the history and religion of this era, as well as the techniques of illumination and the evolution of the codex. Treasures from the Pierpont Morgan Library are magnificently photographed and arranged with artistry in an impressive format. A numbered list of illustrations, a reading list, a glossary, and a list of selected illuminated manuscripts in United States public institutions are included.

The Crusades

425. Bradford, Karleen. **There Will Be Wolves**. New York: Lodestar, 1996. 195p. $15.99. LC 96-1399. ISBN 0-525-67539-6.

An indictment of the First Crusade in 1096, with its violence and fanaticism, is the core of this well-researched and vividly written young adult novel. To escape an unfounded charge of witchcraft, Ursula, a spirited young girl trained in the healing arts, is forced to join the crusade, which consists of many ignorant opportunists and bullies, along with starry-eyed idealists. As supplies dwindle, the crusaders become increasingly ruthless as they pillage and slaughter their way toward Constantinople. A gentle romance tempers the bloodshed.

426. Child, John. **The Crusades**. Biographical History Series. New York: Peter Bedrick Books, 1996. 64p. $17.95. LC 95-44426. ISBN 0-87226-119-0.

This history of the Crusades opens with a comparison of the refined civilization of Islam and the turmoil of Catholic Europe in the eleventh century. Discussed are the First Crusade, launched by Pope Urban II's exhortations to win back Jerusalem for Jesus; the People's Crusade; the Second, Third, Fourth, and Children's Crusades; and other, more minor actions also known as crusades. Thumbnail sketches of prominent figures including Saladin, Richard the Lionheart, and Louis IX, and quotations from primary and secondary sources, further enliven a clear, interesting text. Excellent color artwork and maps illustrate the book.

427. Tate, Georges. **The Crusaders: Warriors of God**. Discoveries Series. New York: Harry N. Abrams, 1996. 192p. $12.95pa. ISBN 0-8109-2829-9.

This comprehensive study begins with the development of Islam, the struggle between the Seljuk Turks and the Byzantine Empire, the division of the Catholic Church into east and west, the emergence of chivalry, and the call by Pope Urban II for the rescue of Jerusalem from the Muslims in 1095. The progress of each crusade is then detailed with chilling factuality. The spiritual quests were drenched with blood and corrupted by a thirst for economic power. The information is well delivered and made appealing by a variety of type sizes, sidebar information, captions, a multitude of colorful illustrations, a reading list, an index, and a list of illustrations.

Cathedrals

428. Erlande-Brandenburg, Alain. **Cathedrals and Castles: Building in the Middle Ages**. New York: Harry N. Abrams, 1995. 174p. $12.95pa. LC 94-77944. ISBN 0-8109-2812-4.

Profusely illustrated with manuscript illuminations, drawings, maps, photographs, and plans of every available aspect of medieval construction, the text is moderately technical but readable. Aspects include machines and tools, workers of various trades, sculptures, interiors and exteriors, models, rose windows, mosaics, and portraits of patrons. Translations of original tenth- and eleventh-century documents dealing with architects, building sites, materials, techniques, and machines add significant interest. A list of great cathedrals, suggestions for further reading, an index, and a list of illustrations are included.

429.   Perdrizet, Marie-Pierre. **The Cathedral Builders**. Ill. Eddy Krehenbuhl. Peoples of the Past Series. Brookfield, CT: Milbrook Press, 1992. 64p. $16.40. LC 91-24233. ISBN 1-56294-162-3.
     Attractively and liberally illustrated with reproductions of lively paintings, this book describes life in the Middle Ages, the purposes the cathedral fulfilled in the community, methods and materials of construction, the master builders and artisans, and ways of worship. Interesting and easy to read, the book includes a list of major European cathedrals, a timeline, a reading list, and an index.

The Pilgrims and Thanksgiving

430.   George, Jean Craighead. **The First Thanksgiving**. Ill. Thomas Locker. New York: Philomel Books, 1993. Unp. $15.95. LC 91-46643. ISBN 0-399-21991-9.
     This skillfully written account emphasizes the crucial role played by Squanto in the Pilgrims' survival, along with the standard material. The book stresses the shared festivities of the Pawtuxet Green Corn Dance and the Harvest Home feast of the Pilgrims, both of which were thanksgiving for bountiful crops. The Pilgrims' trials and triumphs are depicted in full-page reproductions of artistic oil paintings with backgrounds of beautiful landscapes and sea views.

431.   Morris, Gilbert. **The Dangerous Voyage**. Time Navigators Series. Minneapolis, MN: Bethany House, 1995. 104p. $5.99pa. ISBN 1-55661-395-4.
     Christian values are successfully and logically integrated into this time-travel story in which a brother and sister are transported from today to the seventeenth century and onto the *Mayflower*. Because their Recall Unit, the device that returns them to the present, has been stolen by a shipmate, they must go all the way to the New World with the Saints, who seek freedom of worship, and the Strangers, who seek their fortunes. A brisk plot and authentic backgrounds should appeal to upper elementary readers.

432.   Roop, Connie, and Peter Roop. **Pilgrim Voices: Our First Year in the New World**. Ill. Shelley Pritchett. New York: Walker, 1995. 48p. $17.85. LC 95-10114. ISBN 0-8027-8315-5.
     The actual words of Pilgrims have been edited to present a continuous narrative, from August 5, 1610, through November 9, 1621, of the Separatist emigration on the *Mayflower* to Patuxet. The narrative, based on "Mourt's Relation" (presumed to have been written by William Bradford and Edward Winslow) and "Bradford's History of Plymouth Plantation," touches upon the voyage, the first explorations and contacts with the Native Americans, and the harvest festival during which the Pilgrims feasted with Chief Massasoit and ninety of his men. The cooperation between the Pilgrims and the American Indians is stressed. The writing retains a seventeenth-century flavor but is clear and engaging. Reproductions of realistic paintings in bright colors illustrate the

text generously. The book includes a foreword, glossary, index, bibliography, reading list, and source information.

433.   San Souci, Robert. **N. C. Wyeth's Pilgrims**. Ill. N. C. Wyeth. San Francisco: Chronicle Books, 1991. Unp. $13.95. ISBN 0-87701-806-5.
    Reproductions of the murals Wyeth painted for the Metropolitan Life Insurance Company in 1940, which emphasize the beauty of the New England landscape, masterfully illustrate this straightforward, accurate narrative. It traces the experiences of the Saints, seeking religious freedom, and the Strangers, seeking a new life, from their harrowing voyage across the Atlantic through the first desolate winter of suffering, the successful plantings of crops, and the harvest festival shared with Chief Massasoit and members of the Wampanoag.

434.   Stamper, Judith Bauer. **New Friends in a New Land: A Thanksgiving Story**. Ill. Chet Jezierski. Stories of America Series. Austin, TX: Raintree Steck-Vaughan, 1993. 32p. $22.83. LC 92-18072. ISBN 0-8114-7213-2.
    Samoset and Squanto assist the Pilgrims at Plymouth, despite the fact that Squanto was ill-treated by the English, by helping them achieve a treaty with the Wampanoag and improving their agricultural methods. After a bountiful harvest, the Wampanoag and the Pilgrims share in the Thanksgiving feast. The easy-to-read text is illustrated with realistic artwork in subdued colors.

435.   Stein, R. Conrad. **The Pilgrims**. Cornerstones of Freedom Series. Chicago: Children's Press, 1995. 32p. $18.00. LC 95-3292. ISBN 0-516-06628-5.
    The emigration of the Separatist Puritans is described lucidly, from their voyage on the *Mayflower*, through their first year in the New World. An account of their harvest festival in 1621 is included, along with further information about Plymouth in its later days. The book has photographs and artwork, in black and white and color, and a glossary, timeline, and index.

Separation of Church and State

436.   Evans, J. Edward. **Freedom of Religion**. Minneapolis, MN: Lerner, 1990. 88p. $9.95. LC 90-34929. ISBN 0-8225-1754-X.
    This fair and factual history provides a didactic discussion of the development of religious freedom in the United States. It spans from the early intolerance of Anglican and Puritan settlers, through the determined efforts of Roger Williams and Thomas Jefferson to establish freedom of worship, to current problems, such as federal aid to parochial schools and the teaching of evolution and creationism. Black-and-white photographs and art reproductions illustrate the book.

437.   Gay, Kathlyn. **Church and State: Government and Religion in the United States**. Brookfield, CT: Millbrook Press, 1992. 128p. $16.90. LC 91-34753. ISBN 1-56294-063-5.
    The complexities of trying to separate church and state while upholding the First Amendment are carefully and clearly examined. A short account of the first religious groups to settle in this country, many of whom were intolerant of everyone but themselves, is followed by a discussion of the problems of separatist religious communities, parochial school aid, school prayer, observance of the Sabbath, conscientious objectors, tax exemption of churches, the use of peyote

by Native Americans, and so forth. Many interesting specific examples are given. The text is readable, absorbing, timely, well arranged, and illustrated with occasional black-and-white photographs and drawings.

Collective Biography

438.   Meyer, Mary Clemens. **Walking with Jesus: Stories About Real People Who Return Good for Evil**. Ill. Harriet Miller. Scottdale, PA: Herald Press, 1992. 88p. $10.95. LC 92-10912. ISBN 0-8361-3574-1.

Peacemaking and Christian love themes permeate these true-to-life anecdotes, many of which deal with Mennonites. Most take place in the twentieth century and prove that everyday generosity, kindness, and forbearance often exercise a redeeming effect on others. The text is divided into short sections and has simple illustrations.

439.   Rediger, Pat. **Great African Americans in Civil Rights**. Outstanding African Americans Series. New York: Crabtree, 1995. 64p. $14.96. LC 95-24881. ISBN 0-86505-798-2.

Baptist ministers Ralph David Abernathy, Martin Luther King, Jr., and Jessie Jackson; and Malcolm X, a leader in the Nation of Islam, are among the civil rights activists profiled in this book. Their backgrounds, skills, accomplishments, and obstacles overcome are discussed, and black-and-white photographs accompany the text.

Individual Biography

440.   Birch, Beverley. **Father Damien: Missionary to a Forgotten People**. People Who Made a Difference Series. Milwaukee, WI: Gareth Stevens, 1990. 68p. $17.95. LC 89-49751. ISBN 0-8368-0389-2.

This is a gripping account of Father Damien, the Roman Catholic priest who in 1873 volunteered to serve the lepers banished to the island of Molokai. It describes the sixteen years he labored to provide that suffering community with decent housing and food, as well as spiritual guidance, before he himself succumbed to the disease. The book is a revised and abridged version, for younger readers, of *Father Damien* by Pam Brown (Exley, 1987). It is illustrated with black-and-white and color photographs, and has a glossary, reading list, timeline for leprosy in Hawaii, index, and list of leprosy organizations.

441.   Bryant, Jennifer Fisher. **Lucretia Mott: A Guiding Light**. Women of Spirit Series. Grand Rapids, MI: William B. Eerdmans, 1996. 182p. $15.00. LC 95-39373. ISBN 0-8028-5115-0.

Lucretia Mott was an extraordinary woman of the nineteenth century: a devout Quaker minister and dynamic preacher, an outspoken anti-slavery activist, a champion of women's rights, a social reformer, a peacemaker, and an energetic wife and mother. She led a life overflowing with good works and overcame many obstacles. This dynamically written book contains a center section of black-and-white photographs and reproductions of the Motts and other feminists and anti-slavery personalities. An index, list of sources, and suggestions for further reading are included.

442. Jackson, Dave, and Neta Jackson. Ill. Julian Jackson. **Trailblazer Books** series. Minneapolis, MN: Bethany House. $5.99pa.

In these fictionalized biographies, a teenage boy or girl, sometimes based on an actual person, interacts with a Christian hero or heroine, usually a missionary or evangelist. The stories have much action and suspense, well-researched factual backgrounds, vivid settings, and lively dialogue. The titles include:

442.1. **Abandoned on the Wild Frontier**. 1995. 144p. LC 95-10049. ISBN 1-55661-468-3.

A boy joins Peter Cartwright, Methodist evangelist, on a trek to Illinois during the nineteenth century to search for his mother, who has been kidnapped by Native Americans.

442.2. **Attack in the Rye Grass**. 1994. 158p. LC 94-7589. ISBN 1-55661-273-7.

In 1843, the nephew of Marcus and Narcissa Whitman, missionaries to Native Americans, travels to the Oregon territory, where the native peoples are suffering from illnesses and loss of their lands.

442.3. **The Bandit of Ashley Downs**. 1993. 136p. LC 92-46182. ISBN 1-55661-270-2.

After becoming unwittingly involved in a highway robbery, a poor boy in England enters an orphanage run by George Muller, a missionary, in the 1870s.

442.4. **The Betrayer's Fortune**. 1994. 144p. LC 94-32700. ISBN 1-55661-467-5.

In 1543, enemies of Menno Simons, the Anabaptist leader in Holland, tempt a young boy to betray Simons in exchange for his imprisoned mother's freedom.

442.5. **The Chimney Sweep's Ransom**. 1992. 140p. LC 92-546. ISBN 1-55661-268-0.

John Wesley has a role in this story about a Newcastle boy who is helped to rescue his five-year-old brother from being sold as a chimney sweep in the eighteenth century.

442.6. **Danger on the Flying Trapeze**. 1995. 144p. LC 95-10048. ISBN 1-55661-469-1.

In Philadelphia in 1893, a boy and his mother join the circus and meet Dwight L. Moody.

442.7. **Escape from the Slave Traders**. 1992. 135p. LC 92-11170. ISBN 1-55661-263-X.

In 1861, slave traders capture African boys who later encounter David Livingstone.

442.8. **Flight of the Fugitives**. 1994. 144p. LC 94-32699. ISBN 1-55661-466-7.

In 1934, Japanese soldiers threaten Gladys Aylward's missionary orphanage in China.

442.9. **The Hidden Jewel**. 1992. 136p. LC 91-44062. ISBN 1-55661-245-1.

In India in the early twentieth century, Amy Carmichael, an Irish missionary, rescues a runaway girl fleeing marriage to an old man.

442.10. **Imprisoned in the Golden City.** 1993. 155p. LC 92-46181. ISBN 1-55661-269-9.

Although they are Americans, the king of Burma imprisons Adoniram and Ann Judson, missionaries, as English spies during Burma's war with the British in 1824.

442.11. **Kidnapped by River Rats.** 1991. 110p. LC 91-23816. ISBN 1-55661-220-6.

William and Catherine Booth help an orphaned and penniless brother and sister when they come to London seeking their uncle in the 1880s.

442.12. **Listen for the Whippoorwill.** 1993. 144p. LC 93-26837. ISBN 1-55661-272-9.

Slaves associated with Harriet Tubman travel on the Underground Railroad and are rescued by a Quaker boy.

442.13. **The Queen's Smuggler.** 1991. 120p. LC 91-4952. ISBN 1-55661-221-4.

A girl from Antwerp goes to England to serve as a lady-in-waiting to Anne Boleyn, to enlist her support for William Tyndale's translation of the Bible into English.

442.14. **Quest for the Lost Prince.** 1996. 144p. LC 96-9941. ISBN 1-55661-472-1.

Miraculously freed from captivity in the 1890s, Prince Kaboo, also known as Samuel Morris, is converted to Christianity and goes to the United States to study.

442.15. **The Runaway's Revenge.** 1995. 141p. LC 95-43622. ISBN 1-55661-471-3.

A boy whose mother was aboard John Newton's slave ship tracks down Newton to kill him in 1775 but changes his mind after he hears Newton's life story.

442.16. **Shanghaied to China.** 1993. 141p. LC 93-32552. ISBN 1-55661-271-0.

On board a ship in 1853, Hudson Taylor, a missionary, befriends a child who was shanghaied as a cabin boy in Liverpool.

442.17. **Spy for the Night Riders.** 1992. 127p. LC 91-44063. ISBN 1-55661-237-0.

In Wittenberg in 1520, a student and servant of Martin Luther accompanies Luther to Worms.

442.18. **The Thieves of Tyburn Square.** 1995. 141p. LC 95-43826. ISBN 1-55661-470-5.

A brother and sister, imprisoned and stranded in London after their mother is transported to a penal colony for theft, observe Quaker Elizabeth Fry's active ministry to women in Newgate Prison in early-nineteenth-century England.

442.19. **Trial by Poison.** 1994. 144p. LC 94-7587. ISBN 1-55661-274-5.

Mary Slessor, a missionary teacher in Calabar (Nigeria) in the late nineteenth century, helps persuade the king to release Imata's mother.

442.20. **The Warrior's Challenge**. 1996. 144p. ISBN 1-55661-473-X.

The crippled nephew of missionary David Zeisberger dies on the trek west while accompanying displaced Moravian Native Americans in 1772 to a new settlement in Muskingum.

443. Nichols, Joan Kane. **A Matter of Conscience: The Trial of Anne Hutchinson**. Ill. Dan Krovatin. Austin, TX: Raintree Steck-Vaughan, 1993. 101p. $17.98. LC 92-18087. ISBN 0-8114-7233-7.

Anne Hutchinson, her husband, and eleven children were such devotees of John Cotton's preaching of the Covenant of Grace that they followed him from England to the Puritan Massachusetts Bay Colony. She then accused the ministers there of preaching a Covenant of Works and deeply offended the powers that be, to the point that Cotton himself condemned her for her public pronouncements. She was imprisoned and banished. This is a factual, well-researched, unbiased account of narrowminded prejudice and rigidity on both sides.

444. Willard, Nancy. **Gutenberg's Gift: A Book Lover's Pop-Up Book**. Ill. Bryan Leister. Baltimore, MD: Wild Honey, 1995. Unp. $20.00. LC 95-2253. ISBN 0-15-200783-0.

In this poetic and fanciful account, Johannes wants to make a Bible for his wife, Anna; works all year experimenting with iron and wood; makes a lead alphabet and inks it; and produces his gift for Christmas. The well-engineered, forceful, realistic pop-up illustrations show medieval interiors, the press, pages hanging to dry, and so on. A short, factual evaluation of Gutenberg's work by H. George Fletcher of the Pierpont Morgan Library is included.

John Newton

445. Granfield, Linda. **Amazing Grace: The Story of the Hymn**. Ill. Janet Wilson. Plattsburgh, NY: Tundra Books of Northern New York, 1997. Unp. $15.95. ISBN 0-88776-389-9.

This richly conceived, absorbing account of Newton's life emphasizes his participation as a sea captain in the slave trade and his later rejection of slavery and activity as a minister and writer of hymns. The book is illustrated with reproductions of forceful, realistic paintings depicting suffering slaves and storm-tossed ships.

446. Haskins, Jim. **Amazing Grace: The Story Behind the Song**. Brookfield, CT: Millbrook Press, 1992. 48p. $15.40. LC 91-20999. ISBN 1-56294-117-8.

The taut, succinct narrative recounts John Newton's life, from childhood through his irresponsible young adulthood, including his work as captain of a slave ship, call to the ministry, opposition to slavery, and composing of hymns. Additional information about his most famous work, "Amazing Grace," is also given. The book is illustrated with archival artwork and indexed.

Father Junipero Serra and the California Missions

447.   Genet, Donna. **Father Junipero Serra: Founder of California Missions**. Springfield, NJ: Enslow, 1996. 128p. $18.95. LC 95-40199. ISBN 0-89490-762-X.

In this account, the ruthless imposition of Spanish control and culture on Native Americans in Baja and Alta California is not softened, nor is the fact that Spain used the mission to keep them pacified and exploited to establish white settlements and keep the area under Spanish dominance. Nevertheless, Father Serra is portrayed as fiercely dedicated to the mission field since childhood and as having the best of intentions in his goal of converting and civilizing the native peoples as he establishes his "golden chain" of missions from San Diego to San Francisco. This excellent, thorough biography also encompasses the pertinent historical background, including additional information about the fate of the missions and the continuing appreciation and respect in California for Father Serra. It is interestingly written, well organized, and fast-paced for the amount of information it contains.

448.   Gleiter, Jan, and Kathleen Thompson. **Junipero Serra**. Ill. Charles Shaw. Raintree Hispanic Stories Series. Austin, TX: Raintree Steck-Vaughan, 1993. 32p. $19.97. ISBN 0-8114-8482-3.

This easy-to-read version of Miguel Serra's life is illustrated with large, serene watercolors. He was born to illiterate peasants on Majorca, had a brilliant mind, became a Franciscan friar and professor of theology, and followed his dream to become a missionary in the New World. There he converted many, established missions along the California coast, and attracted Spanish settlers. The bilingual text includes Spanish and English versions, and a glossary is included.

449.   Lemke, Nancy. **Missions of the Southern Coast**. California Missions Series. Minneapolis, MN: Lerner, 1996. 80p. $22.95. LC 95-16619. ISBN 0-8225-1925-9.

Although the history of San Diego de Alcala, San Luis Rey de Francia, and San Juan Capistrano is presented in detail, much emphasis is placed on the virtual enslavement of the Native Americans living in the region. The controversy concerning the elevation of Father Serra to sainthood is discussed. Excellent color photographs, old prints, and maps show the progression over the years of the missions and those associated with them. This handsomely presented book includes a glossary, pronunciation guide, chronology, and index.

450.   MacMillan, Dianne M. **Missions of the Los Angeles Area**. California Missions Series. Minneapolis, MN: Lerner, 1996. 80p. $22.95. LC 95-16717. ISBN 0-8225-1927-5.

San Gabriel Arcangel, San Fernando Rey de Espana, and San Buenaventura were founded on territory inhabited by the Chumash and Tongva Native American nations. The fate of these nations at the hands of the Spaniards is a poignant part of this absorbing history of the three missions, from establishment to the present day. The book is generously illustrated with color photographs, maps, and drawings, and contains a glossary, pronunciation guide, chronology, and index.

451.   Van Steenwyk, Elizabeth. **The California Missions**. A First Book Series. New York: Franklin Watts, 1995. 64p. $15.75. LC 95-3847. ISBN 0-531-20187-2.

This factual and interesting overview of Father Serra's life and tireless efforts to build a chain of missions from San Diego to San Francisco is illustrated with excellent color photographs, historical prints, and drawings. The book discusses the friar's difficulties with the Spanish government and military, who wanted the missions primarily as a means to establish settlements in California; the treatment of the Native Americans who converted to Christianity; the completion of the missions by other friars after Serra's death; mission construction and daily life; and the decay of the missions until their recent restoration. A mission timeline, a glossary, current addresses of twenty-one missions, a reading list, and an index supplement the text.

452.   White, Florence Meiman. **The Story of Junipero Serra: Brave Adventurer**. Ill. Stephen Marchesi. Famous Lives Series. Milwaukee, WI: Gareth Stevens, 1996. 100p. $14.95. LC 95-36842. ISBN 0-8368-1460-6.

This well-written biography emphasizes Father Serra's entire life, not just the missions he built that were so integral to his work with Native American peoples. Many interesting, true anecdotes are included to vivify the personality and accomplishments of this diminutive, devoted, determined holy man. Occasional black-and-white drawings, a timeline and map for the missions, lists of related videos and materials for further reading, an index, and highlights of Father Serra's life are included.

453.   White, Tekla N. **Missions of the San Francisco Bay Area**. California Missions Series. Minneapolis, MN: Lerner, 1996. 80p. $22.95. LC 95-8714. ISBN 0-8225-1926-7.

Illustrated with well-reproduced color photographs, maps, historical prints, and drawings, this book presents the history of Santa Clara de Asis, San Jose de Guadalupe, San Francisco de Asis, San Rafael Arcangel, and San Francisco Solano, from their inception through modern restoration. The plight of the local Native Americans, whose hunting grounds and way of life were invaded ruthlessly, is stressed. A glossary, pronunciation guide, chronology, and index are included.

Saints

454.   Armstrong, Carole. **Lives and Legends of the Saints: With Paintings from the Great Art Museums of the World**. New York: Simon and Schuster, 1995. 45p. $17.00. LC 94-43009. ISBN 0-689-80277-3.

Andrew, Apollonia, Catherine of Alexandria, Cecilia, Christopher, Dorothy, Eustace, Francis of Assisi, George, Jerome, Joan of Arc, John the Baptist, Joseph, Lucy, Luke, Martin of Tours, Mary Magdalene, Paul, and Peter are among the saints depicted. The book includes fascinating myths and other material about their lives, and beautiful typography and an interesting arrangement enhance the presentation. Among the artists included are Giotto, Crivelli, Bosch, Memling, Zurburan, and Raphael. The book is indexed by artist and painting and has a calendar of the principal feasts of venerated saints.

455.   Potter, Giselle. **Lucy's Eyes and Margaret's Dragon: The Lives of the Virgin Saints**. Ill. author. San Francisco: Chronicle Books, 1997. 107p. $17.95. LC 97-854. ISBN 0-8118-1515-3.

Told in a simple, straightforward manner, the stories of the unfortunate Saints Ursula, Agnes, Cecilia, Agatha, Lucy, Barbara, Bega, Brigid, Christina, Margaret, Catherine, Joan, and Uncumber almost always include an obdurate pagan father, an importunate suitor smitten by the maiden's beauty, some horrible forms of torture from which the saints emerge miraculously unscathed, and a final beheading, piercing, or stabbing. Only Bega, Brigid, and Christina survived their persecution. The watercolors show wraithlike figures being burned, crucified, sliced, drowned, and otherwise cruelly destroyed.

456.   Waddell, Helen. **Beasts and Saints**. Grand Rapids, MI: William B. Eerdmans, 1996. 132p. $12.00pa. LC 96-16346. ISBN 0-8028-4223-2.

Holy men and women interact lovingly but firmly with all sorts of creatures, from lions and stags to wrens and mice. Their acts of kindness earned them the devoted loyalty of the animals and birds and a happy sharing of the earth. The pre-Franciscan saints, from the fourth through the twelfth centuries, are divided into three groups: the desert fathers, the saints of the west, and the saints of Ireland. Included are Jerome, Columba, Cuthbert, Godric, Brendan, Kevin, and more, with forty-four legends of miraculous communication altogether. The text is divided into short sections and uses sweetly formal, old-fashioned language.

Individual Saints

457.   dePaola, Tomie. **Christopher: The Holy Giant**. Ill. author. New York: Holiday House, 1994. Unp. $15.95. LC 90-49926. ISBN 0-8234-0862-0.

Reprobus, a giant in the land of Canaan, wishes to serve the greatest and most powerful king in the world. First, he chooses the king of the city, and more powerful then the devil. When he learns that the cross frightens the devil away, Reprobus begins a long search for Christ the King, serving others until Christ appears to him in the form of a child and renames the giant Christopher. Christopher lives a holy life and becomes the patron saint of travelers. The simple, dignified text is illustrated with decorative, expressive pictures.

458.   Hodges, Margaret. **St. Jerome and the Lion**. Ill. Barry Moser. New York: Orchard, 1991. Unp. $14.95. ISBN 0-531-05938-3.

This is a beautifully written retelling of the legend of Jerome, patron saint of librarians, and the lion with a thorn-infested paw that came to his monastery, begging for help. Once healed, he became a staunch friend and helper to the monks until he was falsely accused of eating the donkey in his charge. The themes of prejudgment, dishonesty, and atonement are well expressed. The illustrations are elegant, realistic, and powerful.

459.   Roth, Susan L. **Brave Martha and the Dragon**. Ill. author. New York: Dial, 1996. Unp. $14.99. LC 94-41631. ISBN 0-8037-1852-7.

Colorful collages of cut paper and fabric show the action in this Provencal legend of Saint Martha, who supposedly sailed to France circa C.E. 40 and was somehow transported to the Middle Ages. She saves the town of Tarascon from a greedy, green-and-red, smoke-emitting dragon, who has been devouring the villagers' livestock, by roping him with the sash of her garment. The story is told with humor and panache, and the book includes a description of the saint's annual festival and traditions.

460.   Sabuda, Robert. **Saint Valentine**. Ill. author. New York: Atheneum, 1992. Unp. $14.95. LC 91-25012. ISBN 0-689-31762-X.
    A humble physician and herbalist, Valentine was one of a small band of persecuted Christians living in ancient Rome. He treated anyone in need, including the blind daughter of a Roman jailer; the girl miraculously regained her sight when she received a papyrus sent by Valentine from prison. The simple text is illustrated with powerful mosaic-style pictures, and the book includes an explanatory note about Valentine's Day.

Saint Francis of Assisi

461.   Hodges, Margaret. **Brother Francis and the Friendly Beasts**. Ill. Ted Lewin. New York: Scribner, 1991. Unp. $13.95. LC 90-33206. ISBN 0-684-19173-3.
    Illustrated with powerful, realistic watercolors, this sweet, poetic biography describes the life of Saint Francis. Beginning with his childhood as the pampered son of a rich merchant, the story recounts his rejection of materialism and choice of poverty and service to others, his inspiration for the first creche in Greccio, and his glorious "Canticle of the Sun." The underlying theme, however, is his deep love of animals, and theirs of him.

462.   Wildsmith, Brian. **Saint Francis**. Ill. author. Grand Rapids, MI: William B. Eerdmans, 1996. Unp. $20.00. ISBN 0-19-279980-0.
    Highlights of the gentle saint's life, from his early, profligate days through his peaceful death at the small church near Assisi, include his itinerant ministry, his futile trip to the holy land to end the conflict there, the creche at Greccio, the wolf at Gubbio, and his receiving of the stigmata. The celestial glories of his spirituality are reflected in reproductions of lavish, intricately detailed, action-filled paintings, gleaming with color and accented in gold.

Saint Joan of Arc

463.   Dana, Barbara. **Young Joan**. New York: HarperCollins, 1991. 371p. $17.95. LC 90-39494. ISBN 0-06-021422-8.
    This richly imagined, dreamy, mystical, first-person narrative of Joan's early years stresses her strong faith in God; her tenderness toward family, friends, and animals; and her courage. When the saints shatter her quiet rural life with their messages that her mission is to restore the kingdom of France, she is puzzled and overwhelmed, but still obeys. The author successfully integrates Joan's ordinary feelings as a young girl with her intensely spiritual nature, and provides a realistic setting and convincing plot. The language is somewhat stilted but readable and lively.

464.   Garden, Nancy. **Dove and Sword: A Novel of Joan of Arc.** New York: Farrar, Straus & Giroux, 1995. 237p. $17.00. LC 95-920. ISBN 0-374-34476-0.

Although the central character, from Joan's home village of Domremy, is fictional, many of the others in this young adult novel are historical personages. Joan's life is portrayed through the eyes of her friend Gabrielle, who, as a healer ministering to the wounded, follows her into battle. Carefully and vividly written, the text testifies to the miraculous transformation of a simple, pious peasant girl into a fiery warrior. An informative author's note verifies the accuracy of the historical background and Joan's personality.

Saint Patrick

465.   dePaola, Tomie. **Patrick: Patron Saint of Ireland.** Ill. author. New York: Holiday House, 1992. Unp. $15.95. LC 91-19417. ISBN 0-8234-0924-4.

From his capture and sale as a slave in Ireland, through his escape to Britain, his later return to Ireland as a missionary bishop, and his always dangerous travels to perform his good works, Patrick's life unfolds in clear, simple prose. The book is harmoniously illustrated with stylized charm and includes many of the myths associated with the saint's life.

466.   Dunlop, Eileen. **Tales of St. Patrick.** New York: Holiday House, 1995. 125p. $15.95. LC 95-35087. ISBN 0-8234-1218-0.

The tales of Patrick's life are told in an interesting, smoothly flowing union of primary sources from the fifth century, the saint's own writings, and traditions and legends. Included are his capture by Irish raiders, who tear him from a life of comfortable indulgence; his enslavement as a ragged shepherd; his inspiration from God to convert the Irish people; his escape and subsequent preparation as a missionary and priest; and his heroic success in Christianizing pagan Ireland. The narrative features detailed settings, lively dialogue, and a well-developed characterization of Patrick.

467.   Gibbons, Gail. **St. Patrick's Day.** Ill. author. New York: Holiday House, 1994. Unp. $15.95. LC 93-29570. ISBN 0-8234-1119-2.

For young children, this book provides a general introduction to Saint Patrick's life, his mission to Ireland, and the celebration of the holiday honoring him. It includes short accounts of six legends about his miracles and teachings, as well as the origins of such symbols as the harp and the shamrock. Cheerful ink-and-watercolor illustrations range from historical events to the modern parades and parties.

468.   Hodges, Margaret. **Saint Patrick and the Peddler.** Ill. Paul Brett Johnson. New York: Orchard, 1993. Unp. $6.95pa. LC 92-44522. ISBN 0-531-05489-6.

In a charming folktale, a poor but generous peddler in Ballymene shares whatever he has, often giving away his wares in times of difficulty. He thinks that his tiny cottage and old porridge pot probably resemble those of Saint Patrick himself when he was living as a herdsman. When times in Ballymene are truly terrible, the saint appears to the peddler in dreams, sends him to a special bridge over the Liffey River in Dublin, and tells him he will learn something worthwhile there. He obeys, and his reward is surprising and satisfying. The large reproductions of paintings feature lush landscapes and realistic human figures. A short biography of the saint is included.

Contemporary Biography

469.   Coles, Robert. **The Story of Ruby Bridges**. Ill. George Ford. New York: Scholastic, 1995. Unp. $13.95. LC 92-33674. ISBN 0-590-43967-7.

Lest we forget the amazing courage of six-year-old Ruby Bridges, the first African American child to enter a white elementary school in New Orleans, this account of her early days is told clearly and factually. Ruby braved the verbal abuse of frantic whites as she walked to school with an escort of federal marshals. Raised in a strongly religious home, she prayed daily for her tormentors to be forgiven by God, just as Jesus forgave his tormentors. Double-page pictures show a neatly dressed young girl making her way through crowds of jeering adults, praying for them on the street, and studying alone in an empty classroom.

470.   Gourse, Leslie. **Mahalia Jackson: Queen of Gospel Song**. Impact Biography Series. New York: Franklin Watts, 1996. 128p. $17.02. LC 95-49845. ISBN 0-531-11228-4.

This is a detailed and absorbing biography of a woman of great talent and determination who rose from poverty. She always held herself apart from all music she considered secular, and triumphed worldwide with her intense, emotional, gripped-by-the-spirit vocal style. An index, selected discography, and bibliography are included, along with a center section of black-and-white photographs.

Martin Luther King, Jr.

471.   Bray, Rosemary L. **Martin Luther King**. Ill. Malcah Zeldis. New York: Mulberry, 1995. 48p. $5.95pa. LC 93-41002. ISBN 0-688-15219-8.

A clearly written, succinct, and factual text chronicles Dr. King's life from his birth to the declaration of a national holiday celebrating his life, and discusses segregation frankly. Striking, intensely colored, folk-art illustrations invigorate the story. A chronology is included.

472.   Darby, Jean. **Martin Luther King, Jr.** Minneapolis, MN: Lerner, 1990. 144p. $22.00. LC 89-36797. ISBN 0-8225-4902-6.

Thorough, lucid, and absorbing, this biography covers much of the early civil rights movement, as well as Dr. King's life, because they are so closely entwined. His devotion to nonviolence, his steadfastness in the face of danger, and his optimistic Christian faith are stressed. Many quotations from his speeches and writings are included. Black-and-white photographs accompany the text, and a glossary, reading list, and index are included.

473.   Haskins, Jim. **I Have a Dream: The Life and Words of Martin Luther King, Jr.** Brookfield, CT: Millbrook Press, 1992. 112p. $8.95pa. LC 91-42528. ISBN 0-395-64549-2.

This laudatory and well-written biography is illuminated by extensive quotations from Dr. King's writings, which express his principles of nonviolence,

Christian forbearance, and high hopes in the struggle for civil rights. The attractive, large-format paperback has many good black-and-white photographs of the King family and the violent desegregation-related events that happened in the 1960s.

474. Milton, Joyce. **Marching to Freedom: The Story of Martin Luther King, Jr.** Rev. ed. Famous Lives Series. Milwaukee, WI: Gareth Stevens, 1995. 104p. $14.95. LC 95-19272. ISBN 0-8368-1382-0.

The large type and short paragraphs in this factually accurate, fast-paced overview of Dr. King's life and principles make the book easy to read. The dialogue has been excerpted from biographies, writings, and commentaries about this outstanding minister and American hero. The center section contains black-and-white photographs. Also included are a timeline of highlights in Dr. King's life, a list of books and videos for further study, and an index.

Mother Teresa

475. Gray, Charlotte. **Mother Teresa: Servant to the World's Suffering People.** People Who Made a Difference Series. Milwaukee, WI: Gareth Stevens, 1990. 68p. $17.95. LC 89-49750. ISBN 0-8368-0393-0.

Adapted and abridged by Susan Ullstein, this competent survey of Mother Teresa's life, including her work in India and other parts of the world where the poor needed help, is brisk and easy to read. Many favorable quotations from other authors on the subject are cited. The book includes black-and-white and color photographs, maps showing the locations of the Missionaries of Charity worldwide, a list of international charitable organizations, a reading list, a glossary, a chronology of Mother Teresa's life, and an index.

476. Jacobs, William Jay. **Mother Teresa: Helping the Poor.** Gateway Biography Series. Brookfield, CT: Millbrook Press, 1991. 48p. $14.40. ISBN 1-56294-020-1.

Simply but vividly written, this account of Mother Teresa's life includes thorough information about her family and childhood as well as her later ministry. The author's tone is warm and approving. The book contains color and black-and-white photographs, a timeline, a reading list, and an index.

477. Johnson, Linda Carlson. **Mother Teresa: Protector of the Sick.** The Library of Famous Women Series. Woodbridge, CT: Blackbirch Press, 1990. 64p. $15.95. LC 90-47213. ISBN 1-56711-034-7.

Lively and absorbing, this biography emphasizes Mother Teresa's ongoing work with the poor and sick rather than extensive biographical detail. The book discusses the operation of her Missionaries of Charity, and the details of their labors in the Calcutta slums reveal their intense, caring love for all who suffer. Photographs provide adequate illustration, and the book contains a glossary, reading list, and index.

Older and Noteworthy

Additional books about the history of the Christian Church include the Illustrated History of the Church Series by John Drury (Winston, 1979–82), *Life in a Fifteenth Century Monastery* by Anne Boyd (Lerner, 1978), *Rebels of the Heavenly Kingdom* by Katherine Paterson (Dutton, 1983), *The True Cross* by Brian Wildsmith (Oxford, 1977), *Martin Luther* by Judith O'Neill (Lerner, 1975), and *John Wesley* by May McNeer (Abingdon-Cokesbury, 1951).

Cathedrals

Other excellent books about cathedrals include *Cathedral* by David Macauley (Houghton Mifflin, 1973), *Building the Medieval Cathedrals* by Percy Watson (Lerner, 1976), and *Christopher Wren and St. Paul's Cathedral* by Ronald Gray (Lerner, 1982).

The Pilgrims and Thanksgiving

Other recommended books include *The Thanksgiving Story* by Alice Dalgliesh (Scribner, 1954), *Thanksgiving, Feast and Festival* by Mildred Luckhardt (Abingdon, 1966), *Thanksgiving* by Margaret Baldwin (Watts, 1983), *Thanksgiving Day* by Gail Gibbons (Holiday, 1983), *The Pilgrims of Plimoth* by Marcia Sewell (Atheneum, 1986), and *If You Sailed on the Mayflower* by Ann McGovern (Scholastic, 1969).

Separation of Church and State

God and Government by Ann E. Weiss (Houghton Mifflin, 1982) is another worthy resource.

Saints

Other useful books about individual saints include *The Legend of St. Christopher* by J. Jonda (Paulist, 1987), *Story of St. Francis* by Clyde Robert Bulla (Crowell, 1952), *Joan of Arc* by Louis Maurice Boutel de Monvel (Viking, 1980), *Joan of Arc* by Catherine Storr (Raintree, 1985), *St. Patrick and Irish Christianity* by Thomas Corfe (Lerner, 1973), *Saint Patrick* by Ruth Roquitte (Dillon, 1981), and *Thomas More* by Dorothy Smith (Paulist, 1988).

Contemporary Biography

There are many other biographies of Mother Teresa and Dr. King.

Pope John Paul II is the subject of *His Holiness Pope John Paul II* by Thomas Bonic (Grolier, 1984), *Pope John Paul II* by Anthony Di Franco (Dillon, 1983), and *John Paul II* by Robert W. Douglas (Children's Press, 1980).

Bishop Tutu is the subject of *Desmond Tutu* by David Winner (Gareth Stevens, 1989).

Popular titles of the recent past for older children and young adults include *The Man Who Moved a Mountain* by Richard C. Davids (Fortress, 1972), *Joni* by Joni Eareckson (Zondervan, 1976), *Mister God This Is Anna* by Fynn (Ballantine, 1976), *A Walk Across America* by Peter Jenkins (Fawcett, 1979), *The Cross and the Switchblade* by David Wilkerson (Revell, 1963), and *The Hiding Place* by Corrie Ten Boom (Chosen, 1971).

Chapter Eleven

Judaism

478. Chaikin, Miriam. **Menorahs, Mezuzas, and Other Jewish Symbols**. Ill. Erika Weihs. New York: Clarion, 1990. 102p. $14.95. LC 89-77719. ISBN 0-89919-856-2.

This thorough, clear, and absorbing account of a wide variety of Jewish symbols in dress, worship, the home, numbers, holidays, and also the State of Israel includes the Sabbath, circumcision, cleansing in the mikvah, and redeeming the first born. Their history and modern usage are discussed. This excellent reference book has dramatic black-and-white illustrations, notes, a bibliography, and an index.

479. Fine, Doreen. **What Do We Know About Judaism?** What Do We Know About Series. New York: Peter Bedrick Books, 1995. 45p. $18.95. ISBN 0-87226-386-X.

This introduction to the Jewish faith encompasses Jewish identity, the beginnings of the religion, basic beliefs, customs, prayer, the Sabbath, festivals, holy books, holy places, the synagogue, and the division of Jews into Orthodox, Conservative, and Reformed. Many informative, attractive color photographs and drawings accompany the straightforward text. The book includes a timeline, from 2000 B.C.E. to C.E. 1979; a glossary; and an index.

480. Kolatch, Alfred J. **The Jewish Child's First Book of Why**. Ill. Harry Araten. Middle Village, NY: Jonathan David, 1992. Unp. $14.95. LC 91-25352. ISBN 0-8246-0354-0.

In this lively and appealing book, children's questions about shalom, mezuzas, Saturday, challah, the synagogue, the shofar, a sukkah, matzot, Shavuot, and many more topics are answered simply, graciously, and with pride. In the brightly colored illustrations, jolly, button-eyed children and adults interact in the situations posed by the questions.

481.   Penney, Sue. **Judaism**. Discovering Religions Series. Austin, TX: Raintree Steck-Vaughan, 1997. 48p. $16.98. LC 96-33727. ISBN 0-8172-4393-3.

This thorough and simply written overview of Judaism includes sections about the synagogue, the Tanakh, Shabbat, Rosh Hashanah and Yom Kippur, Sukkot and other holidays, Abraham, Moses, anti-Semitism, the State of Israel, the three divisions of Judaism, and customs. Additional information and important prayers are boxed in yellow; new words are boxed in brown. Good color photographs divide the text attractively.

482.   Schanzer, Roz. **My First Jewish Word Book**. Ill. author. Rockville, MD: Kar-Ben Copies, 1992. Unp. $13.95. LC 92-12697. ISBN 0-929371-36-4.

In the style of Richard Scarry, each double-page spread is filled with labeled objects to identify, most of them specifically related to Judaism. Topics include home, community, Shabbat, the holidays, and Israel. In this dictionary of terms from *afikomen* to *yad*, the delightful illustrations show cartoon-style, anthropomorphic animals.

483.   Stoppleman, Monica. **Jewish**. Beliefs and Cultures Series. New York: Children's Press, 1995. 32p. $19.50. LC 95-47345. ISBN 0-516-08077-6.

Included in this simple presentation of the basic facts are the Torah, the Temple, ways of worship, the duties of a Jew, Shabbat, and rites of passage. The section about the Jewish calendar contains short summaries of the major holidays. Colored boxes of text discuss the Hebrew alphabet, kosher foods, the Shema, the Ten Commandments, and other information, as do the captions for the many color photographs. The book also has crafts, recipes, a glossary, and an index.

484.   Topek, Susan Remick. **Ten Good Rules**. Ill. Rosalyn Schanzer. Rockville, MD: Kar-Ben Copies, 1992. 32p. $12.95. LC 91-32109. ISBN 0-929371-30-5.

Although a young boy in a kippah, assisted by a tiny figure of Moses, guides the reader through the ten rules, and although the Sabbath is known as Shabbat, there is no reason why any Judeo-Christian faith could not use this charming, simple, and positive interpretation of the Decalogue. As each commandment is given, the boy raises a stubby pink finger, this work also serves as a counting book. Winsome pastel illustrations accompany the text.

485.   Weiss, Bernard P. **I Am Jewish**. Religions of the World Series. New York: PowerKids Press, 1996. 24p. $13.95. LC 96-733. ISBN 0-8239-2349-5.

A child named David, living in St. Louis, tells about Jewish law, the Sabbath, the synagogue, the Torah, bar mitzvah and bat mitzvah, the High Holy Days, marriage, Passover, Chanukah, and Jerusalem. Each topic has one page of succinct, easy-to-read text, illustrated with color photographs. A glossary and index are included.

486.   Wood, Angela. **Judaism**. World Religions Series. New York: Thomson Learning, 1995. 48p. $16.98. LC 95-1943. ISBN 1-56847-376-1.

This book concentrates more on the history and customs of the Jews as a community rather than upon theology. It includes a timeline summarizing events from the life of Abraham in 2000 B.C.E. to C.E. 1994, the year of peace

agreement between the Israelis and Palestinians; a map showing Jewish popula-
tions throughout the world, by country; a discussion of the Torah; details of Jewish home life; death, birth, marriage, and coming-of-age-customs; and an
excellent informational calendar of feasts and fasts. This well-arranged and interesting book has color photographs, drawings, and reproductions of paintings; sections of special interest and quotations; and a glossary, book list, and
index.

Jewish Life

487.   Barrie, Barbara. **Lone Star**. New York: Delacorte, 1990. 182p. $13.95.
LC 89-78075. ISBN 0-385-30156-1.

In prewar Texas, a ten-year-old Jewish girl clashes with her Orthodox
grandfather, who has come for Hanukkah, over a tiny Christmas tree that her reformed parents have allowed her to cherish in her bedroom. She wants to feel
accepted by her Christian friends, but her grandfather is so offended that he will
not even speak to her, until the terrible news of the Holocaust unites the entire
family. Sharp and telling characterizations and a strong theme that Jewish heritage and religion must be safeguarded, distinguish this novel.

488.   Greene, Jacqueline Dembar. **One Foot Ashore**. New York: Walker,
1994. 196p. $16.95. LC 93-22961. ISBN 0-8027-8281-7.

This fast-moving, historically interesting young adult novel is set in the
seventeenth century at the time of the Inquisition. Catholic friars abduct a Jewish girl from her home in Portugal to ensure that she will not be secretly indoctri-
nated in Judaism. They transport her to Recife, Brazil, as a slave, but she
engineers a daring escape, stows away on a Dutch ship to Amsterdam, and is
helped by Rembrandt Van Rijn in her search for her parents. The book is a sequel
to *Out of Many Waters* by the same author (Walker, 1988).

489.   Lanton, Sandy. **Daddy's Chair**. Ill. Shelly O. Haas. Rockville, MD:
Kar-Ben Copies, 1991. Unp. $12.95. LC 90-44908. ISBN 0-929371-51-8.

Sensitively expressed and psychologically accurate, the simply written text
tells how Michael, a young child, reacts to the death of his father by jealously
guarding Daddy's special chair, with the vague hope that he may return to sit in
it some day. Even though his mother has carefully explained the reality of death,
Michael has to mourn in his own way. The customs of sitting shiva are described
and explained. Softly realistic, sepia watercolors reflect the mood of pensive
mourning.

490.   Miller, Deborah Uchill. **Fins and Scales: A Kosher Tale**. Ill. Karen Os-
trove. Rockville, MD: Kar-Ben Copies, 1990. Unp. $5.95pa. LC 90-24388.
ISBN 0-929371-25-9.

A young Israeli boy and his parents wander through the open-air markets
of Jerusalem and talk about which foods are kosher and why, and the importance of separating meat and dairy products. A lighthearted, rhyming text and
clever, colorful, cartoon-style pictures make the lesson fun as well as informative. End material summarizes what it means to keep kosher.

491.   Oberman, Sheldon. **The Always Prayer Shawl**. Ill. Ted Lewin. Honesdale, PA: Boyds Mills Press, 1994. Unp. $14.95. LC 93-70874. ISBN 1-878093-22-3.

Adam's life turns full circle as he leaves Russia with his grandfather's prayer shawl, emigrates with his family to the United States, prospers, ages, and prepares to pass on the prayer shawl to his grandson, who promises to give it, in turn, to his grandson. Thus, although many things in life change, the heritage of Judaism remains. The vigorous, realistic watercolors, which change from black and white for Adam's youth to color for his maturity, are filled with beauty and reverence.

492.   Schur, Maxine Rose. **When I Left My Village**. Ill. Brian Pinkney. New York: Dial, 1996. 64p. $14.99. LC 94-45799. ISBN 0-8037-1561-7.

In the Gondar province of Ethiopia, a poor village of Beta Israel Ethiopian Jews is feared by Muslims and Christians alike. In a time of severe drought, Menelek and his family decide to brave all dangers and hardships to escape to Israel, even though they have been forbidden to leave the country. This suspenseful and moving story is illustrated with scratchboard artwork in which the agitated lines and somber colors reflect the desperation of their journey.

493.   Syme, Deborah Shayne. **Partners**. Ill. Jeffrey Wiener. New York: United American Hebrew Congregations, 1990. 28p. $8.95. ISBN 0-8074-0435-7.

On a school field trip to a city museum, Josh and Jacob are appalled by the plight of the poor people they pass on the streets. Their rabbi has told the congregation that Jews must be partners with God in healing the world, and consequently the boys plan a number of charitable deeds they can do to help others. Expressive black-and-white drawings illustrate the gently didactic text.

494.   Werlin, Nancy. **Are You Alone on Purpose?** New York: Houghton Mifflin, 1994. 204p. $14.95. LC 93-37653. ISBN 0-395-67350-X.

Against a background of Jewish life in upper-middle-class America, a widowed rabbi struggles with his conscience over how to treat his fourteen-year-old son. Bitter and recalcitrant, the boy is repressing rage and grief over his mother's death. The rabbi also feels that he must refuse to allow an autistic boy to become bar mitzvah. Engaging dialogue and realistic characterization create a poignant novel for young adults.

495.   Zalben, Jane Breskin. **Pearl's Marigolds for Grandpa**. Ill. author. New York: Simon and Schuster, 1997. Unp. $15.00. LC 96-21596. ISBN 0-689-80448-2.

Pearl, an anthropomorphic lamb, plants and tends her marigolds just as she was taught by her beloved grandfather. Remembering all the good things he did for her, Pearl plans to treat her own grandchildren exactly the same way, and is assured that this is how Grandpa can live on through her. Delicate watercolors illustrate a story that describes the universal feelings of grief and remembrance. Short notes at the end of the book describe mourning and burial customs for a number of religions.

Bar Mitzvah

496. Gallant, Janet. **My Brother's Bar Mitzvah**. Ill. Susan Avishai. Rockville, MD: Kar-Ben Copies, 1990. Unp. $4.95pa. LC 90-4879. ISBN 0-929371-21-6.

Eight-year-old Sarah worries about her brother Ben's bar mitzvah. He is still acting like a kid when he is supposed to be becoming a man. When the time comes, however, he makes everyone proud. This sweet story of one of the crowning events of Jewish family life is illustrated with excellent realistic drawings.

497. Kimmel, Eric A. **Bar Mitzvah: A Jewish Boy's Coming of Age**. Ill. Erika Weihs. New York: Viking, 1995. 143p. $15.00. LC 94-34956. ISBN 0-670-85540-5.

This comprehensive and informative study of the ceremony includes chapters about coming-of-age rituals in other cultures, the origin and teachings of Judaism, synagogues, worship, the prayer service, the Torah and bar mitzvah, the tallit and tefillin, and the celebratory parties. Interspersed are varied comments from individuals about their own bar mitzvahs. This excellent summary of the principles of the Jewish faith and the significance of bar mitzvah has a serious and devout tone. It contains a glossary, an index, and black-and-white illustrations.

498. Pushker, Gloria Teles. **A Belfer Bar Mitzvah**. Ill. Judith Hierstein. Gretna, LA: Pelican, 1995. Unp. $14.95. ISBN 1-56554-095-6.

Nine-year-old Toby is thrilled to be invited to her favorite cousin's bar mitzvah. The ceremonies on Friday and Saturday, the traditional gifts, and the joyful celebration afterward are lovingly and reverently detailed and illustrated with splashy, colorful pictures of the joyous events and proud friends and relatives.

Bat Mitzvah

499. Bush, Lawrence. **Emma Ansky-Levine and Her Mitzvah Machine**. Ill. Joel Iskowitz. New York: United American Hebrew Congregations, 1991. 115p. $7.95pa. LC 90-24491. ISBN 0-8074-0458-6.

Twelve-year-old Emma, a child of nonpracticing parents, longs to learn more about her Jewish heritage as she approaches the age of becoming bat mitzvah. An eccentric uncle sends her a mysterious computer that flashes messages about the Torah. These messages begin to influence her behavior in daily life, and by the time her bat mitzvah arrives, she has achieved a mature and sympathetic understanding of what Judaism and Jewishness entail. The illustrations are realistic black-and-white drawings.

500. Goldin, Barbara Diamond. **Bat Mitzvah: A Jewish Girl's Coming of Age**. Ill. Erika Weihs. New York: Viking, 1995. 139p. $14.99. LC 95-22100. ISBN 0-670-86034-4.

This thorough, absorbing discussion begins with a history of Jewish women, from Eve and the matriarchs, prophets, judges, and heroines; to some outstanding figures from talmudic times and the Middle Ages; to the first bat mitzvahs and ordinations of female rabbis. The central themes, however, are the many forms of bat mitzvah; how to prepare for the blessings, the Torah reading, the haftarah, and the Dvar Torah; ways to enrich the ceremony and make it uniquely personal; the service itself; and the party afterward. Anecdotes and quotations from bnot mitzvah, all positive and encouraging, supplement the interesting and inspiring text. Bold black-and-white illustrations, a glossary, source notes, and an index are included.

Prayers

501. Edwards, Michelle. **Blessed Are You: Traditional Everyday Hebrew Prayers**. Ill. author. New York: Lothrop, Lee & Shepard, 1993. Unp. $15.00. LC 92-1666. ISBN 0-688-10759-1.
Thirteen short, lovely prayers are presented in Hebrew, English, and transliterated Hebrew and framed elaborately with bold motifs. Opposite each is a big, bright illustration showing twins and their toddler brother in everyday activities: camping out, baking challah, picking apples, celebrating a birthday, and so on. The explanatory introduction describes how to use each prayer in a traditional manner.

502. Groner, Judyth, and Madeline Wikler. **Thank You, God! A Jewish Child's Book of Prayers**. Ill. Shelly O. Haas. Rockville, MD: Kar-Ben Copies, 1993. Unp. $14.95. LC 93-7550. ISBN 0-929371-65-8.
Short devotions for a variety of occasions encompass bedtime, mealtime, holidays, peace, mourning, appreciation of nature, and deliverance from danger, among others. All are phrased simply and clearly, first in Hebrew, then in phonetic translation, and then in English, with a short explanatory introduction. Delicate watercolors decorate the pages.

Spiritual Stories

503. Aroner, Miriam. **The Kingdom of the Singing Birds**. Ill. Shelly O. Haas. Rockville, MD: Kar-Ben Copies, 1993. Unp. $5.95pa. LC 92-39382. ISBN 0-929371-46-1.
Rabbi Meshulam Zusya, a beloved historical figure in Hasidic folklore known for his gentleness and wisdom, is called upon by his king to solve a problem: Why, despite being given every luxury, does the ruler's large collection of birds refuse to sing? The rabbi's sensible solution is to set them free. Not only do the freed birds sing gloriously, but most of them choose to remain near the palace. The flowing, poetic text is illustrated with misty watercolors.

504. Gershator, Phillis. **Honi's Circle of Trees**. Ill. Mim Green. Philadelphia: Jewish Publication Society, 1994. Unp. $13.95. LC 93-29748. ISBN 0-8276-0511-0.
Honi, a folkloric figure who can talk to the Lord whenever he draws a circle and steps into it, stars in a charming story, perfectly illustrated with gently humorous, black-and-white cartoons. To the amusement of his friends, Honi plants carob seeds to grow trees for future generations, then falls asleep like Rip Van Winkle. He awakes to find his friends gone but his trees bearing fruit for their grandchildren.

505.   Hautzig, Esther. **Riches**. Ill. Donna Diamond. New York: HarperCollins, 1992. 43p. $14.00. LC 89-26904. ISBN 0-06-022259-X.

Samuel has always worked hard and given to charity in his small eastern European town. Upon retirement, he wonders what to do with himself. A wise rabbi suggests that he drive a horse and cart into the country every day, except the Sabbath, of course, for three months. Doing so, Samuel learns an appreciation of nature and the joy of giving of himself, not just his money, to others. The lesson is sweet and gentle, appropriate for any faith, and illustrated with skill in black and white.

506.   Prose, Francine. **Dybbuk: A Story Made in Heaven**. Ill. Mark Podwal. New York: Greenwillow, 1996. Unp. $16.00. LC 95-22825. ISBN 0-688-14307-5.

Forty days before Leah and Chonon are born, the angels decide that they should marry. Nonetheless, Leah's parents attempt to wed her to mean old Benya. Consequently, a dybbuk possesses her on the day of her marriage. The rabbis are unable to exorcise the spirit until Chonon arrives and marries her himself. This mixture of two legends is told with charm and good humor, and illustrated with reproductions of richly colored paintings, spread out in free-flowing lines.

507.   Silverman, Erica. **Gittel's Hands**. Ill. Deborah Nourse Lattimore. Mahwah, NJ: Bridgewater, 1996. Unp. $14.95. LC 96-3625. ISBN 0-8167-3798-3.

In a Rumpelstiltskin-like moral tale, Gittel's father boasts that his daughter has superb skills as an embroiderer, a cook, and a silversmith. A wily creditor offers to forgive the father's debts if she will pass various tests, but she is given no needle, no fire, and only a tiny silver coin. Elijah, impressed by her kindness and goodness, assists her in foiling the creditor and becoming a master silversmith. This gracefully written book is illustrated with reproductions of Chagall-like paintings, depicting hovering figures, tilted houses, and whirling furnishings.

Story Collections

508.   Geras, Adele. **My Grandmother's Stories: A Collection of Jewish Folktales**. Ill. Jael Jordan. New York: Alfred A. Knopf, 1990. 96p. $17.95. LC 90-4309. ISBN 0-679-80910-4.

Ten traditional, instructive folktales are joined together by a narrative in which a young girl visits her beloved grandmother and plays with special possessions that remind her grandmother of old morality stories. Tales include the golden shoes the Chief Sage of Chelm wore on his head so they wouldn't get muddy, the poor farmer who outwitted the tsar and became his chief advisor, and the dove who chose the olive tree as the worthiest in the garden. Biblical themes, humor, trickery, religious customs, the warmth of family relationships, and even a ghost story accentuate themes of ethical living. The musical text is illustrated with forceful, detailed, lively pictures.

509.   Jaffe, Nina. **The Mysterious Visitor: Stories of the Prophet Elijah**. Ill. Elivia Savadier. New York: Scholastic, 1997. 112p. $19.95. LC 96-7534. ISBN 0-590-48422-2.

Elijah, in his role as folkloric miracle worker, healer, and teacher, appears in a variety of settings: in a dream bringing treasure to a poor schoolteacher in Poland; as a magical slave who serves a sultan in Alexandria to benefit a poor farmer; as a pilgrim who grants wishes to three brothers in France; and more. All the stories have a definite lesson: generosity, faithfulness, modesty, obedience, and love are the virtues rewarded. Traditional themes have been adapted with verve and humor. The book is illustrated with lively watercolors, and includes a glossary, notes, a bibliography, and a reading list.

510.   Jaffe, Nina, and Steven Zeitlin. **While Standing on One Foot: Puzzle Stories and Wisdom Tales from the Jewish Tradition**. Ill. John Segal. New York: Henry Holt, 1993. 120p. $6.95pa. LC 93-13750. ISBN 0-8050-5073-6.

These fabulous tales with clever, logical surprise endings are amusing, entertaining, and thought-provoking. A rabbi who outwits the grand inquisitor of Spain; a Jewish jester in the Babylonian court who chooses the manner of his death; Rabbi Hillel, who bests one of Herod's courtiers; and other stories drawn from Jewish folklore and midrashic collections are written in an easy, sprightly style and illustrated with funny black-and-white cartoons. A glossary, source notes, a bibliography, and a list of organizations providing information about Jewish culture are included.

511.   Kimmel, Eric A. **The Adventures of Hershel of Ostropol**. Ill. Trina Schart Hyman. New York: Holiday House, 1995. 64p. $15.95. LC 95-8907. ISBN 0-8234-1210-5.

Ten stories about a poor man who lives mainly by his wits are told spiritedly and illustrated with clever pen-and-ink vignettes. Hershel tricks Rabbi Israel, his rich Uncle Zalman, Count Potocki, and a host of others, as his quick mind devises ways to wring money and food from them for himself and other poverty-stricken Jews. At the end, he even talks himself through the gates of heaven by entertaining God with his smart answers to the recording angel's questions.

512.   Patterson, Jose. **Angels, Prophets, Rabbis, and Kings from the Stories of the Jewish People**. Ill. Claire Bushe. New York: Peter Bedrick Books, 1991. 144p. $24.95. LC 90-23469. ISBN 0-87226-912-4.

This mixture of abbreviated Bible stories and associated Jewish folkloric tales encompasses the Creation; the flood; Abraham, Isaac, Jacob, and Joseph; Moses; Samson, Susanna, and Ruth; Kings David and Solomon; Esther and the Maccabees; and prophets Elijah and Jonah. These are followed by talmudic tales, medieval legends, and stories of rabbis and miracles. All are filled with moral examples of wisdom, persistence, sacrifice, and piety, but are never preachy. Rather, they are exciting and fast-moving adventures. The illustrations are powerful and often eerie. An index is included.

513. Podwal, Mark H. **The Book of Tens**. Ill. author. New York: Greenwillow, 1994. Unp. $15.00. LC 93-43871. ISBN 0-688-12994-3.

Legends, miracles, and images of how the number ten predominates in the biblical history of the Jews include the ten words God used to create the definitive version of the world, ten generations from Adam to Noah, ten plagues in Egypt, ten commandments, ten men needed for a minyan, and more. Each account has an interesting explication and a lively, simply designed, ink-and-watercolor illustration.

514. Prose, Francine. **The Angel's Mistake: Stories of Chelm**. Ill. Mark Podwal. New York: Greenwillow, 1997. Unp. $15.00. LC 96-7465. ISBN 0-688-14905-7.

As the angels are distributing not-so-stupid and not-so-intelligent souls to the towns and cities, the bag holding the latter breaks, and the stupid souls all fall on Chelm. Even the grand rabbi, not to mention the ordinary Jews, cannot think sensibly: for example, the synagogue is roofless so as not to interfere with the upward flight of prayers to heaven. Many other amusing examples of their foolishness are related in lively prose and illustrated with reproductions of brilliantly colored, folk-art-style, gouache paintings.

515. Schwartz, Howard. **Next Year in Jerusalem: 3000 Years of Jewish Stories**. Ill. Neil Waldman. New York: Viking, 1996. 58p. $16.99. LC 95-31213. ISBN 0-670-86110-3.

Tales of magic jewels, a giant ram, talking birds, and a vampire demon are mingled with more mundane stories of ordinary people in extraordinary circumstances in a mixture of historical and legendary themes. The sources are Iraq, Italy, eastern Europe, Israel, Greece, Babylon, Spain, and Poland. Commentaries about interpretations and religious symbolism are given for each story. The book includes a glossary and a list of sources, and delicate, pastel watercolors complement the handsome format.

516. Schwartz, Howard, and Barbara Rush. **The Diamond Tree**. Ill. Uri Shulevitz. New York: HarperCollins, 1991. 120p. $16.95. LC 90-32420. ISBN 0-06-025239-1.

Drawn from a variety of sources, including the Talmud, the Bible, midrashic tales, hasidic lore, eastern European and Middle Eastern folklore, and oral tradition, each of these stories concerns a fundamental teaching of Judaism: honesty, faith, charity, cooperation, and so forth. All the sources are listed and discussed. The occasional full-page illustrations are bright, amusing, and simple.

517. Schwartz, Howard, and Barbara Rush. **The Wonder Child and Other Jewish Fairy Tales**. Ill. Stephen Fieser. New York: HarperCollins, 1996. 66p. $16.95. LC 94-32542. ISBN 0-06-023517-9.

Included are stories of a rabbi and his wife who have a beautiful girl whose soul is in a glowing jewel; a rabbi's son who mistakenly betroths himself to a witch; Og, the giant who survived the flood by riding on the roof of Noah's ark and needs a coat; a kindly rabbi with a cruel wife who is turned into a werewolf; and a nasty dybbuk who inhabits a young boy at Purim. With ingenuity and courage, the problems are overcome in these exciting tales from the oral traditions of Egypt, eastern Europe, and Morocco. The occasional illustrations are full-page reproductions of handsome paintings.

518. Sperber, Daniel, and Chana Sperber. **Ten Best Jewish Children's Stories**. Ill. Jeffrey Allon. New York: Pitspopany, 1995. 47p. $14.95. ISBN 0-943706-58-0.

These short traditional stories that teach moral and ethical values have surprise endings, which often turn hardship, danger, and confusion to joy, as charity and honesty are rewarded. Lively, big, bright illustrations illustrate these straightforward and sprightly retellings.

The Golem

519. Podwal, Mark. **Golem: A Giant Made of Mud**. Ill. author. New York: Greenwillow Books, 1995. Unp. $15.00. LC 94-7865. ISBN 0-688-13811-X.

This is an innovative and delightfully eerie retelling of the legend involving Rabbi Judah Lowe in sixteenth-century Prague. It emphasizes the emperor's fascination with the occult, his friendship with the magical rabbi, his descent into paranoia, the isolation of the Jews into the ghetto, the rabbi's desperate construction of the golem, and the giant's final destructive rampage and mysterious disappearance. The reproductions of brilliant, surrealistic, folk-art-style gouache paintings suit the legend perfectly.

520. Rogasky, Barbara. **The Golem**. Ill. Trina Schart Hyman. New York: Holiday House, 1996. 96p. $18.95. LC 94-13040. ISBN 0-8234-0964-3.

The chief rabbi of Prague, Judah Loew, is frightened by threats to the Jews and, upon God's instructions, creates a huge man of clay to protect them. As the rabbi's servant, the golem thwarts a number of evil schemes against the Jews devised by certain vicious and prejudiced Christians. One Sabbath, however, the golem runs amok and must be deactivated. The gripping, skillfully written text is illustrated with carefully executed, foreboding pictures. Author's and illustrator's notes and a glossary are included.

521. Wisniewski, David. **Golem**. Ill. author. New York: Clarion, 1996. Unp. $15.95. LC 95-21777. ISBN 0-395-72618-2.

Macabre, powerful, cut-paper illustrations in shades of black, brown, red, and gold energize the ancient tale of Jews in 1580 Prague. After being accused of using the blood of Christian children to make Passover matzot, the chief rabbi, in desperation, creates the golem, a mighty giant made of clay, using the holy name of God. The giant's job is to protect the Jews at night and serve in the synagogue by day. He does his work so well that the emperor is forced to guarantee the Jews' safety. The writing is evocative and compelling, suitable to a tale of vengeance and supernatural strength run amok.

Jewish and Christian Ecumenism

522. Cohen, Barbara. **Make a Wish, Molly**. Ill. Jan Naimo Jones. New York: Delacorte, 1994. 40p. $14.95. LC 93-17901. ISBN 0-385-31079-X.

In this sequel to *Molly's Pilgrim* by the same author (Lothrop, 1983), a classic Thanksgiving book, Molly, an immigrant child from Russia living in New Jersey, is crushed when her mother tells her that because it is Passover she cannot have any of the glorious pink birthday cake at her friend Emma's party. Her reason for not eating is misunderstood by the Christian girls, and one says cruel, untrue things about Jewish customs. In the end, however, the mistakes are explained, and they all eat rugelach on Molly's birthday. The touching story is illustrated with soft-lined but realistic black-and-white drawings.

523. Cohn, Janice. **The Christmas Menorahs**. Ill. Bill Farnsworth. Morton Grove, IL: Albert Whitman, 1995. 40p. $16.95. LC 95-2053. ISBN 0-8075-1152-8.

Based on a true incident that occurred in Billings, Montana, in 1993, the somewhat fictionalized story about the Schnitzer family tells of a hate group involved in breaking windows and destroying Hanukkah menorahs throughout the city. The incensed townspeople, unwilling to let prejudice and vandalism hold sway, retaliate by placing large pictures of menorahs in all their front windows in support of their Jewish neighbors and freedom of religion. The illustrations are reproductions of thoughtful, realistic oil paintings.

524. Kuskin, Karla. **A Great Miracle Happened There: A Chanukah Story**. Ill. Robert Andrew Parker. New York: HarperCollins, 1993. Unp. $15.00. LC 92-17909. ISBN 0-06-023617-5.

A young Jewish boy explains the significance of the menorah, the blessings, the dreidel, and the latkes and doughnuts to his Christian friend. The boy's mother tells them the history of the holiday. The sketchy, dreamy, ink-and-watercolor illustrations are mostly of the Maccabees, and the text is serious, simple, and engaging.

525. Meyer, Carolyn. **Drummers of Jericho**. San Diego, CA: Gulliver Books, 1995. 308p. $11.00. LC 94-36105. ISBN 0-15-200441-6.

In this young adult novel, a small-town Fundamentalist Christian community becomes intensely prejudiced against a Jewish girl. She has joined the high school marching band but she objects to the band director's program of Christian hymns, climaxed by a cross-shaped formation. Surprisingly, a decent but rather inarticulate boy, also in the band and a traditional Baptist, agrees with her objection in the controversy that ensues. No one really wins. Legal issues force the cancellation of the program; the girl returns to New York; and the boy is ostracized by his friends. Still, the boy never regrets his decision to support what he believes to be right.

526. O'Keefe, Susan Heyboer. **A Season for Giving**. Ill. Pamela T. Keating. Mahwah, NJ: Paulist, 1990. 28p. $2.95pa. LC 89-78239. ISBN 0-8091-6592-9.

In this school story for middle elementary ages, Aloysius, a Roman Catholic, and Ezekiel, a Jew, share the humiliation of unusual names, which make them objects of derision among their classmates. At first hostile and defensive with each other, they become friends, and Ezekiel's grandfather suggests that the boys stress similarities rather that differences. He clarifies his point by describing how the ways of celebrating Christmas and Hanukkah have become similar, even though the holidays have very different meanings, and the boys incorporate the lesson successfully at school. The large-print text is easy to read and illustrated with black-and-white drawings.

527. Polacco, Patricia. **Mrs. Katz and Tush**. Ill. author. New York: Little Rooster, 1992. Unp. $15.00. ISBN 0-553-08122-5.

The newly widowed, elderly, and sorrowful Mrs. Katz is befriended by Larnel, a young black boy, who brings her a kitten to love. He also helps her celebrate the Passover seder and say kaddish for Myron, her late husband, at the cemetery. She soon becomes a beloved honorary bubee for Larnel, and then for his family when he is an adult. The tone is loving and ecumenical. Animated, large, warmly colored illustrations are filled with unique personalities.

528. Polacco, Patricia. **The Trees of the Dancing Goats**. Ill. author. New York: Simon and Schuster, 1996. Unp. $16.00. LC 95-26670. ISBN 0-689-80862-3.

While in the midst of their joyful preparations for Hanukkah, a Jewish farm family in Michigan discovers that many of their neighbors are seriously ill with scarlet fever and will be unable to celebrate Christmas. Babushka and Grampa decide to create a happy holiday for these friends by cutting down tiny evergreen trees and decorating them with hand-carved toys, and packing baskets of chicken, latkes, and Hanukkah candles (to give them the protective light of God) for their dinners. The double-page illustrations are as warm, bright, and lively as the story.

529. Pushker, Gloria Teles. **Toby Belfer Never Had a Christmas Tree**. Ill. Judith Hierstein. Gretna, LA: Pelican, 1991. Unp. $13.95. LC 91-14514. ISBN 0-88289-855-8.

Toby is a young Jewish girl growing up among Christians in a small Southern town. At holiday time, she shares with her many friends the special Hanukkah customs of her family and the story of the Maccabees. She also participates in their carol singing and tree trimming. The illustrations are bold, detailed, and bright.

530. Pushker, Gloria Teles. **Toby Belfer's Seder: A Passover Story Retold**. Ill. Judith Hierstein. Gretna, LA: Pelican, 1994. Unp. $14.95. LC 93-5585. ISBN 0-88289-987-2.

In a simple, sweet story, Toby, the only Jewish girl in a small Louisiana town, invites her best friend, Donna, a Christian, to the family Passover seder. After they assist with the cooking and cleaning and help prepare the table, Toby explains the significance of the blessings, the four questions, and all the other traditional festivities. Passover and Easter parallels are cited, and a glossary and bibliography are included. Big, lively pictures reflect the happy mood.

531. Rosen, Michael J. **Elijah's Angel: A Story for Chanukah and Christmas**. Ill. Aminah Brenda Lynn Robinson. San Diego, CA: Harcourt Brace Jovanovich, 1992. Unp. $13.95. LC 91-37552. ISBN 0-15-225394-7.

A touching story based upon actual characters tells of the friendship between Elijah, an octogenarian black barber and woodcarver, who is filled with Christian love, and Michael, an observant nine-year-old Jewish boy. When Elijah gives Michael one of his precious carved angels as a Christmas gift, Michael fears that it may be a forbidden "graven image." Joyfully, his parents declare it to be an angel of friendship, which encompasses all religions. The vivid text is illustrated with unusual, distorted, brightly colored pictures.

Older and Noteworthy

Other titles of interest about Judaism include *Your Neighbor Celebrates* by Arthur Gilbert (Friendly House, 1957), *Celebrating Life* by Malka Drucker (Holiday, 1984), *Ima on the Bima* by Mindy Portnoy (Kar-Ben, 1986), and *The Old Synagogue* by Richard Rosenblum (Jewish Publication Society, 1989).

Jewish Life

Additional excellent books about Jewish life include *The Empty Chair* by Bess Kaplan (Harper, 1975); *Chernowitz!* by Fran Arrick (Bradbury, 1981); *The Murderer* by Felice Holman (Scribner, 1978); *How Yossi Beat the Evil Urge* by Miriam Chaikin (Harper, 1983), and other Yossi books; *Lower, Higher, You're a Liar* (Harper, 1984), and other Molly books by Miriam Chaikin; *All-of-a-Kind Family* by Sydney Taylor (Dell, 1966), and other books in this series; and *Inside the Synagogue* by Joan G. Sugarman (United American Hebrew Congregations, 1984).

For more information about bar mitzvah and bat mitzvah, read *Bar Mitzvah* by Howard Greenfeld (Henry Holt, 1981), and *Bar Mitzvah, Bat Mitzvah* by Bert Metter (Clarion, 1984), as well as the novels *Does Anyone Know the Way to Thirteen?* by Stephen Kaufman (Houghton Mifflin, 1985), *About the B'nai Bagels* by E. L. Konigsburg (Dell, 1969), *Good If It Goes* by Gary Provost (Bradbury, 1984), and *My Bar Mitzvah* by Richard Rosenblum (Morrow, 1985).

Spiritual Stories

Another legend to consider is *Elijah the Slave* by Isaac Bashevis Singer (Farrar, Straus & Giroux, 1970). An additional worthy collection of stories is *A Treasury of Jewish Literature* by Gloria Goldreich (Henry Holt, 1982). Other tales about the golem include *The Golem* by Beverly Brodsky (Lippincott, 1976) and *The Golem* by Isaac Bashevis Singer (Farrar, Straus & Giroux, 1982).

Other recommended titles about Judaism and Christianity include *Are You There, God? It's Me, Margaret* by Judy Blume (Bradbury, 1970), *There's No Such Thing As a Chanukah Bush, Sandy Goldstein* by Susan Sussman (Whitman, 1981), and *A Boy of Old Prague* by Sulamith Ish-Kishor (Scholastic, 1963).

Chapter Twelve

Jewish Holidays

Holiday Collections

532.   Blue, Rose. **Good Yontif: A Picture Book of the Jewish Year**. Ill. Lynne Feldman. Brookfield, CT: Millbrook Press, 1997. Unp. $16.95. LC 96-31054. ISBN 0-7613-0142-9.

This wordless picture book follows one family through Rosh Hashanah, Yom Kippur, Sukkot, Simhat Torah, Hanukkah, Purim, Passover, Shavuot, and Shabbat with the typical warmth of celebratory joy. The brilliantly colored, stylized illustrations are full of life. End notes describe each holiday.

533.   Drucker, Malka. **The Family Treasury of Jewish Holidays**. Ill. Nancy Patz. Boston: Little, Brown, 1994. 180p. $22.95. LC 93-7549. ISBN 0-316-19343-7.

This outstanding, thorough presentation of the major religious holidays includes Rosh Hashanah, Yom Kippur, Sukkot, Simhat Torah, Hanukkah, Tu B'Shvat, Purim, Pesach, Shavuot, and Shabbat. An easy-to-read and gracefully written description of the traditions and origins of each is given, with several appropriate stories, special recipes, crafts, games, prayers, and songs. Isaac Bashevis Singer, Sadie Rose Weilerstein, David Adler, and Barbara Cohen are among the authors whose works are used to add creative warmth and interest. The book has lively ink-and-watercolor pictures, a glossary, a reading list, and an index.

534.   Drucker, Malka. **A Jewish Holiday ABC**. Ill. Rita Pocock. San Diego, CA: Harcourt Brace Jovanovich, 1992. Unp. $6.00pa. LC 90-36791. ISBN 0-15-201366-0.

 A is for *afikoman*, *D* for *dreidel*, *G* for *grogger*, *R* for *rabbi*, *Y* for *yarmulke*, and so on, in this charming alphabet book. A capsule description of each holiday is given, and a glossary is included. The illustrations are reproductions of bright collages and colored-pencil drawings.

535.   Foy, Don. **Israel**. Festivals of the World Series. Milwaukee, WI: Gareth Stevens, 1997. 32p. $13.95. LC 96-31953. ISBN 0-8368-1684-6.

 The history and celebratory customs of Pesach, Sukkot, Shemini Atzeret, Simhat Torah, Hanukkah, and Purim are discussed. Such activities as how to dance the hora, how to construct a megillah, and how to bake hamentashen are included. The book contains a reading list, a glossary, an index, a holiday calendar for Jewish and Muslim holidays (although the latter are not discussed), and many color photographs.

536.   Gross, Judith. **Celebrate: A Book of Jewish Holidays**. Ill. Bari Weissman. All Aboard Books Series. New York: Platt and Munk, 1992. Unp. $2.95pa. ISBN 0-448-40302-1.

 This inexpensive and clear guide to Rosh Hashanah, Yom Kippur, Sukkot, Simhat Torah, Hanukkah, Tu Bishvat, Purim, Passover, and Shavuot explains the holidays in a colorful, informal way, and includes short retellings of the associated Bible stories. Lively, cartoon-style illustrations add charm and fun.

537.   Jaffe, Nina. **The Uninvited Guest and Other Jewish Holiday Tales**. Ill. Elivia Savadier. New York: Scholastic, 1993. 72p. $16.95. LC 92-36308. ISBN 0-590-44653-3.

 These stories of Rosh Hashanah, Yom Kippur, Sukkot, Hanukkah, Purim, Passover, and Shabbat are sweet and sprightly, and have funny and clever surprise endings. A description of each holiday's significance, comments about each story, and a calendar, glossary, bibliography, and reading list are included. The watercolor and crayon illustrations are witty and bright.

538.   Lepon, Shoshana. **Hillel Builds a House**. Ill. Marilynn Barr. Rockville, MD: Kar-Ben Copies, 1993. Unp. $5.95pa. LC 92-39383. ISBN 0-929371-41-0.

 A young boy who loves to build himself houses tries to fit his construction work into a variety of Jewish holidays and is constantly frustrated. At Hanukkah, for example, he cannot light candles in his house for fear of fire; and at Purim, his cardboard costume shaped like a house is ruined by the rain. This continues throughout the year, until Sukkot arrives at last. The story is happily pictured in scenes of the family's holiday celebrations.

539.   Pearl, Sydelle. **Elijah's Tears: Stories for the Jewish Holidays**. Ill. Rossitza Skortcheva Penney. Redfeather Books Series. New York: Henry Holt, 1996. 63p. $14.95. LC 96-15399. ISBN 0-8050-4627-5.

 Charming, folkloric, original stories tell of the mythical prophet as in his associations with Shabbat, Passover, Succot, Hanukkah, and Yom Kippur. Often in the guise of an old man, Elijah rewards those who take pity on him. One story deals with his sister Eliora, who weaves tallises, challah covers, glove menorahs, and other items to help Jews throughout the world celebrate Hanukkah. The book has line drawings and a glossary.

540. Ross, Kathy. **The Jewish Holiday Craft Book**. Ill. Melinda Levine. Brookfield, CT: Millbrook Press, 1997. 96p. $25.90. LC 96-31002. ISBN 0-7613-0055-4.

Handsome, brightly colored, cut-paper illustrations give step-by-step procedures for constructing simple but clever decorations for Shabbat, Rosh Hashanah, Yom Kippur, Sukkot, Simchat Torah, Hanukkah, Tu B'Shevat, Purim, Passover, and Shavuot. A short description of each holiday is included. Tzedakah boxes, kiddush cups, shofars, Torah pins, and Purim puppets are among the items easily created.

541. Silverman, Maida. **The Glass Menorah: And Other Stories for Jewish Holidays**. Ill. Marge Levine. New York: Four Winds, 1992. 64p. $14.95. LC 91-13890. ISBN 0-02-782682-1.

Mild, instructive short stories for eight Jewish holidays describe how Ben and Molly, often with the help of their friend Mr. Yomtov, overcome obstacles and conceive new ways to celebrate properly. Simple and colorful pictures are scattered throughout, and a glossary of holiday terms is included.

542. Silverman, Maida. **My First Book of Jewish Holidays**. Ill. Barbara Garrison. New York: Dial, 1994. 32p. $14.99. LC 93-20370. ISBN 0-8037-1427-0.

The Sabbath, Rosh Hashanah, Yom Kippur, Sukkot, Simchat Torah, Hanukkah, Tu BiShevat, Purim, Passover, and Shavuot are commemorated in an exclamatory, free-verse style. The history and traditions of each holiday are described briefly and enthusiastically and illustrated with primitive, intaglioed pictures with watercolor washes.

543. Wood, Angela. **Jewish Festivals**. Celebrate Series. Crystal Lake, IL: Heinemann Library, 1997. 48p. $13.95. LC 96-29764. ISBN 0-431-06962-X.

In a lively, well-researched text, Shabbat, the High Holy Days, Sukkot, Simchat Torah, Hanukkah, Tu B'Shevat, Purim, Passover, Yom Hashoah, Shavuot, and Tisha B'Av are explained, and the celebratory practices of each are discussed. The section about Shabbat is outstanding. Many well-captioned color photographs and comments by Jewish children enhance the information. The book contains a glossary, reading list, and index.

544. Yolen, Jane. **Milk and Honey: A Year of Jewish Holidays**. Ill. Louise August. New York: Putnam, 1996. 80p. $21.95. LC 93-44474. ISBN 0-399-22652-4.

The history and celebration of the holidays Rosh Hashanah, Yom Kippur, Sukkot, Chanukah, Purim, Pesach, Shavuot, and the Sabbath are described. Appropriate folktales, poems, traditional songs with musical scores, personal reminiscences, and a Purim play accompany the discussion. This yearlong guide to holidays is illustrated with bold, decorative folk art.

545. Zeldin, Florence. **A Mouse in Our Jewish House**. Ill. Lisa Rauchwerger. Los Angeles: Torah Aura Productions, 1990. Unp. $11.95. LC 89-40362. ISBN 0-933873-43-3.

This clever counting book, illustrated in black and white with paper sculptures, concerns a rakish mouse who celebrates the various holidays by nibbling on the appropriate foods. For example, the mouse eats one challah for Shabbat, two honey-dipped apple slices for Rosh Hashanah, eight hamantashen for Purim, nine matzot for Passover, and so on. The meaning of each holiday is briefly discussed.

Individual Holidays

546. Rael, Elsa Okon. **When Zaydeh Danced on Eldridge Street**. Ill. Marjorie Priceman. New York: Simon and Schuster, 1997. Unp. $16.00. LC 96-35045. ISBN 0-689-80451-2.

A charming and joyful celebration of Simchas Torah is set on the Lower East Side of Manhattan in the 1930s. Zeesie's stern Zayde (grandfather) relaxes his rigidity when he takes his young granddaughter to his beautiful synagogue for the enthusiastic dancing parade that marks the ending of the past year's reading of the Torah and the beginning of the next. To see Zayde dance, to have him kiss her and praise her appreciation of the Torah, is a perfect moment in Zeesie's life. Expressive, folk-art-style watercolors reflect the exuberant mood.

547. Zalben, Jane Breskin. **Pearl Plants a Tree**. Ill. author. New York: Simon and Schuster, 1995. Unp. $14.00. LC 94-38404. ISBN 0-689-80034-7.

Tu B'Shvat, the New Year of trees, is celebrated as Pearl plants an apple seed in a pot, nurtures it during the winter, and finally plants it outdoors with the help of her amused grandfather. The book includes notes about other tree-celebrating holidays, a description of Tu B'Shvat customs, two midrashim, and directions for how to grow a tree. The delicate, framed illustrations show anthropomorphic sheep.

Hanukkah

548. Backman, Aidel. **One Night, One Hanukkah Night**. Ill. author. Philadelphia: Jewish Publication Society, 1990. Unp. $14.95. LC 90-4965. ISBN 0-8276-0368-1.

Hanukkah candles lit in an heirloom silver menorah are shown in a modern home and in the home of the family's grandparents in an eastern European shtetl in alternate scenes to emphasize the permanence and joy of the traditions. This counting book with a repetitive, rhythmic text shows the candles accumulating one by one and tells the meanings of associated words, such as *shamash*, *gelt*, *dreidel*, and *Maccabees*. The two families pictured in the large watercolors are charming and lively.

549. Chaikin, Miriam. **Hanukkah**. Ill. Ellen Weiss. New York: Holiday House, 1990. Unp. $14.95. LC 89-77512. ISBN 0-8234-0816-7.

Action-filled, expressive, primitive-style line drawings washed with pale watercolors illustrate the history of the holiday, plainly recounted, and the modern celebration.

550.   Feder, Harriet K. **Judah Who Always Said "No!"** Ill. Katherine Janus Kahn. Rockville, MD: Kar-Ben Copies, 1990. Unp. $12.95. LC 90-4854. ISBN 0-929371-14-3.

Judah was always stubborn, from the time he was a young boy in a loin-cloth, when he carried a wooden sword and refused to take a nap, through adulthood, when he vigorously rejected Antiochus's edicts and led his Maccabees to victory. Clever, lively illustrations complement the delightful text.

551.   Hoyt-Goldsmith, Diane. **Celebrating Hanukkah**. New York: Holiday House, 1996. 32p. $16.95. LC 96-5110. ISBN 0-8234-1252-0.

This excellent resource has a history of the holiday; short and informative discussions of the Hebrew language; discussions of holiday celebrations at home, in the synagogue, and at a private Jewish school; and many insights about the practice of Judaism. It is illustrated with excellent color photographs and includes suggestions for an eight-night celebration, a glossary, and an index.

552.   Kalman, Bobbie. **We Celebrate Hanukkah**. Holiday and Festivals Series. New York: Crabtree, 1993. 56p. $14.36. LC 93-27382. ISBN 0-86505-045-7.

Although this book describes the history of the holiday, as well as menorah ceremonies, special foods, and other customs, it emphasizes crafts, recipes, poems, stories, and games. Black-and-white and color illustrations accompany the text.

553.   Koralek, Jenny. **Hanukkah: The Festival of Lights**. Ill. Juan Wijngaard. New York: Lothrop, Lee & Shepard, 1990. 29p. $13.95. LC 89-8064. ISBN 0-688-09329-9.

A serious treatment of the historical events, this book discusses the desecration of the Temple in Jerusalem by Antiochus's soldiers; the long, determined struggle of the Maccabee forces to drive them out; the purification of the Temple; and the miraculous oil that burned for eight days in the menorah. Muted yet powerful and dramatic, full-page pictures are formally framed in columned arches. The writing is simple and effective.

554.   Modesitt, Jeanne. **Songs of Chanukah**. Ill. Robin Spowart. Boston: Little, Brown, 1992. 32p. $15.95. LC 90-27455. ISBN 0-316-57739-1.

Fourteen songs, new as well as traditional, praise God, celebrate the candle lighting, tell of holiday fun with dreidels and latkes, and relate the story of the Maccabees. The scores are arranged for voice, piano, and guitar, with lyrics in Hebrew and in English. A short, simple, informational text about the history of the holiday and ways of its celebration accompanies the music. Reproductions of warm, softly colored acrylic paintings show anthropomorphic mice and bunny families enjoying the holiday.

555.   Wax, Wendy. **Hanukkah, Oh, Hanukkah: A Treasury of Stories, Songs, and Games to Share**. Ill. John Speirs. New York: Parachute Press, 1993. Unp. $12.95. ISBN 0-533-09551-X.

This treasury includes a melange of songs with musical scores; memories and stories by such children's authors as Jack Prelutsky, Shari Lewis, and Eric Kimmel; instructions for dancing the hora and how to play the dreidel game;

crafts; a latke recipe; blessings; poetry by Myra Cohn Livingston, Sadie Rose Weilerstein, Aileen Fisher, and Sylvia Rouss; and a fingerplay. All are illustrated with cheerful, active watercolors.

Family Celebration Stories

556.   Adler, David A. **One Yellow Daffodil: A Hanukkah Story**. Ill. Lloyd Bloom. San Diego, CA: Gulliver Books, 1995. Unp. $16.00. LC 94-31374. ISBN 0-15-200537-4.

An elderly Holocaust survivor, a flower merchant living alone in a small apartment, always treats his customers with great generosity. Two children who come regularly for Sabbath arrangements discover that he no longer celebrates Shabbat or Hanukkah and invite him to their home for the traditional menorah lighting. Many memories of his childhood and the horrors of Auschwitz, where he lost his family, are reawakened, but the Becker family welcomes him so warmly that he is able to join reverently and joyfully in their celebrations. The sympathetic, unpretentious text is impressively illustrated with reproductions of somber, moving paintings.

557.   Conway, Diana Cohen. **Northern Lights: A Hanukkah Story**. Ill. Shelly O. Haas. Rockville, MD: Kar-Ben Copies, 1994. Unp. $5.95pa. LC 94-25831. ISBN 0-929371-80-1.

When Sara and her physician father are grounded by an Alaskan blizzard in a Yupik Eskimo village, she is sad because she will miss Hanukkah at home for the first time in her life. After telling her new Yupik friends the story of the holiday, Sara finds that she can celebrate using a seal-oil lamp for a little menorah and the northern lights for a big one. The story is beautifully illustrated with dramatic watercolors.

558.   Drucker, Malka. **Grandma's Latkes**. Ill. Eve Chwast. San Diego, CA: Gulliver Books, 1992. Unp. $13.95. LC 91-50086. ISBN 0-15-200468-8.

Molly helps Grandma prepare latkes according to Grandma's grandmother's recipe (included in the book). As they work together in the kitchen, Molly learns the history of Hanukkah and how the oil in which the latkes are fried represents the miracle at the Temple. The unusual, flat illustrations are prints of woodcuts painted with watercolors.

559.   Katz, Bobbi. **A Family Hanukkah**. Ill. Caryl Herzfeld. New York: Random House, 1992. Unp. $7.99. LC 91-51093. ISBN 0-679-43240-8.

A lively text and reproductions of warmly realistic paintings portray Jonathan, Rachel, and their cousins preparing gifts, visiting their grandparents in the country, hearing the story of the Maccabees from their grandfather, feasting, opening presents, and enjoying holiday traditions.

560.   Kimmelman, Leslie. **Hanukkah Lights, Hanukkah Nights**. Ill. John Himmelman. New York: HarperCollins, 1992. 25p. $4.95pa. LC 91-15633. ISBN 0-06-446164-5.

In this progressive story, traditional activities and games are pictured as each menorah candle is lit: relatives come, grandmothers sip chicken soup, aunts chant holiday blessings, nieces play dreidels, nephews fight like Maccabees, and so on. Cartoon-style watercolors reflect the fun and love of the holiday season. The text is simple, and a short history of Hanukkah is included.

561. Levine, Arthur A. **All the Lights in the Night**. Ill. James E. Ransome. New York: Tambourine, 1991. Unp. $14.95. LC 90-47496. ISBN 0-688-10107-0.

The heart-stopping journey of two young brothers, from persecution in their Russian shtetl to freedom with their older brother in Palestine in 1914, is illuminated by reproductions of dark, strong oil paintings. The boys sustain their courage by celebrating Hanukkah, wherever they happen to be on their perilous journey, using a little old lamp of their grandmother's. Miraculously, though they have only a tiny bit of oil, the lamp continues to burn.

562. Moss, Marissa. **The Ugly Menorah**. Ill. author. New York: Farrar, Straus & Giroux, 1996. Unp. $14.00. LC 95-33260. ISBN 0-374-38027-9.

After Rachel's grandfather dies, she is sent to keep her grandmother company during Hanukkah. Rachel wonders why Grandma's menorah is just a plain wooden board with tin cups for the candlesticks, and not a beautiful silver candelabra. Grandma explains that during the Great Depression, they were so poor that they had to use a crude homemade menorah, and she treasures it as a link with the happy past. This sweetly sentimental story is illustrated with light-filled, full-page watercolors of endearing, round-faced people.

563. Rosenberg, Amye. **Melly's Menorah**. Ill. author. New York: Little Simon, 1991. Unp. $2.95pa. ISBN 0-671-74495-X.

The Gophers have just moved into a new house and are preparing to celebrate Hanukkah. Melly wants to clean, decorate, make cards, and cook, but family members think that she is too young. Finally, she concocts a menorah out of cookie dough. When the real menorah cannot be found, the family uses hers, with praise. Cheerful pictures show the animals enjoying traditional holiday activities.

564. Rothenberg, Joan. **Inside-Out Grandma**. Ill. author. New York: Hyperion, 1995. Unp. $14.95. LC 94-23677. ISBN 0-7868-2092-6.

Rosie's grandmother wears her clothes inside out to remind herself to buy oil. The complicated series of associations that leads to this behavior begins with Rosie's daddy, who often hurried his dressing so much that he put on his clothes incorrectly, and ends with the preparation of lots of latkes for the family and needing oil. Holiday customs, family love, and the joy of the occasion are blended into a winning story, illustrated with bold, bright, clever pictures.

565. Rouss, Sylvia A. **Sammy Spider's First Hanukkah**. Ill. Katherine Janus Kahn. Rockville, MD: Kar-Ben Copies, 1993. Unp. $5.95pa. LC 92-39639. ISBN 0-929371-46-1.

Sammy, a tiny spider, sits in a web, watches the Shapiro family light the Hanukkah candles night by night, and admires the colored dreidels given to young Josh each time. Sammy longs for one of his own. On the eighth night, his mother surprises him with socks in eight colors, with dreidels on every toe. This is a counting and color identification book, as well, and has lively, one-dimensional pictures.

566.   Schnur, Steven. **The Tie Man's Miracle: A Chanukah Tale**. Ill. Stephen T. Johnson. New York: Morrow, 1995. Unp. $16.00. LC 94-39854. ISBN 0-688-13463-7.

Poorly dressed and cold, the man selling ties from door to door is warmly welcomed by a young boy and his sympathetic family to their Chanukah celebration. Afraid of intruding, he agrees reluctantly to join them, and they discover that he has lost all of his family in the Holocaust. After telling them that a wish made on the final night of Chanukah is magic, the man goes back out into the snow. The young boy wishes that the tie man might rejoin his family and suddenly hears voices calling "Papa." The tie man is never again seen. Realistic, moving watercolors illustrate this well-written story.

567.   Schotter, Roni. **Hanukkah!** Ill. Marylin Hafner. Boston: Little, Brown, 1990. Unp. $13.95. LC 88-28426. ISBN 0-316-77466-9.

Mama, Papa, Grandma Rose, and five children, the youngest of whom is Moe, a toddler just learning to pronounce the word *Hanukkah*, happily immerse themselves in holiday preparations, consume a huge Hanukkah feast, and celebrate love and the light of the candles with affectionate joy. Setting the mood are warmly shaded, exuberant watercolors depicting a jolly, comfortable family. An endnote explains the historical circumstances of the holiday.

568.   Weiss, Nicki. **The First Night of Hanukkah**. Ill. author. New York: Grosset and Dunlap, 1992. 48p. $3.95pa. LC 91-32147. ISBN 0-448-40387-0.

As family members cook and polish in preparation for the celebration, Uncle Dan tells the story of King Antiochus trying to force the Jews to worship his gods, the destruction of the Temple, the resistance of Mattathias and his family, the battle at Modin won by Judah Maccabee's troops, the restoration of the Temple, and the miracle of the oil. This simple, clear, and complete story is illustrated with watercolor cartoons.

569.   Zalben, Jane Breskin. **Papa's Latkes**. Ill. author. New York: Henry Holt, 1994. Unp. $5.95. LC 93-37986. ISBN 0-8050-3099-9.

In an anthropomorphic family of bears, Mama is tired of making latkes, and everyone else in the family tries to help. The results are amusingly misshapen, raw, lumpy, oily, and so forth, until Papa steps in to create huge stacks of perfect potato pancakes. Then the Chanukah celebration can continue. This tiny picture book for very young children has the score of "O Chanukah," the family's favorite song.

Folktales

570.   Adler, David A. **Chanukah in Chelm**. Ill. Kevin O'Malley. New York: Lothrop, Lee & Shepard, 1997. Unp. $16.00. LC 96-53127. ISBN 0-688-09952-1.

The synagogue caretaker in Chelm, the city of foolish Jews, struggles with the task of providing a table for the Chanukah menorah, and finally succeeds in a hilarious and convoluted manner. The funny plot is augmented by bold illustrations caricaturing the credulous townspeople who tell, in comic-strip-style dialogue balloons, unintended bad jokes and go about their tasks with great seriousness while a smart-aleck cat makes comments.

571.   Jaffe, Nina. **In the Month of Kislev: A Story for Hanukkah**. Ill. Louise August. New York: Penguin Puffin, 1992. 32p. $4.99pa. LC 91-45804. ISBN 0-14-055654-0.

In this charming cautionary tale, a rich merchant wants to charge the daughters of a poor peddler for merely smelling the aroma of latkes cooking in his kitchen. He drags them to court, where the wise rabbi says that the peddler may pay with the mere sound of Hanukkah gelt clinking in a bag. Abashed, the merchant mends his ways. The stylized prints of woodcuts, rhythmic and expressive, portray the sprightly humor perfectly. An explanatory note about the holiday is included.

572.   Kimmel, Eric A. **The Chanukah Guest**. Ill. Giora Carmi. New York: Holiday House, 1990. Unp. $14.95. LC 89-20073. ISBN 0-8234-0788-8.

Aroused from hibernation by the savory smell of frying latkes, Old Bear invades Bubba Brayna's cottage and gobbles stacks and stacks. The nearsighted old lady, Bubba Brayna, willingly serves the bear, thinking that he is the rabbi, whom she is expecting, in a fur coat. The amusing plot is well developed and illustrated with bold, caricatured pictures of merrymaking villagers.

573.   Kimmel, Eric A. **The Magic Dreidels: A Hanukkah Story**. Ill. Katya Krenina. New York: Holiday House, 1996. Unp. $15.95. LC 96-2405. ISBN 0-8234-1256-3.

Jacob accidentally flips his new brass dreidel into a well. The well's goblin, a dapper merman with a lorgnette and a braided green beard, gives him a magic wooden dreidel, which spins out latkes, then a silver dreidel, which spins out Hanukkah gelt, and finally an iron dreidel, which spins out fleas, to punish the unscrupulous woman who has tricked Jacob into giving her the first two dreidels. This cleverly conceived and brightly written story has amusing watercolor caricatures with a wintry setting.

574.   Kimmel, Eric A. **The Spotted Pony**. Ill. Leonard Everett Fisher. New York: Holiday House, 1992. 70p. $14.95. LC 91-24214. ISBN 0-8234-0936-8.

Delightful stories and fables, two for each night of Hanukkah, are thoughtful, humorous, witty, mysterious, clever, and ethical. They deal with those who are not only quick-witted but righteous, honoring God and their fellow human beings. The occasional black-and-white illustrations are bold and expressive.

575.   Manushkin, Fran. **Latkes and Applesauce**. Ill. Robin Spowart. New York: Scholastic, 1990. Unp. $12.95. LC 88-38916. ISBN 0-590-42261-8.

Just before the potatoes are to be dug and the apples picked, a tremendous snowstorm rages, and the Menashe family has no latkes and applesauce for Hanukkah. Although the blizzard continues and the food supply dwindles, they take in two starving animals and are unexpectedly rewarded for their kindness. Misty, gently glowing pictures contrast the warmth of the cozy cottage with the cold, blue-white outdoors. A reading list and explanatory material concerning the history of the holiday are included.

576.   Penn, Malka. **The Miracle of the Potato Latkes: A Hanukkah Story**.
Ill. Giora Carmi. New York: Holiday House, 1994. Unp. $15.95. LC 93-29921.
ISBN 0-8234-1118-4.

Each year at Hanukkah, Tante Golda, a poor but generous woman, provides the most delicious latkes in all of Russia to her friends and neighbors. After a severe drought, however, she has only one tiny potato left. She shares it
with a poor beggar on the first night of Hanukkah. Subsequently, more and
more potatoes appear mysteriously each morning, enabling her once again to
feed everyone. Watercolors with vigorous caricatures of Russian peasants add
zest to the story.

High Holy Days

577.   Fishman, Cathy Goldberg. **On Rosh Hashanah and Yom Kippur**. Ill.
Melanie W. Hall. New York: Atheneum, 1997. Unp. $16.00. LC 96-23258.
ISBN 0-689-80526-8.

A serious and meaningful text discusses the customs and symbols of Rosh
Hashanah and Yom Kippur, as experienced by a modern Jewish family. As God
inscribes names in the Book of Life, the New Year begins, the world's birthday is
celebrated, and the foods, synagogue services, tashlich, shofar, tzedakah, fasting, and prayer are explained. The flowing lines, odd angles, and soft colors of
the distinctive illustrations reinforce the mood of contemplation and holiness.
The book includes a glossary.

578.   Goldin, Barbara Diamond. **The World's Birthday: A Rosh Hashanah
Story**. Ill. Jeanette Winter. San Diego, CA: Harcourt Brace Jovanovich, 1990.
32p. $13.95. LC 89-29208. ISBN 0-15-299648-6.

When Daniel realizes that Rosh Hashanah is the time when God's creation
is celebrated, he wants to have a birthday party for the whole world. Despite his
family's doubts, he buys the bakery's biggest cake, makes a birthday card, and
envisions the perfect setting for his party. The gentle, ingenuous story is illustrated with bold, bright watercolors.

579.   Kimmel, Eric A. **Days of Awe: Stories for Rosh Hashanah and Yom
Kippur**. Ill. Erika Weihs. New York: Viking, 1991. 47p. $14.50. LC 91-50198.
ISBN 0-670-82772-X.

After an explanatory introduction, three didactic stories from traditional
folkloric and talmudic sources are retold. They depict the virtues associated
with the High Holy Days: charity, prayer, and repentance. The topics are a poor
couple who share what little they have with others in need, a simple shepherd so
devout that his prayers are more acceptable to God than those of the learned
rabbis, and a rabbi who begs forgiveness from someone he has unthinkingly in-
sulted. Expressive folk art illustrates the lively storytelling, and the book includes source notes.

580.   Weilerstein, Sadie Rose. **K'tonton's Yom Kippur Kitten**. Ill. Joe
Boddy. Philadelphia: Jewish Publication Society, 1995. Unp. $12.95. LC
95-8541. ISBN 0-8276-0541-2.

This sympathetically told story captures the High Holy Days' spirit of repentance and forgiveness. The day after Rosh Hashanah, K'tonton, the Jewish

Tom Thumb, allows a stray kitten to take the blame for spilling honey that he himself has overturned. To atone, he fasts, gives his money to charity, and finally confesses to his father. The kitten is once again welcomed inside the house, and K'tonton asks its forgiveness. The book has pleasant black-and-white drawings and a glossary.

Passover

581. Bat-Ami, Miriam. **Dear Elijah: A Passover Story**. New York: Farrar, Straus & Giroux, 1995. 96p. $14.00. LC 94-29941. ISBN 0-374-31755-0.

Five weeks before Passover, twelve-year-old Rebecca begins writing letters addressed to the prophet Elijah, who is an unseen presence at every seder meal (and more approachable than God). In the letters, she expresses her feelings of fear about her father, who has a serious heart problem, her doubts about God's existence, her questions about Orthodox rules, and her uncertainty about the future. She also records her joy about being Jewish and her appreciation of Passover and all its customs. The author's sympathetic insights into Rebecca's emotions and dilemmas make the book authentic and moving.

582. Fishman, Cathy Goldberg. **On Passover**. Ill. Melanie W. Halla. New York: Atheneum, 1997. Unp. $16.00. LC 91-43110. ISBN 0-689-80528-4.

The sights of the special dishes and pots and pans; the smells of chicken soup and spicy apples; the tastes of matzah, bitter herbs, and salt water; the sounds of the Haggadah; and the textures of the silk matzah cover and Elijah's silver cup, are dear and familiar parts of Passover. The book includes swirling, sophisticated, mixed-media illustrations and a glossary.

583. Goldin, Barbara Diamond. **The Magician's Visit: A Passover Tale**. Ill. Robert Andrew Parker. New York: Viking Press, 1993. 32p. $13.99. LC 92-22903. ISBN 0-670-84840-9.

In this simple and moving retelling of a story by I. L. Peretz, a couple experiencing difficult times give their last few pennies to charity and have no money to prepare for Passover. Still, they believe that God will somehow provide a seder. When a mysterious magician lavishes food and furnishings upon them, however, they are afraid of him and hurry to their rabbi for counsel. The rabbi calms their fears by explaining that their feast has been provided by heaven and Elijah. Prints of unusual, rough, colored etchings express the power and majesty of the text, and an explanatory afterword is included.

584. Goldin, Barbara Diamond. **The Passover Journey: A Seder Companion**. Ill. Neil Waldman. New York: Puffin, 1994. 56p. $5.99pa. LC 93-5133. ISBN 0-14-056131-5.

Part I, which includes stories from the Midrash, is a clear, vivid retelling of Moses' exploits, from birth to the exodus through the Sea of Reeds (the Red Sea). Part II is a thorough explication of the traditional ways to prepare for Passover, the seder foods, the fourteen steps of the Haggadah and the Four Questions during the Maggid, and the singing of "Dayenu" and "One Little Goat." Also discussed are customs from other lands, and the Warsaw Ghetto versus the Nazis in 1943. The book provides excellent coverage; stylized, decorative illustrations; and a glossary.

585.   Kimmelman, Leslie. **Hooray! It's Passover!** Ill. John Himmelman. New York: HarperCollins, 1996. Unp. $12.95. LC 94-18685. ISBN 0-06-024674-X.

A large, cheerful, extended family, shown in appealing watercolor cartoons, gathers around the seder table and observes the special traditions, such as dipping parsley in salt water, asking the Four Questions, and singing "Dayenu." Then they feast on chicken soup and gefilte fish, followed by a rousing hunt for the afikomen. The book includes an explanatory note about Passover.

586.   Manushkin, Fran. **The Matzah That Papa Brought Home**. Ill. Ned Bittinger. New York: Scholastic, 1995. Unp. $14.95. LC 94-9952. ISBN 0-590-47146-5.

In a lilting, cumulative, rhymed text based on "This Is the House That Jack Built," three generations of a handsome family celebrate the seder, with its matzah ball soup, afikoman, open door for Elijah, bitter herbs, ten plagues, and "Dayenu." The text is illustrated with idealized realism, full of love and comfort, and includes explanatory notes about the foods and their significance, as well as other Passover traditions.

587.   Oppenheim, Shulamith Levey. **Appleblossom**. Ill. Joanna Yardley. San Diego, CA: Harcourt Brace Jovanovich, 1991. 28p. $14.95. LC 89-24575. ISBN 0-15-203750-0.

Eight-year-old Naphtali and his mother long for a cat, but Papa refuses. The clever Appleblossom, who wants to be their pet, befriends Papa by marching in boldly when the door is opened for Elijah at Passover and settling down beside his chair. The Passover preparations are accomplished in an atmosphere of close family love, adding to the sweetness of this short story. Luminous watercolors complement the text.

588.   Portnoy, Mindy Avra. **Matzah Ball: A Passover Story**. Ill. Katherine Janus Kahn. Rockville, MD: Kar-Ben Copies, 1994. Unp. $5.95pa. LC 93-39402. ISBN 0-929371-68-2.

In this lively sports story, Aaron discovers that because it is Passover, he must take a suitable lunch to the Orioles-Rangers game and eschew all the ballpark junk food that he loves. After his friends have gone to the concession stand, leaving Aaron alone, an old man sympathizes with him and talks of the old days at Ebbets Field but vanishes mysteriously after Cal Ripken hits a home run and Aaron catches the ball. Was he Elijah? The bright, active pictures are full of life and fun.

589.   Schnur, Steven. **The Koufax Dilemma**. Ill. Meryl Treatner. New York: Morrow, 1997. 186p. $15.00. LC 96-18049. ISBN 0-688-14221-4.

Twelve-year-old Danny is angry and upset when he is forbidden to pitch in the crucial opening game of his baseball league, because it has been scheduled for the night of the Passover seder. Even remembering that Sandy Koufax sat out a World Series game on Yom Kippur hardly helps, especially because Danny's best friend and his coach, although they are also Jewish, plan to participate in the game anyway. The importance of Passover as a time when Jews throughout the world celebrate together is stressed throughout, as various people try to soothe Danny's distress. The result is a spirited story with a triumphant conclusion, and a celebration of Passover traditions, as well.

590. Schotter, Roni. **Passover Magic**. Ill. Marylin Hafner. Boston: Little, Brown, 1995. Unp. $14.95. LC 93-20053. ISBN 0-316-77468-5.

All the relatives cram the house for the holiday. Everyone helps cook the seder meal in the kitchen; they enjoy the meal, hunt the afikoman, and dance; and Uncle Harry entertains with his clever magic tricks. Warmth, joy, and family love fill the story and the charming watercolor illustrations.

591. Simon, Norma. **The Story of Passover**. Ill. Erika Weihs. New York: HarperCollins, 1997. Unp. $14.95. LC 95-41201. ISBN 0-06-027062-4.

This newly illustrated reprint of *Passover* (previously published by Crowell in 1965) describes and explains all the important elements of the holiday: the Exodus; preparations, including table settings and Haggadot; the order of the seder; the afikoman; and the special foods. The richly colored, decorative pictures have cartoon-style figures.

592. Wohl, Lauren L. **Matzoh Mouse**. Ill. Pamela Keavney. New York: HarperCollins, 1991. Unp. $13.95. LC 90-31976. ISBN 0-06-026580-9.

Nine-year-old Sarah's love of chocolate-covered matzot is her undoing during the family's joyous preparations for and celebration of Passover. Although no one is to touch the holiday sweets, only one is left to serve at the seder, and everyone suspects who the nibbling little matzoh mouse might be. The meaning and ceremonies of Passover are described and pictured in a loving, middle-class family setting.

593. Zalben, Jane Breskin. **Happy Passover, Rosie**. Ill. author. New York: Henry Holt, 1990. Unp. $13.95. LC 89-19979. ISBN 0-8050-1221-4.

Cheerful, warmly colored illustrations of the bear relatives gathered for the seder reinforce this happy tale of young Rosie. She is allowed to ask the Four Questions and also finds the afikoman, but is frightened when Grandpa pretends to be Elijah's ghost. The meanings of the food on the seder plate and the significance of the Four Questions are discussed at the end of the book.

Purim

594. Goldin, Barbara Diamond. **Cakes and Miracles: A Purim Tale**. Ill. Erika Weihs. New York: Viking, 1991. Unp. $13.95. LC 90-42048. ISBN 0-670-83047-X.

Although blind, Hershel is an active, imaginative child who longs to do something more for his widowed mother than bring wood and water into the house. On the eve of Purim, he dreams of an angel who urges him to make what he sees inside his head. He creates beautiful cookies, to the amazement of his mother, for her to sell along with the traditional hamantashen. This touching tale is colorfully illustrated with reproductions of primitively-styled oil paintings and includes a short description of the holiday and its history.

595. Zalben, Jane Breskin. **Goldie's Purim**. Ill. author. New York: Henry Holt, 1991. Unp. $13.95. LC 90-43153. ISBN 0-8050-1227-3.

Cute, anthropomorphic bears begin their Purim celebration by baking hamantashen (the recipe is included). Then, when Goldie is about to begin her part as Queen Esther in the synagogue's Purim play, she suffers from sudden stage fright. Luckily, she thinks of Esther's bravery and follows her example by step-ping forward boldly. Afterward, Papa reads the megillah, and the celebrations continue. The easy-to-read text of this happy story is illustrated with bright pictures of a contented, loving family.

Shabbat (the Jewish Sabbath)

596.   Greene, Patricia Baird. **The Sabbath Garden**. New York: Lodestar, 1993. 215p. $15.99. LC 93-19561. ISBN 0-525-67430-6.

A teenage African American girl, Opal, and an elderly Jew, Solomon, live in the same shabby Lower East Side apartment building in New York City. The girl is self-destructive and comes from a dysfunctional family; the man, fussy and ethical, is the remnant of a once-thriving Jewish neighborhood. Despite their differences, though, Solomon welcomes Opal into his home during a time of stress and danger in her life, and he introduces her to the peace and beauty of the Sabbath celebration. A fast-moving, exciting plot; a rich variety of characters; and a vivid setting combine to make an outstanding novel for young adults.

597.   Manushkin, Fran. **Starlight and Candles: The Joys of the Sabbath**. Ill. Jacqueline Chwast. New York: Simon and Schuster, 1995. Unp. $15.00. LC 94-20232. ISBN 0-689-80274-9.

Jake and Rosy love all the Sabbath traditions: the baking of the challah loaves, the lighting of the candles, dinner with their grandparents, worship at the synagogue, and the fragrant spices that signal the end of the celebration. The Sabbath is an ongoing reminder of God's covenant with the Jews. Thick black lines and brilliant colors distinguish the bold illustrations.

598.   Rosman, Steven M. **The Bird of Paradise and Other Sabbath Stories**. Ill. Joel Iskowitz. New York: United American Hebrew Congregations, 1994. 168p. $8.95pa. LC 94-10414. ISBN 0-8074-0529-9.

Rabbi Rosman delightfully adapts fifty-four stories from a fertile variety of sources, including chasidic lore, the Midrash, the Talmud, and Yiddish folklore. Verses from the sidrah preface each story, and many feature wise and ingenious rabbis coping with difficult situations. Never heavily didactic, the tales are filled with humor, love, morality, and, of course, religious devotion. These edifying lessons in the form of entertaining stories spanning many centuries are appropriate for any reader.

599.   Schur, Maxine Rose. **Day of Delight: A Jewish Sabbath in Ethiopia**. Ill. Brian Pinkney. New York: Dial, 1994. Unp. $15.99. LC 93-31451. ISBN 0-8037-1413-0.

Setting aside their cares and worries, the people of a Beta Israel village high in the Ethiopian mountains stop their work before the sun sets and return to their huts to bathe and prepare for the Sabbath meal. The next morning, the high priest leads their worship, which is followed by a welcome day of rest and play. Although their way of life is primitive and difficult, they know that they are God's chosen people and rejoice in their knowledge of this truth. The vividly de-tailed text is illustrated with scratchboard pictures that give the Beta Israel peo-ple an aura of peace and dignity. The book includes a pronunciation guide, glossary, and explanatory note.

600.   Schwartz, Howard, and Barbara Rush. **The Sabbath Lion: A Jewish Folktale from Algeria**. Ill. Stephen Fieser. New York: HarperCollins, 1992. Unp. $14.00. LC 91-35766. ISBN 0-06-020853-8.

Yosef, only ten years old and the son of a poor widow with seven young children, volunteers to travel the formidable distance from Algiers to Cairo to collect an inheritance his mother has received. Because the unscrupulous caravan leader refuses to stop to rest on the Sabbath, even though he promised to do so, Yosef stays behind in the desert to celebrate properly. During the night, a magnificent lion, sent by the Sabbath Queen, appears to guard him and, after the holy day, carries him to Cairo and back to Algiers to complete his mission. The story is illustrated with reproductions of expressive, exciting paintings.

601.   Schweiger-Dmi'el, Itzhak. **Hanna's Sabbath Dress**. Ill. Ora Eitan. New York: Simon and Schuster, 1996. Unp. $15.00. LC 94-12819. ISBN 0-689-80517-9.

Hanna, who has a new white dress for the Sabbath, is very careful to keep it clean, until she meets an elderly charcoal burner in the forest and helps him carry his heavy sack. Weeping because her dress is covered by black smudges but still happy that she helped the old man, she is rewarded when the moon sends down cleansing beams to purify her dress and make it radiant. This simple, poetic story is illustrated with blocky, brightly colored shapes.

602.   Snyder, Carol. **God Must Like Cookies, Too**. Ill. Beth Glick. Philadelphia: Jewish Publication Society, 1993. Unp. $16.95. LC 92-26886. ISBN 0-8276-0423-8.

A young red-haired girl attends Shabbat services with her grandmother. Though she appreciates all the elements of worship, she also daydreams about things she and her grandmother have done together and takes a little nap. At the Oneg Shabbat, she enjoys cookies and attention from adults. The softly shaded watercolors portray her lovely experience at the temple.

Sukkot

603.   Goldin, Barbara Diamond. **Night Lights: A Sukkot Story**. Ill. Louise August. San Diego, CA: Gulliver, 1995. Unp. $15.00. LC 94-27109. ISBN 0-15-200536-6.

Daniel and Naomi are to sleep in a succah booth and fear that wolves and bears will creep through the roof of branches. After a jolly family supper in the hut, decorated with fruits and paper chains, they are left alone. Looking up at the night lights of the stars and moon, and knowing that these are the same lights their ancestors saw centuries ago while fleeing Egypt, dispels their fears as they cuddle together closely. Big, splashy illustrations show wondrous night monsters. An explanatory note is included.

604.   Polacco, Patricia. **Tikvah Means Hope**. Ill. author. New York: Bantam Doubleday Dell, 1996. Unp. $5.99pa. ISBN 0-440-41229-3.

Justine and Duane, and Tikvah, their cat, are enjoying their neighbor's sukkah when a terrible fire sweeps down the Oakland hills, forcing everyone to flee from their homes. Tikvah cannot be found. When the fire has subsided, they return to find everything burned to the ground, except, miraculously, the sukkah, from which Tikvah emerges unharmed. The happiness, fear, and sorrow of the events are portrayed poignantly in bright, detailed, gently humorous illustrations.

605.   Zalben, Jane Breskin. **Leo and Blossom's Sukkah**. Ill. author. New York: Henry Holt, 1990. Unp. $13.95. LC 89-24596. ISBN 0-8050-1226-5.

The bear children decide to build their own sukkah, but they hang so much fruit on it that their decorations crash down upon them. After their parents help them rebuild the sukkah, the children celebrate their harvest feast in comfort. The simple text and active pictures radiate family love and holiday cheer. Sukkot is explained in an endnote.

Older and Noteworthy

Holiday Collections

Other excellent collections include *A Picture Book of Jewish Holidays* by David Adler (Holiday, 1981), *Jewish Holidays* by Judith E. Greenberg (Watts, 1984), *Holiday Tales of Sholom Aleichem* by Sholom Rabinowitz (Atheneum, 1979), and *The Best of K'tonton* by Sadie Rose Weilerstein (Jewish Publication Society, 1980).

Individual Holidays

For more general information about Hanukkah, see *A Picture Book of Hanukkah* by David A. Adler (Holiday, 1982), *Light Another Candle* by Miriam Chaikin (Clarion, 1981), *Hanukkah* by Malka Drucker (Holiday, 1980), and *Chanukah* by Howard Greenfeld (Henry Holt, 1976).

Additional sources for Hanukkah folktales include *Hanukkah Money* by Sholem Aleichem (Greenwillow, 1978), *The Power of Light* by Isaac Bashevis Singer (Farrar, Straus & Giroux, 1980), and *The Chanukah Tree* (Holiday, 1988) and *Hershel and the Hanukkah Goblins* (Holiday, 1989) by Eric A. Kimmel.

More useful material about the High Holy Days includes *Rosh Hashanah and Yom Kippur* by Howard Greenfeld (Holt, Rinehart, and Winston, 1979), *Rosh Hashanah and Yom Kippur* by Malka Drucker (Holiday, 1981), *Yussel's Prayer* by Barbara Cohen (Lothrop, Lee & Shepard, 1981), *A Sound to Remember* by Sonia Levitin (Harcourt, 1979), and *Sound the Shofar* by Miriam Chaikin (Clarion, 1986).

Additional worthwhile titles about Passover include *Ask Another Question* by Miriam Chaikin (Clarion, 1985), *A Picture Book of Passover* by David A. Adler (Holiday, 1982), *Passover* by Malka Drucker (Holiday, 1981), *Passover* by Howard Greenfeld (Henry Holt, 1978), *The Carp in the Bathtub* by Barbara Cohen (Lothrop, Lee & Shepard, 1972), *The Magician* by Uri Shulevitz (Macmillan, 1973), and *But This Night Is Different* by Audrey Friedman Marcus (United American Hebrew Congregations, 1980).

For more information about Purim, see *Make Noise, Make Merry* by Miriam Chaikin (Clarion, 1983) and *Purim* by Howard Greenfeld (Henry Holt, 1982).

Other valuable material concerning Shabbat includes *The Seventh Day* by Miriam Chaikin (Doubleday, 1980), *Shabbat* by Malka Drucker (Holiday, 1983), *The Remembering Box* by Eth Clifford (Houghton Mifflin, 1985), *Mrs. Moskowitz and the Sabbath Candlesticks* by Amy Schwartz (Jewish Publication Society, 1983), and *Joseph Who Loved the Sabbath* by Marilyn Hirsh (Viking, 1986).

Chapter Thirteen

Native American Religions

Beliefs

606.   Bruchac, Joseph. **The Circle of Thanks: Native American Poems and Songs of Thanksgiving**. Ill. Jacob Murv. Mahwah, NJ: Bridgewater Books, 1996. 32p. $14.95. LC 95-41175. ISBN 0-8167-4012-7.

Simple, expressive, and moving short poems based on the songs and prayers of the Micmac, Mohawk, Papago, Cherokee, Kwakiutl, Hopi, Pima, Navajo, Osage, and Pawnee give thanks for the fertile earth, the life-giving rain, medicinal plants, cedar trees, the sun and stars, and the gifts of the Great Creator. They are displayed upon double-page spreads of dramatic folk art, showing the various Native American nations in their daily life. Notes on each poem are included.

607.   Campbell, Maria. **People of the Buffalo: How the Plains Indians Lived**. Ill. Douglas Tait and Shannon Twofeathers. How They Lived in Canada Series. Buffalo, NY: Firefly Books (U.S.), 1995. 47p. $7.95pa. ISBN 0-88894-329-6.

In this explication of the spirituality of such nations as the Paigan, Cheyenne, Arapaho, Blackfoot, Kiowa Apache, Pawnee, Shoshone, Ute, Crow, and Osage, all things have souls, from human beings to plants and insects, and must be treated with respect and dignity. Life is a circle of birth, living, and dying. Death, after which the body enriches the earth, is not feared. Fasting and meditation are used to contact the spirits for help. Sacred rites and vision quests are also discussed. Pen-and-ink drawings illustrate the book.

608.   Hucko, Bruce. **A Rainbow at Night: The World in Words and Pictures by Navajo Children**. San Francisco: Chronicle Books, 1996. 44p. $14.95. ISBN 0-8118-1294-4.

The rainbow, symbolizing the spirits of the Navajo who guard and bless the people, appears in much of the dynamic, full-page artwork by Navajo children aged five through thirteen. Using all types of media, from watercolor and tempera to markers and chalks, they have pictured essential areas of their lives, which include such subjects as yei-bi-cheis, the grandfather spirits; sacred animals, birds, and reptiles; chiindis, the demonic beings who practice witchcraft; a peyote church ceremony; and a powwow round dance. Their styles vary from simple stick figures to sophisticated semi-abstraction, but all the illustrations are arresting and vividly colored. Each work has a quotation from the artist and a descriptive note by the author.

609.   Liptak, Karen. **North American Indian Ceremonies**. A First Book Series. New York: Franklin Watts, 1992. 64p. $5.95pa. LC 91-30263. ISBN 0-531-20100-7.

Straightforward and compact, this overview includes an introduction explaining how ceremonies are a form of worship and then briefly describes rituals and dances for birth, naming, coming of age, marriage, initiation into a secret society, death, hunting, harvesting, fertility, thanksgiving, healing, and going to war. The Hopi, Sioux, Apache, Navajo, Cherokee, Nootka, and Tlingit are among the nations discussed. The book is illustrated in color, and contains a glossary, reading list, and index.

610.   McConkey, Lois. **Sea and Cedar: How the Northwest Coast Indians Lived**. Ill. Douglas Tait. How They Lived in Canada Series. Buffalo, NY: Firefly Books (U.S.), 1995. 30p. $7.95pa. ISBN 0-88894-371-7.

Although religion is more peripheral among the Tlingit, Tsimshian, Haida, Bella Coola, Kwakiutl, Nootka, and Coast Salish nations, with whom displaying and passing on wealth is central to prestige, they believe that each person has a soul, which becomes a ghost upon death, as well as a guardian spirit. Their shamans have the power to drive away ghosts, lest they return to haunt the living. Black-and-white illustrations accompany the text.

611.   Monroe, Jean Guard, and Ray A. Williamson. **First Houses: Native American Homes and Sacred Structures**. Ill. Susan Johnston Carlson. Boston: Houghton Mifflin, 1993. 150p. $14.95. LC 92-34900. ISBN 0-395-51081-3.

The building of homes and places to celebrate rituals is a sacred act in Native American tradition, done upon instructions from the gods themselves. Because the people's physical and spiritual lives are so closely entwined, provisions for both are made in their dwellings. The structures described include the Iroquois longhouse, the Navajo hogan, the Pueblo kiva, the Pawnee earth lodge, the Delaware big house, and the sweatlodges common to a number of nations. Many of these structures are still in use today. The test is scholarly, absorbing, and clear, enlivened by many myths and legends, and illustrated with black-and-white pen-and-ink drawings and decorations. A pronunciation glossary of nations and terms, a reading list, a bibliography referenced by subject, and an index are included.

612. Rendon, Marcie R. **Powwow Summer: A Family Celebrates the Circle of Life**. Minneapolis, MN: Carolrhoda, 1996. 48p. $21.50. LC 95-36777. ISBN 0-87614-986-7.

The teaching of the Anishinabe (also known as Ojibway or Chippewa) that the circle of life is endless, as the human spirit passes from the spirit world to birth and the springtime of life, to the growth of the summer season, to the maturation of autumn, and to the winter of rest, old age, and death, is expressed in their powwow ceremonies of singing and dancing. The book follows the Downwind family as they attend a summer of powwows and discusses the social and spiritual significance of the ceremonies. Outstanding color photographs illuminate the text.

613. Ridington, Jillian, and Robin Ridington. **People of the Longhouse: How the Iroquoian Tribes Lived**. Ill. Ian Bateson. How They Lived in Canada Series. Buffalo, NY: Firefly Books (U.S.), 1995. 47p. $7.95pa. ISBN 1-55054-221-4.

Divinely inspired by the god Dekaniwedah, the Huron, Petun, Neutral, Iroquois, and Erie leagues were formed to enable nations to live together in peace; to guarantee such freedoms as speech, hunting, and worship; and to establish beneficial laws. Their supreme being created the sky and earth spirits, which in turn control everything, and the shaman can employ their forces through his dreams. Black-and-white drawings illustrate descriptions of the leagues' festivals and ceremonies.

614. Ridington, Robin, and Jillian Ridington. **People of the Trail: How the Northern Forest Indians Lived**. Ill. Ian Bateson. How They Lived in Canada Series. Buffalo, NY: Firefly Books (U.S.), 1995. 40p. $7.95pa. ISBN 0-88894-412-8.

For the Kutchin, Hare, Tutchone, Kaska, Dogrib, Yellowknife, Chipewyan, Sekani, Beaver, Cree, Northern Ojibwa, Montagnais, and Naskapi nations, all living things have spirits that must be respected. The shaman, who sings and drums to call spirit helpers, conducts significant rituals at birth and death and calls for changes in the weather, the return of game, and fertility. Illness and death are caused by evil spirits or supernaturally powerful enemies. Precise black-and-white drawings illustrate the text.

615. Roessel, Monty. **Kinaalda: A Navajo Girl Grows Up**. We Are Still Here: Native Americans Today Series. Minneapolis, MN: Lerner, 1993. 48p. $19.95. LC 92-35204. ISBN 0-8225-2655-7.

The Navajo coming-of-age ceremonies for girls experiencing the onset of menarche are described in the experiences of thirteen-year-old Celinda. Because the ceremony was given to the Navajo by the Holy People, and the first to undergo it was Changing Woman, it is a deeply spiritual rite, not only for the young woman, but also for her friends and family, who participate in the rituals. Simply and movingly written, Celinda's story is beautifully photographed in color by the author. A glossary and reading list are included.

616.   Seattle, Chief. **Brother Eagle, Sister Sky: A Message from the Words of Chief Seattle**. Ill. Susan Jeffers. New York: Dial, 1991. Unp. $15.00. LC 90-27713. ISBN 0-8037-0969-2.

Although this book has been criticized as inaccurately portraying its subject matter, it is true in spirit to Native American ideals. A central belief of Native American spirituality is that a sacred and inseparable bond exists among the earth and all its creatures, humankind included. In this poetic adaptation of the address by Chief Seattle (of the Suquamish) to the white government's treaty negotiators, these beliefs are beautifully expressed and gorgeously pictured in spectacular views of mounted Native Americans in the unspoiled wilderness, followed by scenes of logging devastation.

617.   Siska, Heather Smith. **People of the Ice: How the Inuit Lived**. Ill. Ian Bateson. How They Lived in Canada Series. Buffalo, NY: Firefly Books (U.S.), 1995. 47p. $7.95pa. ISBN 0-88894-404-7.

Among the Nunivak, Bering Sea, North Alaskan, Nunamint, Mackenzie, Copper, Caribou, Netsilik, Iglulik, Baffin, Polar, East and West Greenland, Ungava, and Labrador Inuit peoples is the belief that everything has a soul. Upon death, that soul can enter another living creature. Shamans can converse with the spirits, which both help and trick the people. Protective amulets are of paramount importance and give specific powers to the wearer. Taboos and other rituals are also discussed. Black-and-white illustrations accompany the text.

618.   Swamp, Chief Jake. **Giving Thanks: A Native American Good Morning Message**. Ill. Erwin Printup. New York: Lee and Low Books, 1995. Unp. $14.95. LC 94-5955. ISBN 1-880000-15-6.

This celebratory, beautifully expressed prayer, composed by a Mohawk and based upon the "Thanksgiving Address of the Iroquois Nations," appreciates Mother Earth for her bounty of food, water, and healing herbs; animals, trees, and birds; winds, rain, Elder Brother Sun, and Grandmother Moon; the Spirit Protectors of past and present, who teach peace and harmony; and the Great Spirit. The handsome, decorative illustrations by a Cayuga/Tuscarora artist enhance the mystery, beauty, and reverence of the prayer.

619.   Wood, Nancy C. **Shaman's Circle**. Ill. Frank Howell. New York: Delacorte, 1996. 80p. $22.50. LC 95-52387. ISBN 0-385-32222-4.

Inspired by traditional Pueblo beliefs and rituals concerning the seasons, puberty, marriage, coming of age, and all other such essentials of life, these poems reflect, positively and beautifully, the deep spirituality and respect for all living things inherent in their culture. The reproductions of unusual, mystical, richly colored paintings of Native American men and women with flowing hair and strong, meditative faces are a perfect accompaniment.

620.   Wood, Nancy C. **Spirit Walker**. Ill. Frank Howell. New York: Doubleday, 1993. 80p. $19.95. LC 92-29376. ISBN 0-385-30927-9.

The Taos Pueblo belief that all parts of nature are closely connected and equally valuable, be it mountain, desert, animal, or human being, is evident in this collection of poems. Written in a chantlike cadence, they celebrate the beneficences and beauties of Mother Earth, the wisdom of elders, and the circle of life. The luminously colored illustrations are powerful portraits of Native American women with streaming hair and serene faces.

Spiritual Stories

621. Bernhard, Emery. **The Tree That Rains: The Flood Myth of the Huichol Indians of Mexico**. Ill. Durga Bernhard. New York: Holiday House, 1994. Unp. $15.95. LC 93-8296. ISBN 0-8234-1108-7.

An upstanding, hard-working man clears, plants, weeds, and harvests his fields. In one field, though, a huge fig tree suddenly begins growing back each night after having been cut down the previous day. Mystified, the man hides one night to watch and sees that Great-Grandmother Earth rises from the soil. She warns him that a great flood will come because the people have forgotten the gods. The man is told to collect seeds and build a boat, in which he drifts for five years before he finds dry land again and can plant his seeds. Then the magic fig tree reappears to shower the seeds with rain. The tree stands on the shore of Lake Chapala and is worshipped today at the Huichol harvest festival of thanksgiving to the divine Earth Mother and rain goddesses. The story is enhanced by handsome, large, folk-art illustrations.

622. Bruchac, Joseph. **Between Earth and Sky: Legends of Native American Sacred Places**. Ill. Thomas Locker. San Diego, CA: Harcourt Brace, 1996. Unp. $16.00. LC 95-10862. ISBN 0-15-200042-9.

The full-page reproductions of spectacular, formal oil paintings, filled with majesty and beauty, depict holy sites such as Gay Head, sacred to the Wampanoag; Lake Champlain, to the Abenaki; Niagara Falls, to the Seneca; the Great Smoky Mountains, to the Cherokee; and so on. Sacred places are found in all seven directions—east, north, south, west, above, below, and within—to give balance to life. A legend pertaining to each site tells a significant moral or spiritual lesson, and a map of Native American nations in the United States is included.

623. Bruchac, Joseph. **Four Ancestors: Stories, Songs, and Poems from Native North America**. Ill. S. S. Burrus, Jeffrey Chapman, Murr Jacob, and Duke Sine. Mahwah, NJ: Bridgewater Books, 1996. 96p. $18.95. LC 95-15250. ISBN 0-8167-3843-2.

In many Native American traditions, earth, fire, air, and water are considered to be the materials from which everything, including human beings, was created. These tales and poems from many nations, including Mohawk, Osage, Penobscot, Micmac, and Navajo, are divided into four sections, one for each ancestor, and powerfully illustrated by the four artists. Notes at the end of the book give further information.

624. Courlander, Harold. **People of the Short Blue Corn: Tales and Legends of the Hopi Indians**. Ill. Enrico Arno. New York: Henry Holt Owlet, 1996. 184p. $9.95pa. LC 95-37318. ISBN 0-8050-3511-7.

Trickster and humor tales are intermingled with religion and morality themes in legends of Spider Grandmother, the spirit of Mother Earth; the mischievous twins Pokanghoya and Polongahoya, who helped during creation;

Moski, the land of the dead; the belief that all forms of living creatures are closely akin; and the calling of the Hopi people by Masauwu, Lord of the Upper World and Guardian of the Dead, to rise from the Lower World and settle in their new homeland on earth. This simply and well-written book has a few black-and-white drawings, a glossary, and lengthy explanatory notes.

625.   Cusler, Leigh. **The Boy Who Dreamed of an Acorn**. Ill. Shonto Begay. New York: Philomel, 1994. Unp. $15.95. LC 92-44902. ISBN 0-399-22547-1.

Three Chinook boys go on their vision quest. One dreams of a bear, one of an eagle, and one of an acorn. The bear boy is strong; the eagle boy is a skilled hunter; but the acorn boy plants a tree that gives food and shelter freely when it matures, just as he gives wise counsel, peace, and happiness to his people. The rhythmic, mythic story is illustrated with strong, colorful human forms.

626.   Duncan, Lois. **The Magic of Spider Woman**. Ill. Shonto Begay. New York: Scholastic, 1995. Unp. $14.95. LC 95-17366. ISBN 0-590-46155-9.

Expressive of the need for a well-balanced life, an important concept of Navajo culture, the story tells of the animals and insects making their way from the flooded Third World to the beautiful Fourth World, so lovely that the Spirit Being created the Dineh (Navajo) to share it with them. Then the Spirit Being teaches the people everything, including the Blessing Way, to keep them healthy and in harmony with nature. When one woman becomes so obsessed by the beauty of her weaving that she loses the Middle Way, only Spider Woman can release her spirit and save her. The book is lavishly and mystically illustrated by a Navajo artist.

627.   Gerson, Mary-Joan. **People of the Corn: A Mayan Story**. Ill. Carla Golembe. Boston: Little, Brown, 1995. Unp. $15.95. LC 94-18140. ISBN 0-316-30854-4.

Drawn from the sacred book of the Maya, these creation stories, which are still told in Guatemala today, center on the gods' desire to form creatures who will thank and praise their creators. The animals they make cannot talk. The wooden people they make have no hearts to rejoice. Finally, the Grandmother of Light causes white and yellow corn to grow, and from that the gods Plumed Serpent and Heart of Sky create human beings. Handsome, brightly colored pictures displaying a folk-art technique have motifs from Mayan glyphs and cloth.

628.   Goble, Paul. **Remaking the Earth: A Creation Story from the Great Plains of North America**. Ill. author. New York: Orchard Books, 1996. Unp. $15.95. LC 96-4243. ISBN 0-531-08874-X.

The Algonquin "Earth Diver" creation myth describes how the First World was flooded with water, and how the surviving water birds and animals begged the Earth Maker (the Creator, Great Spirit, or God) to again form land. Taking a bit of mud from the depths, brought up by the tiny coot, he re-created the world on the back of Grandmother Turtle and produced all of its glories: mountains, plains, lakes, plants, animals, thunderbirds, and so on; and, last of all, man and woman. Earth Maker then promised the people that he would be with them always but that only earth can remain forever. The dignified narrative is reinforced by sweeping, emotional, masterful illustrations.

629.   Jackson, Ellen. **The Precious Gift: A Navaho Creation Myth**. Ill. Woodleigh Marx Hubbard. New York: Simon and Schuster, 1996. Unp. $16.00. LC 94-16709. ISBN 0-689-80480-6.

When the first people come up to earth from the underworld, they have no water. First Man sends various animals to search for some, but each becomes distracted, fails, and is punished by having to live in some particular way forever after. Finally, the lowly snail succeeds and is rewarded with a lovely, protective shell. This entertaining pourquoi story has large, colorful, stylized pictures and an author's note that discusses Navaho creation and evolution myths.

630.   Pijoan, Teresa. **Healers on the Mountain: Traditional Native American Stories for Cleansing, Healing, Testing, and Preserving the Old Ways**. Little Rock, AR: August House, 1993. 219p. $10.00pa. LC 93-29465. ISBN 0-87483-269-1.

The importance of spiritual harmony is the basis for healing in these stories from many cultures, among them Cherokee, Pueblo, Hopi, Pima, Iroquois, and Navajo. They are divided into sections concerning dreams and medicine, myths, chants, vision quests, and healing myths. The clear, lively text is written in the matter-of-fact, condensed style of the Native American storyteller. All the stories are short and to the point. The introductory material and story notes are excellent.

631.   Rodanas, Kristina. **Dance of the Sacred Circle: A Native American Tale**. Ill. author. Boston: Little, Brown, 1994. Unp. $14.95. LC 93-19626. ISBN 0-316-75358-0.

Inspired by a Blackfoot myth and illustrated with reproductions of sweeping paintings with vigorous lines, the creation of the horse as a companion and helper for the Plains Native Americans by the Great Chief in the Sky is retold as the story of an orphan boy. When the buffalo herds wander away from the hunting ground, he goes alone to seek aid from the Great Chief. Impressed by the child's courage, the Great Chief molds a creature from mud and calls upon the trees, birds, and animals to give it some of their special qualities. It becomes a noble horse, which multiplies instantaneously to provide swift mounts for all the buffalo hunters.

632.   Rodanas, Kristina. **The Eagle's Song: A Tale from the Pacific Northwest**. Ill. author. Boston: Little, Brown, 1995. Unp. $15.95. LC 94-6596. ISBN 0-316-75375-0.

Ermine, a young Native American boy, is given a drum by a wise, giant mother eagle, who bemoans the isolation and selfishness of his people. This gift creates a hypnotic music, drawing the scattered groups together, inspiring them to dance and feast, and encouraging them to celebrate their blessings and share in life. Reproductions of powerful, action-filled paintings add power and meaning to the story.

633.   Taylor, Carrie J. **Bones in the Basket: Native Stories of the Origin of People**. Ill. author. Plattsburgh, NY: Tundra Books of Northern New York, 1994. 32p. $17.95. LC 94-61786. ISBN 0-88776-327-8.

How human life on earth began is interpreted by the Zuni, Mandan, Cree, Chuckchee, Osage, Mohawk, and Modod nations, inhabitants of the United States, Canada, and Siberia. Creation methods vary in each myth, but all emphasize that the earth was prepared especially for people, who consequently have a responsibility to preserve the land and its animals. The creator is known by many names: Wisagatcak, Giant Beaver, Big Raven, Spider Woman, or Grandfather Sun. The storyteller-style narrative is illustrated with reproductions of dramatic, mysterious paintings.

634.   Taylor, Carrie J. **How We Saw the World: Nine Native Stories of the Way Things Began**. Ill. author. Plattsburgh, NY: Tundra Books of Northern New York, 1993. 32p. $8.95pa. LC 92-83960. ISBN 0-88776-373-1.

The sacred relationship of Native Americans to the creator and to nature is at the heart of these myths from the Algonquin, Tohono, O'oodhan, Bella Coola, Micmac, Blackfoot, Oneida, Kiowa, Mohawk, and Cheyenne nations. The origins of natural beauties, such as Niagara Falls and butterflies; disasters, such as tornadoes and endless winters; and faithful servants, such as the horse and dog, are among the subjects. Reproductions of eerie, spectacular paintings illustrate the dignified text.

635.   Young, Ed. **Moon Mother**. Ill. author. New York: Willa Perlman Books, 1993. Unp. $15.00. LC 92-14981. ISBN 0-06-021301-9.

In this Native American creation story, a spirit man sees earth's beauty and decides to live there. Being lonely, he creates all types of animals, birds, and fish. Then he fashions men in his own image and teaches them living skills. A spirit woman also descends from the sky, and eventually she and the spirit man return to the house of the spirit people, leaving behind a baby girl to marry the chief of the men and found the human race. The spirit woman becomes the moon. Double-page illustrations in rich pastels reflect the mood of supernatural mystery.

Older and Noteworthy

Other helpful titles about Native American spirituality include *Waterless Mountain* by Laura Adam Armer (Longmans, Green, 1931); *And Me, Coyote* by Betty Baker (Macmillan, 1982); *A God on Every Mountaintop* by Byrd Baylor (Scribner, 1981); *The Sacred Path* by John Bierhorst (Morrow, 1983); *The Legend of the Bluebonnet* by Tomie dePaola (Putnam, 1983); *Buffalo Woman* (Bradbury, 1984), *The Gift of the Sacred Dog* (Bradbury, 1980), *The Great Race* (Bradbury, 1985), and *Star Boy* (Bradbury, 1983) by Paul Goble; *The Boy Who Made Dragonfly* by Tony Hillerman (University of New Mexico Press, 1986), *Arrow to the Sun* by Gerald McDermott (Viking, 1974), and *Ceremony—In the Circle of Life* by White Deer of Autumn (Raintree, 1983).

Chapter Fourteen

Buddhism

636.   Demi. **Buddha**. Ill. author. New York: Henry Holt, 1996. Unp. $18.95. LC 95-16906. ISBN 0-8050-4203-2.

In a lovely blend of myth and historical fact, Siddhartha's life unfolds: his unusual birth, erupting from the right side of Queen Mahamaya, after a prophetic dream; his exemplary childhood, marriage to a beautiful princess, decision to leave his family and seek truth, and enlightenment under the bodhi tree; his Four Noble Truths and Noble Eightfold Path; his life as a begging monk with his disciples; and his entry into nirvana at death. All this is interwoven with stories of miraculous events and wisdom tales. The delicately detailed illustrations, inspired by Indian miniature paintings and other Asian art, shine like jewels.

637.   Erricker, Clive, and Jane Erricker. **Buddhist Festivals**. Celebrate Series. Crystal Lake, IL: Heinemann Library, 1997. 48p. $13.95. LC 97-2413. ISBN 0-431-06965-4.

Buddhism and its general precepts are described in a thorough introductory section. The festivals are separated by locale and type of Buddhism (Theravada, Mahayana, Tibetan, Japanese, and Western Buddhist Order) and include Uposatha Days; Wesak, or Visakha; Poson and Asala Days in Sri Lanka; Kathina, Hana Matsuri, Obon, and Higan in Japan; Buddha, Dharma, and Sangha Days in the Western Buddhist Order; and more. Good color photographs supplement the clear text. A glossary, reading list, and index are included.

638.   Ganeri, Anita. **Buddhist**. Beliefs and Cultures Series. New York: Children's Press, 1997. 32p. $19.50. LC 96-4409. ISBN 0-516-08086-5.

This attractive presentation includes short sections about the biography of the Buddha; Buddhist theology, with the Four Noble Truths, the Middle Path, and the Three Jewels; the Theravada Mahayana, Tantric, and Zen branches of Buddhism; worship, especially in Tibet; monastic life; sacred places and scriptures; festivals; a Jataka tale; and crafts. The color photographs are excellent, and the format is varied and interesting. A glossary and index are included.

639. Hewitt, Catherine. **Buddhism**. World Religions Series. New York: Thomson Learning, 1995. 48p. $16.98. LC 95-1942. ISBN 1-56847-375-3.

A more thorough description of the life of monks and nuns inside and outside the monastery, and a more extensive examination of Buddhist theology distinguish this book from the others cited. It also includes a short history of the faith, a biography of the Buddha, a discussion of the various branches of Buddhism, and a description of the festivals. Helpful color photographs, sidebars of additional information, and a glossary, reading list, and index are included.

640. Kalman, Bobbie. **Tibet**. The Lands, Peoples, and Cultures Series. New York: Crabtree, 1990. 32p. $14.36. LC 93-27371. ISBN 0-86505-213-1.

Because Tibet is the home of Lamaist Buddhism, religion is the cornerstone of Tibetan culture, despite the Chinese incursion and the exile of the Dalai Lama. The history of Lamaist Buddhism, marriage customs, the sacred altar in every home (even a nomad's tent), prayer flags, thangkas, mandalas, the monastic life, the Dalai Lama, and traditional festivals are briefly described. The book has appealing color photographs, a glossary, and an index.

641. Penney, Sue. **Buddhism**. Discovering Religions Series. Austin, TX: Raintree Steck-Vaughan, 1997. 48p. $16.98. LC 96-3733. ISBN 0-8172-4395-X.

This informative, understandable, overall survey examines Buddhist teaching, including the Three Jewels, the three signs of being, the Four Noble Truths, the Noble Eightfold Path, and nirvana; Mahayana, Zen, Pure Land, and Tibetan Buddhism; places of worship; symbols; monks and nuns; customs; and festivals held specifically in Thailand, Sri Lanka, and Japan. Significant teachings and quotations are set off in yellow boxes; new words are set off in brown boxes. The book has good color photographs and an index.

642. Roth, Susan L. **Buddha**. New York: Doubleday, 1994. 32p. $15.95. LC 93-8240. ISBN 0-385-31072-2.

In a legendary tone and poetic language, the story of Siddhartha's life is chronicled: his luxurious upbringing, his beautiful wife, his protection from the ills of the world, his discovery of suffering and death, his shedding of all the trappings of wealth, and his search for inner peace. His kindness, gentleness, and love are stressed. The illustrations, inspired by Buddhist manuscripts, are cut-paper collages, bright and primitive in feeling.

643. Zerner, Amy, and Jessie Spicer Zerner. **Zen ABC**. Boston: Charles Tuttle, 1993. Unp. $14.95. ISBN 0-8048-1806-1.

Each alphabet letter is associated with a Zen-related word, which is then described by a haiku, koan, or quotation from Zen classical literature and illustrated with a reproduction of a painting or collage. The artwork is beautifully framed and creative. The concepts are difficult, however, and would require adult assistance in their interpretation. Included are such terms as *awakening, cadence, enlightenment*, and *nirvana*.

Dalai Lama

644.   Gibb, Christopher. **The Dalai Lama: The Exiled Leader of the People of Tibet and Tireless Worker for World Peace**. People Who Have Helped the World Series. Milwaukee, WI: Gareth Stevens, 1990. 68p. $13.95. LC 89-43119. ISBN 0-8368-0224-1.

The Dalai Lama's exceptional intelligence, humanitarianism, respect for all peoples and religions, dedication to nonviolence, and desire for peace and harmony are stressed in this factual, uplifting biography. A capsule history of Tibet, including its oppression by the Chinese; a discussion of how the dalai lamas are chosen; and an overview of Buddhism are included. The book has a bibliography of books and magazine articles, a list of United States organizations concerned with Tibet, a glossary, a chronology, and an index.

645.   Pandell, Karen, and Barry Bryant. **Learning from the Dalai Lama: Secrets of the Wheel of Time**. New York: Dutton, 1995. 40p. $16.99. LC 95-6984. ISBN 0-525-45063-7.

Included in this work are discussions of the beliefs of Buddhism, the life of Siddhartha, the search for and discovery of the Fourteenth Dalai Lama, monks and nuns, the sand mandala ceremony and the significance of its parts, and the twelve-day ceremony with the Dalai Lama himself as the Ritual Master. The book contains elucidative color photographs, a glossary, and an index.

646.   Stewart, Whitney. **The 14th Dalai Lama: Spiritual Leader of Tibet**. Minneapolis, MN: Lerner, 1996. 128p. $23.95. LC 95-17221. ISBN 0-8225-4926-3.

The personal contact of the author with his subject gives warmth and authority to this suspenseful and absorbing biography, illustrated with photographs. It covers the birth of the Dalai Lama, Tenzin Gyatso, in a cow shed in 1933 to an ordinary Tibetan farm family, through his work today, liberalizing and reorganizing his government-in-exile and awaiting the day when Tibet is free from China. The history of the dalai lamas is discussed, and extensive quotations from the Dalai Lama's writings are included.

Jataka Tales

The Jataka tales are stories about the Buddha's previous incarnations or ones told by the Buddha. They were originally considered as part of the canon of Buddhist scriptures.

647.   Crofts, Trudy, and Ken McKeon. **The Hunter and the Quail**. Ill. Rachel Garbett. Jataka Tales Series. Berkeley, CA: Dharma, 1993. Unp. $7.95pa. ISBN 0-89800-250-8.

The Sage, a wise quail, instructs his fellow birds to cooperate when the hunter's net is thrown over them and escape by all flapping their wings at once. The scheme works perfectly until some of the quail begin complaining and criticizing one another. The Sage and the birds who continue to trust one another depart, and the quarrelers are easily netted. The vivid text has bold, bright illustrations and a helpful introduction.

648. Demi. **Buddha Tales**. Ill. author. New York: Henry Holt, 1997. Unp. $16.95. LC 96-31253. ISBN 0-8050-4886-3.

In a stunning presentation, the moral fables "The Lion King," "The Turtle and the Geese," "The Black Bull," "The Beautiful Parrots," "The Cunning Wolf," "The Little Grey Donkey," "The Clever Crab," "The Monkey King," "The Golden Goose," "The Magic Pig," and "The Magic Elephant" are gorgeously illustrated with spirit and delicacy. Both pictures and text are presented in two colors, gold against midnight blue.

649. Ernst, Judith. **The Golden Goose King: A Tale Told by the Buddha**. Ill. author. Chapel Hill, NC: Parvardigar Press, 1995. Unp. $19.95. LC 94-74107. ISBN 0-9644362-0-5.

This story of the Buddha's incarnation as king of a huge flock of golden geese describes how he is captured by a fowler at the behest of the king and queen of Benares. Forgiving them, the Buddha/Goose King instructs the rulers on moral law and righteousness before returning to his flock. The tale is told with beauty and dignity, and illustrated with reproductions of elegant gouache paintings. The book contains an excellent foreword.

650. Harman, Michael, ill. **The Parrot and the Fig Tree**. Jataka Tales Series. Oakland, CA: Dharma, 1990. Unp. $7.95pa. LC 86-19769. ISBN 0-89800-142-0.

In a Job-like story, a parrot demonstrates the quality of loyal friendship by remaining with a fig tree that once nourished him but has been devastated by Shakra, king of the heavenly beings, to test his devotion. Unmoved by the advice of Shakra, who has assumed the form of a goose, the parrot refuses to seek a home elsewhere and leave his friend. Pleased by the parrot's selflessness, Shakra restores the tree to its former fruitfulness. The illustrations are simple and colorful.

651. Hodges, Margaret. **The Golden Deer**. Ill. Daniel San Souci. New York: Scribner, 1992. Unp. $14.95. LC 90-42873. ISBN 0-684-19218-7.

This charming, tender legend of the Buddha, who was reputed to have come to earth at many times and in many shapes before he came as a man, tells of a magnificent stag, the Banyan Deer, whose herd is captured and confined to provide hunting for a powerful king. When the stag comes to sacrifice himself in the place of a pregnant doe and pleads in a human voice for the lives of all creatures, the king is so affected that he vows to protect all of them. The pictures are beautiful and dreamy.

652. Meller, Eric, ill. **The Rabbit Who Overcame Fear**. Jataka Tales Series. Oakland, CA: Dharma, 1991. Unp. $7.95pa. LC 90-48400. ISBN 0-89800-211-7.

In a story similar to "Chicken Little," with plain but pleasant illustrations, a rabbit is awakened by a thump, fears the earth is breaking, and panics many other animals into running after him. A wise lion stops them, identifies the thump as a fallen mango, and counsels them to investigate first before giving in to fright and flight.

653.   Meller, Eric, ill. **The Value of Friends**. Jataka Tales Series. Berkeley, CA: Dharma, 1990. Unp. $7.95pa. LC 86-24164. ISBN 0-89800-154-4.

More than 2,000 years ago, the Buddha told this story to illustrate respect for the bonds of friendship, compassion, and goodness. A lady and gentleman hawk have young children who are threatened by hungry men trying to smoke them out of their nest. Fortunately, the hawks have an osprey, a turtle, and a lion as caring friends, and they quench the fire and drive away the men. The formal, didactic text is sumptuously illustrated with gleaming colors, highlighted in gold.

654.   Mipham, Lama. **Great Gift and the Wish-Fulfilling Gem**. Ill. Terry McSweeney. Jataka Tales Series. Oakland, CA: Dharma, 1990. Unp. $7.95pa. LC 86-19767. ISBN 0-89800-157-9.

A compassionate young man, appalled by the conditions of the poor, sets out to find a wish-fulfilling gem to provide for them. On his journey, he overcomes snakes, cannibals, and the Naga monsters by the power of his loving kindness. He returns with the magic jewel and teaches the people kindness and generosity. Colorful, primitively styled pictures accompany the smoothly flowing text.

655.   Stone, Karen. **Golden Foot**. Ill. Rosalyn White. Jataka Tales Series. Berkeley, CA: Dharma, 1993. Unp. $7.95. ISBN 0-89800-252-4.

When the golden-coated Royal Stag is snared by a hunter, his mate offers her own life as his ransom. Deeply affected, the hunter frees both of them. Cautioning the hunter never to harm any living creature, the Royal Stag rewards him with three wish-fulfilling gems. Large, two-dimensional pictures illustrate this simply written tale.

Older and Noteworthy

Two other recommended books concerning Buddhism are the young adult novel *The Eternal Spring of Mr. Ito* by Sheila Garrigue (Bradbury, 1985) and *First Snow* by Helen Coutant (Knopf, 1974), a book for young children.

Chapter Fifteen

Ɦinӄuism

656.   Easwaran, Eknath. **The Monkey and the Mango: Stories of My Granny**. Ill. Ilka Jerabek. Tomales, CA: Nilgiri Press, 1996. 29p. $14.95. ISBN 0-915132-82-6.

Hindu precepts are presented simply and beautifully in the stories a wise grandmother in Kerala, South India, tells her grandson. Tales of native animals, such as elephants, red ants, and cobras, teach lessons about creation, trust in God, patience, kindness, and so on. Dreamy, softly colored illustrations suit the half-fantastic subject matter.

657.   Ganeri, Anita. **Hindu**. Beliefs and Cultures Series. New York: Children's Press, 1996. 32p. $19.50. LC 94-47344. ISBN 0-516-08076-8.

This discussion of Hinduism is presented in large print and illustrated generously. It includes summaries of the basic beliefs, the principal gods and goddesses, worship, sacred writings, festivals, and customs. Crafts, a recipe, a calendar, a glossary, and an index supplement the book.

658.   Ganeri, Anita. **What Do We Know About Hinduism?** New York: Peter Bedrick, 1996. 45p. $18.95. LC 95-51827. ISBN 0-87226-385-1.

In a text suitable for middle elementary ages, this overview of Hinduism includes discussion of its origin and extent, the influence of Aryan gods, basic beliefs, principal deities, family life, worship, holy men, sacred scriptures and places, festivals, medicine, art, music, and dance. Small blocks of text are separated by color photographs, drawings, maps, and artwork. The book has an excellent timeline, glossary, and index.

659.   Godden, Rumer. **Premlata and the Festival of Lights**. Ill. Ian Andrew. New York: Greenwillow, 1997. 60p. $15.00. LC 96-2756. ISBN 0-688-15136-1.

In this novel of India for middle elementary ages, a poor widow has had to sell almost everything, including her deepas, the tiny clay lamps used to celebrate Diwali. Prem, her seven-year-old daughter and a fervent devotee of Kali, is determined to somehow buy more deepas to honor the goddess and has a series of frightening and exciting adventures on her quest, which culminates in a happy ending. Belief in Kali's power suffuses Prem's life, and Hindu ways of worship, even in the humblest home, are described. Soft-lined, black-and-white pencil drawings suit the mood of the story.

660. Kadodwala, Dilip, and Paul Gateshill. **Hindu Festivals**. Celebrate Series. Crystal Lake, IL: Reed, 1997. 48p. $13.95. LC 97-2412. ISBN 0-431-06966-2.

This thorough discussion of the major holidays includes Divali, Holi, Raksha Bandhan, Mahashivaratri, Durgapuja, Ramnavami, Janmashtami, Ratha Yatra, Vasant Panchami, and Ganesha Chaturti. Also discussed are the deities and certain myths associated with each holiday, and ways of celebration and decoration. Many eye-catching color photographs add to the joyful spirit. A glossary, reading list, and index are included.

661. Kadodwala, Dilip. **Hinduism**. World Religions Series. New York: Thomson Learning, 1995. 48p. $16.98. ISBN 1-56847-377-X.

In this account of Sanatan dharma (the eternal religion), a Hindu is born into a tradition, a way of life, and certain beliefs and practices. To facilitate worship, Brahma, the Supreme Being, is given many forms or images because he is everywhere. The principles of karma, samsara, and moksha are discussed, along with the sacred places, holy scriptures, stages of life, mandirs and puja, festivals, and customs. A short review of Hindu history is given as well, but with little mention of the principal deities. The book has good color photographs, a glossary with a pronunciation guide, a book list, and an index.

662. Kadodwala, Dilip. **Holi**. A World of Holidays Series. Austin, TX: Raintree Steck-Vaughan, 1997. 31p. $14.98. LC 96-42308. ISBN 0-8172-4610-X.

This festival, in which Hindus thank the gods for the upcoming harvest and welcome spring, is celebrated with light and fire, such as bonfires and diva lamps, and fun and mischief, such as tricking family and friends and throwing colored powders upon them. In some areas, fairs, feasts, and parades take place. Vishnu, especially in his avatar of Krishna, is a central figure. Good color photographs complement the lively text; and crafts, a glossary, a reading list, and an index are included.

663. Kagda, Falaq. **India**. Festivals of the World Series. Milwaukee, WI: Gareth Stevens, 1997. 32p. $13.95. LC 96-27330. ISBN 0-8368-1683-8.

A large-print text with many color photographs features Divali, Holi, and Ponggal, and describes the ways of celebrating them. Included are lights, colored powders, and decorated cows, and the traditional stories associated with each. A game, a craft, a recipe, a reading and video list, a glossary, an index, and a holiday calendar are included.

664. Krishnaswami, Uma. **The Broken Tusk: Stories of the Hindu God Ganesha**. Ill. Maniam Selven. North Haven, CT: Linnet Books, 1996. 101p. $19.95. LC 96-22410. ISBN 0-208-02242-5.

Legends of the elephant-headed deity include how he is created by Parvati, how he gets his head, how he learns kindness, how he chastises Chandra the moon for ridiculing him, how he fights with demons, and so on. Written in an easy, folkloric style, the stories are short and lively, and illustrated with witty pen-and-ink drawings. Excellent introductory material discusses Ganesha and Hindu mythology. The book contains a glossary, a list of sources, a pronunciation guide, a list of Ganesha's various names, and a who's who of gods, demons, kings, and people.

665.   Penney, Sue. **Hinduism**. Discovering Religions Series. Austin, TX: Raintree Steck-Vaughan, 1997. 48p. $16.98. LC 96-6981. ISBN 0-8172-4397-6.

Among the topics covered are identification of the principal gods and goddesses; the holy books; worship at home and in the temple; holy places and rivers; basic beliefs about dharma, reincarnation, karma, and moksha; yoga; important festivals; castes; and birth, marriage, death, and other customs. Scripture quotations, prayers, new words, and other information are set apart in boxes for a more readable format. The book contains useful color photographs and an index.

Older and Noteworthy

Other worthy titles about Hinduism include *Yougga Finds Mother Teresa* by Kirsten Bang (Seabury, 1983), *The Adventures of Rama* by Milo Beach (Freer Gallery of Art, 1983), *Ganesh* by Malcolm A. Bosse (Crowell, 1981), *Seasons of Splendor* by Jeffrey Madhur (Atheneum, 1985), and *The Slaying of the Dragon* by Rosaline Verven (Andre Deutsch, 1987).

Chapter Sixteen

Islam

666.   Chazi, Suhaib Hamid. **Ramadan**. Ill. Omar Rayyan. New York: Holiday House, 1996. Unp. $15.95. LC 96-5154. ISBN 0-8234-1254-7.

Illustrated with soft, lush charm, the pleasant text follows the holiday celebration as experienced by Hakeem, a young boy, and his family. Although they do not live in an Arabic setting, they demonstrate that Ramadan has the same meaning and practice throughout the Islamic world. Daytime fasting, prayer and worship, cleaning and purifying the mind and body, forgiving and asking forgiveness, and donating to charity strengthen and unite the community.

667.   Child, John. **The Rise of Islam**. Biographical History Series. New York: Peter Bedrick Books, 1995. 64p. $17.95. LC 94-37633. ISBN 0-87226-116-6.

Quoting primary and secondary sources for added interest and enrichment, this overview of the Islamic world includes biographical information about Muhammad, Umar, Ali, Ayesha, Saladin, Suleiman, and many more important historical figures, ending with Muhammar Gaddafi. Tracing the ebb and flow of Muslim influence, the briskly written text is arranged in blocks for easy readability, illustrated with many color photographs and maps, and indexed.

668.   Husain, Sharukh. **What Do We Know About Islam?** What Do We Know About Series. New York: Peter Bedrick Books, 1996. 45p. $18.95. ISBN 0-87226-388-6.

In an eye-appealing format generously illustrated with color photographs and artwork, many aspects of the Muslim religion and culture are discussed. Included are sections about the Qurun, Islamic law, Sunna, the Five Pillars, and Ramadan; the origin and spread of the faith; prayer and worship; the haj; art and calligraphy; the calendar; and daily living. The text is clear and interesting, and the book contains a glossary and an index.

669. Kerven, Rosalind. **Id-ul-Fitr**. A World of Holidays Series. Austin, TX: Raintree Steck-Vaughan, 1997. 31p. $14.98. LC 96-42307. ISBN 0-8172-4609-6.

Excellent color photographs reflect the solemnity, beauty, and joy of not only Ramadan and its climactic celebration of Id-ul-Fitr, but also of the Islamic faith. The cheerful, easy-to-understand text discusses all aspects of the holiday: greeting cards, foods, feasting, new clothes, special fairs, and entertainment. Crafts, a reading list, an index, and a glossary are included.

670. Knight, Khadijah. **Islam**. World Religions Series. New York: Thomson Learning, 1995. 48p. $16.98. LC 95-30445. ISBN 1-56847-378-8.

Fact-filled, handsomely presented, and illustrated with good color photographs, this overview discusses the tenets of Islam, its history and geographic distribution, Sunnis and Shiites, the Koran and other writings, prayer, Ramadan, customs, dietary laws, mosques and imams, and the haj. The writing is firm and uncompromising, and the book includes a timeline, the yearly calendar, a glossary, a book list, and an index.

671. Knight, Khadijah. **Islamic Festivals**. Celebrate! Series. Crystal Lake, IL: Heinemann Library, 1997. 48p. $13.95. LC 96-53257. ISBN 0-431-06964-6.

Material about the Islamic faith, including its Five Pillars, the Koran and hadith (sayings of Muhammad), and salah (prayer), precedes the descriptions of the holidays, many of which are associated with events in Muhammad's life. These include Maulid, Laylat-ul-Isra, wal Mi'raj, and Laylat-ul-Barat. Ramadan, Laylat-ul-Qadr, and Id-ul-Fitr are also discussed, along with the hajj pilgrimage and other events and aspects of the faith. The text is easy to read and has a serious, laudatory tone. The book is illustrated with good color photographs, and includes a glossary, reading list, and index.

672. MacMillan, Dianne M. **Ramadan and Id al-Fitr**. Best Holiday Books Series. Springfield, NJ: Enslow, 1994. 48p. $16.95. LC 93-46185. ISBN 0-89490-502-3.

A summary of Muhammad's life, the Five Pillars of Islam, the Koran, and ways of worship introduces the material on Ramadan, its meaning, and observance, and Id al-Fitr, the festival that follows Ramadan. The easy-to-read text is well illustrated with black-and-white and color photographs. The book includes a helpful pronunciation guide to Arabic terms and an index.

673. Matthews, Mary. **Magid Fasts for Ramadan**. Ill. E. B. Lewis. New York: Clarion Books, 1996. 48p. $15.95. LC 95-10452. ISBN 0-395-66589-2.

Seven-year-old Magid wants with all his heart to fast. He secretly promises Allah that he will, despite the fact that he is too young and his parents will disapprove. After his sister finds him giving his lunch to the geese, she tattles. The adults chastise Magid for being dishonest and disobedient but praise his desire to practice Islam fully. The sympathetic narrative for early elementary children explains Ramadan and gives warm insight into Muslim family life. The book is illustrated with large, thoughtful, realistic watercolors, and includes a note about the Islamic faith and an excellent glossary.

674.   Oppenheim, Shulamith Levey. **And the Earth Trembled: The Creation of Adam and Eve**. Ill. Neil Waldman. San Diego, CA: Harcourt Brace, 1996. Unp. $16.00. LC 95-30829. ISBN 0-15-200025-9.

God, feeling lonely, decides to fashion a companion with flesh like an animal and a brain like an angel. Fearing that this creation, man, will be a killer and despoiler, the angels warn against him, the earth cries out in anguish as the clay is wrested out, and the soul cringes when ordered to enter man's body. Nevertheless, all obey God, whose purpose is to prepare the way for Muhammad, his messenger, to lead all humankind to truth. Adam and Eve marry and live 500 years in paradise. The impressionist illustrations resemble the work of van Gogh in their mystery and power.

675.   Oppenheim, Shulamith Levey. **The Hundredth Name**. Ill. Michael Hays. Honesdale, PA: Boyds Mills Press, 1995. Unp. $14.95. LC 94-72255. ISBN 1-56397-183-6.

In a tenderly told story, a seven-year-old Muslim boy living in Egypt is sad because the family camel, his faithful friend, always looks downcast and unhappy. Because men can know only the ninety-nine names of Allah but not the hundredth, the boy prays one night that Allah will reveal the hidden name to the camel and make him special. The next morning, the camel's head is high, and his expression happy and wise. The pictures are misty and softly colored.

676.   Oppenheim, Shulamith Levey. **Iblis: An Islamic Tale**. Ill. Ed Young. San Diego, CA: Harcourt Brace Jovanovich, 1994. Unp. $15.95. LC 92-15060. ISBN 0-15-238016-7.

Iblis (Satan) has been trying to enter paradise for 500 years. With a promise of eternal life and beauty, he tricks a peacock into slipping him in, with the aid of a serpent. Iblis appears to Eve as a gorgeous angel and offers her the same rewards if she will eat a wheat tree branch. Her delight in it convinces Adam, who eats also, and they are cast out of paradise by God. The artwork is brilliant and mystical.

677.   Penney, Sue. **Islam**. Discovering Religions Series. Austin, TX: Raintree Steck-Vaughan, 1997. 48p. $16.98. LC 96-3729. ISBN 0-8172-4394-1.

This thorough, factual overview includes sections about Muhammad's life; the Koran; the mosque, worship, and the hajj; Ramadan and other celebrations; family life and customs; and the history and influence of the religion. Dividing the text are boxes with new words and their definitions, prayers, quotations from the Koran, and other information, as well as color photographs and maps. An index is included.

678.   Tames, Richard. **Muslim**. Beliefs and Cultures Series. New York: Children's Press, 1995. 32p. $19.50. LC 94-47347. ISBN 0-516-08078-4.

This readable and informative overview of Islam for middle elementary ages includes a biography of Muhammad, as well as information about the Five Pillars and the Koran; prayers, mosques, and the pilgrimage to Mecca; holy days; and family customs. A few craft projects relating to Islam and many good color photographs add to the interest. The book is indexed.

679.   Tames, Richard. **The Rise of Islam**. History Through Sources Series. Crystal Lake, IL: Rigby Interactive Library, 1996. 48p. $13.95. LC 95-20616. ISBN 1-57572-010-8.

After an introduction that briefly describes the religion, a condensed history of its spread proceeds from Muhammad through the decline of Isfahan in the 1700s. Topics include the Umayyads, Abbasid, the Crusades, Suleiman the Magnificent and the Ottoman Empire, and the Mughal emperors. Islamic scientific and cultural contributions to the world and ways of life over the centuries are part of the additional information, augmented by quotations from primary and secondary historical sources. The book has excellent color photographs, maps, and art reproductions, as well as a timeline, glossary, and index.

680.   Wormser, Richard. **American Islam: Growing Up Muslim in America**. New York: Walker, 1994. 130p. $16.85. LC 94-12335. ISBN 0-8027-8344-9.

This is an absorbing combination of the history of Islam and extensive quotations from young American Muslims about the value of their religion and the prejudice they have experienced. Part I deals with Muslims in general, and Part II with the African American community, including the Nation of Islam. Complementing a well-organized and clear presentation are an index, bibliography, and black-and-white illustrations.

Older and Noteworthy

Additional titles of interest about Islam are a history book, *The Sword of the Prophet* by Robert Goldston (Dial, 1979), and a young adult novel, *Shabanu* by Suzanne Staples (Knopf, 1989).

Chapter Seventeen

Other Religions

Maori

681.   Lattimore, Deborah Nourse. **Punga the Goddess of Ugly**. Ill. author. San Diego, CA: Harcourt Brace Jovanovich, 1993. Unp. $14.95. LC 92-23191. ISBN 0-15-292862-6.

Twin Maori girls are learning to do the haka dance, trying to feel fierce and powerful as they stick out their tongues and try not to seem silly or ugly. Punga, the goddess of everything ugly, captures those who do not dance the haka beautifully and seriously. The girls encounter Punga in the forest and dance so forcefully that they rescue Lizard and Mudfish from her dominion by inspiring them also to dance with grace and beauty. Lizard and Mudfish are freed to rejoin their own deities, Tane, god of the earth, and Tangeroa, god of the sea. The illustrations are swirling and eerie. Notes and a glossary are appended.

African Religions

682.   Dee, Ruby. **Tower to Heaven**. Ill. Jennifer Bent. New York: Henry Holt, 1991. Unp. $14.95. LC 90-34131. ISBN 0-8050-1460-8.

The relationship between a talkative old woman and the great god of the sky, at a time when he was still close to earth, is the subject of this amusing folktale from Ghana. Because the woman continuously pokes him carelessly with her pestle as she is grinding grain, he flees high and higher into the heavens, but even then she continues to shout up to him as she stands on a shaky tower of mortar bowls. Bright, primitively styled pictures enliven the story.

683.   Gerson, Mary-Joan. **How Night Came from the Sea: A Story from Brazil**. Ill. Carla Golembe. Boston: Little, Brown, 1994. Unp. $15.95. LC 93-20054. ISBN 0-316-30855-2.

The Candomble religion of Bahia worships Iemanja (a form of the deity Yemoja, revered by the Yorubas of West Africa), a sea goddess who links the former black slaves in Brazil to their African heritage. In this myth about the beginning of time, when there was only daylight, Iemanja's daughter, who has married an earth man, longs for some restful darkness to relieve the constant brilliance of the sun. Her husband sends emissaries into the ocean to appeal to Iemanja for a "bag of night," which she willingly supplies. Brilliant folk-art illustrations further animate the story.

684.   Knappert, Jan. **Kings, Gods, and Spirits from African Mythology**. Ill. Francesca Pelizzoli. World Mythology Series. New York: Peter Bedrick Books, 1993. 92p. $24.95. LC 93-12903. ISBN 0-87226-916-7.

Creation stories from throughout the continent include those from the Yoruba of Nigeria, the Bakuba of Zaire, the Pangwe of Cameroon, the Zulu of South Africa, the Swahili of East Africa, and many more. Stories of the earth; human beings; the sun, moon, and stars; divine beings, such as the Moonprince of the Basotho and Heise of the Bushmen; the spirit world; and the land of the dead are told with animation and powerfully illustrated in color and black and white. The book includes explanations of the symbolism, source material, and an index.

Chinese Religions

685.   Nomura, Nokiko. **I Am Shinto**. Religions of the World Series. New York: PowerKids/Rosen, 1996. 24p. $13.95. LC 96-6979. ISBN 0-8239-2380-0.

Yaskuko of Honolulu tells of Kami spirits of ancestors and nature; shrines and Kami Dana, or ancestor worship, at home; the New Year celebration; marriage customs; the 7-5-3 Festival, which celebrates the health and future of a child; and Seijin-no-Hi, or coming of age. The book is illustrated with photographs and includes a glossary and index.

686.   Sanders, Tao Tao. **Dragons, Gods, and Spirits from Chinese Mythology**. Ill. Johnny Pau. World Mythology Series. New York: Peter Bedrick Books, 1994. 132p. $24.95. LC 94-8354. ISBN 0-87226-922-1.

These vividly told tales are amalgams of the pre-Buddhist Chinese religions of many gods, representing various aspects of nature and the mysteries of the universe; Confucianism, which concerns human relationships; mystical Taoism; and Buddhism. Themes include creation and creators, gods, heroes and heroines, spirits, demons, ghosts, and morality. The book is elegantly illustrated in the Chinese artistic tradition, with subtle colors and high-quality black-and-white drawings, and includes the sources and symbolism of the stories and an index.

687.   Zhang, Song Nan. **Five Heavenly Emperors: Chinese Myths of Creation**. Ill. author. Plattsburgh: Tundra Books of Northern New York, 1994. 36p. $17.95. LC 93-61794. ISBN 0-88776-338-3.

Stories of the gods are retold with dignity. Included are Yang, Yin, and Pangu, creators of the universe; the five heavenly emperors and the forces they control; Nuwa, the goddess who made human beings from clay; Youchao, the god who taught people to build homes; Shennong, who brought plants to feed people; Suiren, who gave fire to people; and other mythical figures. The beautiful, decorative illustrations are based on Chinese pottery and artwork.

Sikhism

688.   Chambers, Catherine. **Sikh**. Beliefs and Cultures Series. New York: Children's Press, 1996. 32p. $19.50. LC 94-47348. ISBN 0-516-08079-2.

With large type, simple writing, and many color photographs and maps, this thorough overview is readable and informative. Discussed are the history of Sikhism, methods of worship, festivals, and ways of life. The book includes crafts, a glossary, and an index.

689.   Coutts, John. **Sikh Festivals**. Celebrate Series. Crystal Lake, IL: Heinemann Library, 1997. 48p. $13.95. LC 96-52641. ISBN 0-431-06963-8.

Because Sikh holidays celebrate the lives and activities of its principal leaders—Guru Nanak, Guru Gobind Singh, Guru Har Gobind, and Guru Arjan—all the essentials of Sikhism are included in this discussion of its festivals. Baisakhi, or New Year, celebrates Guru Goband Singh's founding of the Khalsa and the Five Ks, and Hola Mohalla honors his teaching that Sikhs must keep fit. Divali commemorates the freeing from prison of Guru Har Gobind and the fifty-two princes holding his coattails. The birthdays of the first and tenth gurus and the martyrdom of Guru Arjan are also remembered. Legends, prayers, and hymns enrich the text. Color photographs and artwork, a glossary, a reading list, and an index are included.

690.   Dhanjal, Beryl. **What Do We Know About Sikhism?** What Do We Know About Series. New York: Peter Bedrick Books, 1996. 45p. $18.95. ISBN 0-87226-387-8.

This survey is plentifully illustrated with color photographs, drawings, and maps, which divide the text into succinct, nonintimidating segments. Discussion includes the history of Sikhism, the Khalsa, the Guru Granth Sahib and the religion's system of beliefs and worship, family life and ceremonies, music and dance, and more. This clear, interesting book includes a timeline, glossary, and index.

691.   Kaur-Singh, Kanwaljit. **Sikhism**. World Religions Series. New York: Thomson Learning, 1995. 48p. $16.98. LC 95-4711. ISBN 1-56847-379-6.

Although circumscribed in their social customs, particularly their dress, the Sikhs have religious beliefs that are all-embracing: one God, eternal and imageless; the equality of all human beings, male and female; the acceptance of all faiths; and the importance of service to others. The history of the gurus, the creation of the Khalsa, the problems facing the Punjab, ways of worship, homes and families, festivals, and obligations are discussed. This well-varied, easy-to-read book is generously illustrated with good color photographs. It contains a glossary with a pronunciation guide, a reading list, and an index.

692.   Penney, Sue. **Sikhism**. Discovering Religions Series. Austin, TX: Raintree Steck-Vaughan, 1997. 48p. $16.98. LC 96-12379. ISBN 0-8172-4398-4.

The youngest monotheistic and probably the most tolerant of the world's major religions is described in detail. Sections discuss the Five Ks; worship in the gurdwara; the Guru Granth Sahib; the ten gurus of the religion; the Khalsa; holy places and festivals; ways of living; and birth, marriage, and death customs.

Prayers, hymns, poems, quotations, and definitions of new words are set off in boxes to vary the format of this lucid text. The book has excellent color photographs and an index.

Older and Noteworthy

Children's books about Bahaism may be obtained from the Bahai Publishing Trust and Kalimat Press. Material about the Australian Aboriginal beliefs is contained in *The Rainbow Serpent* by Dick Roughsey (Gareth Stevens, 1988) and *Gidja the Moon* by Percy Trezise (Gareth Stevens, 1988), both part of an excellent series (Stories of the Dreamtime—Tales of the Aboriginal People) about this people.

Numbers refer to entry numbers

Subject Index

Numbers refer to entry numbers

A

Abbasid, 679
Abel. *See also* Cain and Abel
  and prayer, 409
Abenaki people
  and Lake Champlain, 622
Abernathy, Ralph David, 439
Abigail
  in art, 116
  stories about, 151, 152
Abraham, 102, 104, 119, 123, 130, 138,
    343, 412, 481
  in African-American spirituals, 369
  family of, 91
  and sacrifice of Isaac, 122
  stories about, 133, 142, 145, 149, 150,
    512
  timeline of events of lifetime of, 486
Abram. *See* Abraham
Activity books
  on Bible, 102
Acts of the Apostles, 57, 117, 126
Adam, 106, 513
  stories about, 163
Adam and Eve, 91, 104, 162, 171, 343
  in Islamic stories, 674, 676
  painting of fall of, 148
  stories about, 118, 122, 128, 133, 137, 149
  verses about, 147
Advent, 341. *See also* Christmas
  candles, 302
  mealtime prayers during, 73
Adventures
  in Bible, 143
Aelia Capitolina, 114
Afikomen (Passover), 585, 586, 591
Africa
  holy places and sacred sites in, 22
  parables and folktales from, 6
  prayers from, 81, 82
  religion and spirituality in, 20
  spirit religions in, 8
African American folk art
  Holy Family in, xiii
African Americans
  Christmas anthology by and about, 271
  churches of, 388–391
  in civil rights movement, 349, 439,
    469, 471–474

creation stories of, 15, 166
friendships between Jews and, 531
and Gospel music, 367
Muslim community, 680
prayers of, 83
songs and hymns of, 366–369
spirituals of, 366–369
in stories about Shabbat, 596
African art
  Nativity, 289
African religions, 682–684
Africans
  coming-of-age rituals, 27
  creation myths of, 19
  deities of, 10
Afterlife, 32
Agatha, Saint, 455
Agnes, Saint, 455
Agricultural customs, 35
Agrippa, 89
Ahasueurus, King, 158
Ain Ghazal, 88
Alaska
  Christmas customs in, 270
  Hanukkah story in, 557
Alcoholics
  children of, 352, 354
Alcoholism
  Christian perspective on, 352, 354
Alexander the Great, 114
Algeria
  Jewish folktale from, 600
Algonquin nation
  creation stories of, 628, 634
Ali, 667
All Saints' Day, 341, 415
All Souls' Day, 415
Alphabet books
  for Jewish holidays, 533
  on Zen Buddhism, 642, 643
Alphabets
  and Bible, 105, 106
  Christmas, 272
  Hebrew, 483
"Amazing Grace"
  story of, 445, 446
Amazonia youth
  coming-of-age, 27

G

K

Kachina spirits (Hopi), 20
Kaddish, reciting of, 527
Kali, 659
Karma, 661, 665
Kaska nation
    spiritual beliefs of, 614
Kathina festival (Buddhist), 637
Keller, Helen
    prayers of, 85
Kesada offering (Hindu), 34
Kevin, Saint, 456
Khalsa, the (Sikhism), 689, 691, 692
Kidderminster Kingdom tales
    and New Testament parables, 256, 257
Kiddush cups, 540
Kilauwea, 22
Kindness, 305, 438, 654, 656, 664
    of Buddha, 642
King, Martin Luther, Jr., 439
King James Version of Bible
    and Genesis, 170
    masterwork paintings and selections
        from, 148
King Leonard the Lion
    and workers in vineyard parable, 256
Kiowa Apache nation
    creation stories of, 634
    spirituality of, 607
Kiva
    Pueblo, 611
Koalas
    eyes of, 52
Koan
    Zen Buddhist, 641
Koran, 668, 670–672, 677, 678
    Muslim study of, 29
Kosher foods, 483
Koufax, Sandy, 589
Krishna, 662
K'tonton (Jewish Tom Thumb), 580
Kutchin nation
    spiritual beliefs of, 614
Kwakiutl nation
    beliefs of, 610
    thanksgiving songs and prayers of, 606

L

Labrador Inuit people
    spiritual beliefs of, 617
Lagerlof, Selma, 319
Lake Champlain
    and Abenaki people, 622

Lamaist Buddhism
    in Tibet, 640
Landscapes
    and Bible, 96, 98
Laos
    That Luang in, 34
Las Posadas custom (Mexico), 28
    of Christmas, 298, 322
Last Supper, 225
    story adaptation with animal charac-
        ters, 255
    washing of feet at, 236
Latin America
    Christmas songs from, 326
Latino Day of the Dead, 20
Latkes, 524
    and Hanukkah, 555, 558, 564, 571,
        572, 575, 576
La Vie de Jesus, 238
Laylat-ul-Barat (Islam), 671
Laylat-ul-Isra (Islam), 671
Laylat-ul-Qadr (Islam), 671
Lazarus
    resurrection of, 223, 225
Leah
    in art, 116
    stories about, 151, 152
Learning
    value of, 71
Lee, Mother Ann
    and Shakers, 420
Legends
    about St. Patrick, 467
    Native American, 611, 622, 624
    and number ten in biblical history of
        Jews, 513
    of saints, 456
    in Sikhism, 689
Lent, 341, 408
    mealtime prayers during, 73
Letters
    to God, 41
"Let Us Go, O Shepherds," 333
Leviticus, 139
Librettos
    on The Messiah, 244
Life after death
    Christian assurance of, 345
Lilith, 153
Lions
    eyes of, 52
Lippi, Fra Filippo, 116
    Christmas art by, 275
    paintings on Christ's life by, 243
Liturgical prayer, 409

Money
    in Bible, 102
Monks and monasteries
    Buddhist, 639, 641, 645
    in Vietnam, 12
Montagnais nation
    spiritual beliefs of, 614
Moody, Dwight L., 442.6
Moon Festival (China), 26
Moonies, the, 5
Moravian community
    during Revolutionary War, 384
Mordecai
    stories about, 144
Mormons and Mormonism, 5, 8, 387
Morning prayers, 86
Morocco
    Jewish oral tradition from, 517
Moroni (angel), 387
Morris, Samuel, 442.14
Moses, 7, 97, 139, 140, 412, 481
    in African-American spirituals, 369
    and burning bush, 189
    in Egypt, 191, 193
    life of, 141, 189
    in Old Testament/Hebrew Bible,
        189–193
    painting of, 148
    stories about, 117, 122, 128, 133, 137,
        142, 144, 149, 150, 512
    stories for Passover, 584
    verses about, 147
Mosques, 670, 677
Mother Teresa, 475–477
    prayers of, 85
Mott, Lucretia, 441
Mountains, 50
    biblical, 50
Mount Ararat, 50
    and Noah's Ark, 197, 200
Mount Moriah, 50
    and Ark of the Covenant, 112
Mount Nebo
    and death of Moses, 189, 190
Mount Sinai, 50
Mourning and remembrance, 32, 495
    Jewish prayers for, 502
"Mourt's Relation"
    and Pilgrim's emigration, 432
Mughal emperors, 679
Muhammad, 667, 674, 679
    escape from Mecca, 7
    events in life of, 671, 672, 677
    and hadith, 671
Muhammar Gaddafi, 667

Mulleer, George, 442.3
Multiethnic stories
    about angels, 380
    about Christmas, 305, 306
    Christian, 349
Murillo, Bartolomé, 274
Music. See also Hymns; Songs
    in Bible, 99, 108
    Christian, 361–371
    Christmas, 323–337
    Gospel, 367
    Hindu, 658
    Sikh, 690
    story of "Amazing Grace," 445, 446
Muslim religion
    celebrations in, 35
    marriage in, 25
    prayers in, 81
Muslims
    African American community, 680
    birth customs of, 31
    and Crusades, 427
    death customs of, 32
    and Ethiopian Jews, 492
    holiday calendars for, 535
    and Indian culture, 11
    and Jerusalem, 110, 112, 114
    pilgrimages and journeys by, 30
    religion and culture of, 668
Mustard seed parable, 253
Myanmar
    Schwedagon Pagoda Festival in, 33
Myra, Nicholas of, 333
Myths
    African, 684
    Blackfoot, 631
    Chinese, 686, 687
    Native American, 611, 630
    worldwide, 19

N

Naamah
    stories about, 207
Naboth's vineyard, 102
Nam
    return to, 32
Names and naming
    of animals, 163
    about God, 61
    Native American rituals for, 609
Naomi
    in art, 116
    stories about, 137, 144
Nash, Ogden
    prayers of, 85

O

P